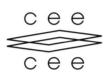

Cee Cee Berlin No.2

DISTANZ

Intro
06

Foreword
08

Index
12

Borderless
16

Hidden Gems
44

Classics
72

Scenic Berlin I
90

New Classics
102

Shortlist
120

Grey Sky
128

Blue Sky
144

Born & Bred
160

Live & Learn
182

Perfect Day
194

Scenic Berlin II
218

Nightfall
230

Perspectives
248

Kaleidoscope
262

A-Z
284

Artists & Courtesy
287

Publishing Details
288

CONTENTS

Intro

Als wir mit Cee Cee starteten, haben wir – Nina und Sven, die Herausgeber dieses Buches – uns selten gesehen. Damals, 2011, war Cee Cee ein rein digitales Projekt und mehr als einen Computer mit Internetverbindung brauchten wir nicht, um unseren Newsletter zu erstellen. In Berlin, dieser sich ewig wandelnden Stadt, waren wir natürlich trotzdem viel unterwegs. Kaum gingen wir aus dem Haus, stießen wir auf ein neues Café, einen kleinen Shop, hörten über Bekannte von einem Opening oder einer Party an einem noch nie bespielten Ort. Daran hat sich bis heute nichts geändert, denn Berlin ist noch immer die Stadt für alle Erlebnishungrigen, und unsere Tipps teilen wir nach wie vor jeden Donnerstag mit Euch.

Aber eines ist inzwischen anders: Aus unseren sporadischen Treffen und dem kleinen Nebenprojekt ist mehr geworden. Heute sitzen wir beide am gleichen Ort – in unserem eigenem Studio in einem Plattenbau in Mitte. Mit uns arbeitet ein talentiertes, internationales Team aus Designern, Fotografen, Redakteuren, Autoren und Projektmanagern. Zusammen sind wir die Agentur Cee Cee Creative und machen jeden Tag das, was wir lieben: Konzepte, Design, Content, Workshops und Events. Und natürlich Neues entdecken – in Berlin und auf der ganzen Welt. Für Kunden und für unsere eigenen Projekte, wie dieses Buch.

Im Jahr 2014 ist der erste Band erschienen. Mit dieser zweiten Ausgabe wollen wir noch mehr Lieblingstipps des Cee Cee Teams und von ausgewählten Gastautoren teilen. Schön gedruckt und mit vielen Abbildungen ist dieser Band nicht nur ein Handbuch, sondern auch ein Zeitdokument: „Cee Cee Berlin No.2" zeigt unser Berlin im Hier und Jetzt. Gedacht ist das Buch für zuhause und die Karte für unterwegs – denn erreichen wollen wir schließlich, dass Ihr hinausgeht in unsere vielfältige Stadt, unsere Tipps testet und eigene Entdeckungen macht, die wir irgendwann dann in unserem Newsletter oder nächsten Buch vorstellen ...

XX,
Nina Trippel, Sven Hausherr & das Cee Cee Team

Intro

When Cee Cee took its first steps, we, Nina and Sven, only saw each other from time to time. Cee Cee was a digital project back in 2011, and we didn't need much more than our computers and an internet connection to compile our weekly newsletter. But we were out there a lot, exploring Berlin, this vibrant city. We just needed to step outside our front doors to spot a new café or lovely little stores, while friends informed us about openings and parties at places we'd never been to.

Nothing has changed since then: Berlin is still an amazing location for anyone on the hunt for excitement, and we still share our recommendations every Thursday.

But one thing has changed: we've outgrown occasional meetings and working on it as a side project. Nowadays, we sit together in the same office in a Berlin-Mitte Plattenbau with a talented team of designers, photographers, editors, writers, and project managers. Together, we are Cee Cee Creative and we do what we love best: design concepts, create content, consult clients, conduct work-shops, or organize events. And, of course, discover new things to see and do all over Berlin for our readers and clients alike, as well as for our own projects – such as this book.

In 2014, the first Cee Cee Berlin book was published. In our second edition, we're once again sharing some of our favorite tips from our team and select guest writers. Printed on fine paper with lots of inspirational images, this book is not merely a compen-dium, but a vivid snapshot of our Berlin today.

"Cee Cee Berlin No.2" is meant for you to read at home, with a convenient on-the-go map enclosed. That's what we want you to do, after all: explore the city on your own and connect with its makers and shakers – or even better, discover new spots that we can share later in our newsletter or our next book ...

XX,
Nina Trippel, Sven Hausherr & the Cee Cee Team

Vorwort

Wie Berlin sich in den vergangenen Jahren verändert hat, lässt sich an vielen Beispielen zeigen. Als ich Ende der Neunzigerjahre in die Stadt kam, gab es etwa kaum beschreibenswerte Gastronomie. Das stimmt natürlich nicht ganz: Es gab Klassiker wie die beiden Café Einstein, drei, vier Sternerestaurants in Hotels, einige gute Kiez-Lokale, aber viel mehr nicht. Dann machte das Maxwell auf, das erste Restaurant in Mitte mit besonderer Küche und zeitgenössischer Kunst an den Wänden. Plötzlich wurde klar, dass Berlin dabei war, sich neu zu erfinden: Die Mischung aus Lebenslust, Genuss und Kunst ist bis heute der Grund, warum sich die Stadt immer noch freier anfühlt, als alle anderen großen Städte der Welt.

Um zu begreifen, wie sich Berlin verändert hat, reicht es deshalb zu erzählen, dass das Maxwell regelmäßig mit Stinkbombenattentaten malträtiert wurde. Besondere Küche kombiniert mit Kunst: das galt damals als Feindbild.

Wie sich Berlin verändert hat, lässt sich auch an seinen Medien erzählen. Als ich hierher zog, um beim Tagesspiegel zu arbeiten, gab es neben den Tageszeitungen zwei große Stadtmagazine und die Sozialen Medien waren noch nicht erfunden. Wenn mir damals jemand prophezeit hätte, dass ich mich im Jahr 2016 jede Woche von einem Newsletter informieren lassen würde, welche neuen Restaurants, Bars und Ausstellungen gerade empfehlenswert sind, hätte ich ihn ausgelacht.

Deshalb steht auch die Geschichte von Cee Cee für die Veränderung Berlins: Der Newsletter versorgt mit seinen mittlerweile über 30.000 Abonnenten alle, die sich für die schönen Seiten der Stadt interessieren, mit den kleinen und großen Orten und Ideen, die es zu entdecken gibt. Entstanden ist Cee Cee Berlin aus einem privaten E-Mail-Wechsel zwischen den beiden Gründern Nina Trippel und Sven Hausherr, die sich gegenseitig darüber informieren wollten, was gerade los ist, und diese E-Mails nach einer Weile auch an ihren Freundeskreis verschickten. Dieser persönliche Tonfall ist bis heute geblieben, und er hat so gar nichts von dem Trendgehabe manch anderer deutschen Stadtmagazine.

Heute schreiben auf Cee Cee Freunde der beiden Gründer ihre Empfehlungen, Journalisten, Kuratoren, Lektoren, Leute, die sich auskennen, ohne damit anzugeben.

Cee Cee veröffentlicht seine Beiträge selbstverständlich auf Deutsch und Englisch, denn Berlin ist die internationale Stadt geworden, von der früher immer behauptet wurde, dass sie es wäre. In manchen Stadtteilen wird mindestens so viel Englisch gesprochen wie Deutsch. Das hat auch die Gastronomie- und die Kunstszene auf den Kopf gestellt – die isländische Spitzenköchin Victoria Eliasdóttir und ihr Restaurant sind dafür das beste Beispiel. Sie kam in die Stadt, um in der Kantine ihres Bruders, des Künstlers Olafur Eliasson, zu kochen. Heute ist ihr Dóttir einer meiner Lieblingsorte in Berlin. Cee Cee hat früh über ihre Küche geschrieben.

Das Maxwell musste nach ein paar Jahren schließen, aber heute befindet sich dort das Katz Orange, ein weiteres jener Restaurants, über die Cee Cee früher als andere berichtet hat. Der Macher Ludwig Cramer-Klett hat inzwischen ein neues Restaurant eröffnet, das Panama, in einem Hinterhof in der Potsdamer Straße. Das Panama hat eine besondere internationale Küche, exzeptionelle Drinks, Kunst von Alicja Kwade, Julius von Bismarck und Björn Dahlem hängt an den Wänden.

Als ich zum ersten Mal dort war, wurde ich für einen Moment sentimental. Direkt nebenan hatte der Tagesspiegel einst seinen Sitz, die Zeitung, für die ich vor 17 Jahren nach Berlin gekommen war. Damals war die Gegend um die Potsdamer Straße heruntergekommen, an manchen Ecken gefährlich. Heute befinden sich dort der Concept Store von Andreas Murkudis, die Galerien von Tanya Leighton und Tanja Wagner, das Oliv Eat, der Park am Gleisdreieck. Und so dachte ich an diesem Abend im Panama wieder einmal darüber nach, wie sehr sich Berlin verändert hat und was das auch mit meinem eigenen Leben gemacht hat. Aber das ist eine andere Geschichte.

Christoph Amend,
Chefredakteur ZEITmagazin

Foreword

There are many examples of how much Berlin has changed in the past years. When I arrived in the city in the late nineties, there was little good food worth mentioning. Well, that's not quite true: there were classics like both of the Café Einstein, three or four star restaurants in hotels, and some good local spots, but not much more. Then came Maxwell, Mitte's first restaurant with a specialized kitchen and contemporary art decorating its walls. Suddenly it became clear that Berlin was about to reinvent itself: the mixture of joie de vivre, culinary delight, and art that is the reason that Berlin feels freer than any other capital in the world today was beginning to form.

The fact that Maxwell's was regularly assaulted by stink bombs is important to understanding how much Berlin has changed. Fine cuisine combined with art: back then, many saw this as an enemy concept. As Berlin has changed, its media has changed with it. When I came to the city in the late nineties to work at Tagesspiegel, there were only two big city magazines. Social media hadn't been invented. And if someone had told me that in 2016, I'd be getting tips on the best new restaurants, bars, and exhibits to visit around the city from a newsletter, I would have laughed.

That's why the story of Cee Cee Berlin parallels that of the city that gives it life: the newsletter, with its 30,000 subscribers, aids intrepid adventurers by directing them to spots worth discovering. Cee Cee is the result of the private emails between its founders, Nina Trippel and Sven Hausherr, who wanted to tip each other off about interesting things to do around the city. The email exchange expanded to include their friends. The intimate, personal tone hasn't changed, which is why the newsletter has escaped the trend-posturing that many German city magazines used to engage in. Today, friends of both the founders write about their recommendations for Cee Cee, alongside journalists, curators, and editors: people who are in the know but don't need to shout about it.

The story of Berlin's change can also be told in the language of Cee Cee. Cee Cee publishes its suggestions in both German and

English – because Berlin has become the international city its inhabitants always maintained it was.

There are parts of the city where English is spoken just as much as German, and the international influence has turned the culinary and art scenes upside down. Icelandic top chef Victoria Eliasdóttir and her restaurant are the best example: she came to the city to work in the studio kitchen of her brother, artist Olafur Eliasson, and today her restaurant, Dóttir, is one of my favorite spots in Berlin. Cee Cee discovered and recommended her cooking early on.

Maxwell had to close after a couple of years, but now the space is occupied by Katz Orange, another restaurant that Cee Cee discovered early. Its creator, Ludwig Cramer-Klett, has just opened a new restaurant, the Panama, in a Potsdamer Straße backyard. The Panama has delicious cuisine, exceptional drinks, and art by Alicja Kwade, Julius von Bismarck, and Björn Dahlem.

When I went for the first time, I had a sentimental moment. The Tagesspiegel offices, which had drawn me to Berlin 17 years ago, used to be right next door. At that time, the area was dilapidated, even dangerous. Today, it houses the concept store Andreas Murkudis, the galleries of Tanya Leighton and Tanja Wagner, the Park am Gleisdreieck, and Oliv Eat. And so even that night out at the Panama made me think of how much Berlin has changed – along with my own life. But that's another story.

Christoph Amend,
Editor-in-Chief ZEITmagazin

BO RD ER LE SS

INDEX

Park am Gleisdreieck
29

Panama Restaurant & Bar
45

Sexauer Gallery
60

Harry Lehmann
74

Arirang Two
32

Smac
48

Il Kino
62

Café Einstein Stammhaus
76

Osmans Töchter
17

Dóttir
33

Bergschloss
49

Einsunternull
63

Bohazel
20

Barbershop Kücük Istanbul
36

Bonanza Roastery Café
51

Bootsbau Köpenick
68

Teehaus im Englischen Garten
80

Madame Ngo
22

Ryoko
38

Savvy Contemporary
52

Father Carpenter Coffee Brewers
70

Der Goldene Hahn
82

Lode & Stijn
23

House of Small Wonder
39

Woltersdorfer Straßenbahn
56

CL AS SI CS

Freiluftkino Hasenheide
83

Akroum Snack
26

Gordon Café & Recordstore
42

Eins44
58

Körnerpark
84

HID DEN GE MS

Bellman Bar
73

Sammlung Scharf-Gerstenberg
86

Studio Niculescu
59

Chicha
28

Joseph Roth Diele
87

YamYam
114

The Good Store
133

Hebbel am Ufer 1
142

Spreehafen Burg
154

Schaubühne am Lehniner Platz
88

Andreas Murkudis Möbel +
Architektur
116

The Feuerle Collection
134

B L U E S K Y

The Klub Kitchen
156

N E W C L A S S I C S

Fine Bagels
136

California Pops
145

Beuster Bar
118

Knödelwirtschaft
137

Liebermann-Villa
157

The Store x Soho House Berlin
103

Kapelle auf dem
Dorotheenstädtischen Friedhof
138

Urbanhafen
148

I N D E X

Habermannsee
158

G R E Y S K Y

Mandy's Cocktail Bar
140

Café zum Löwen
150

B O R N & B R E D

Schwarzhogerzeil
106

Ora
129

Harry Hurtig & Müritzhof
151

Le Bon
108

Black Sheep Café
132

Lichtblick Kino
141

Michael Sontag Shop
161

Bar Milano
110

Café-Restaurant Wintergarten im
Literaturhaus
152

Edition Block
164

I N D E X

Laden Buchholzberlin
165

Felicious
176

Hallmann & Klee
177

Westberlin Coffeebar & Mediashop
183

Das Hotel
198

Distrikt Coffee
210

District Berlin
168

Accidental Concrete
178

Bender Keramik
186

Museum für Naturkunde
187

The Bread Station
199

Peppikäse
211

Nobelhart & Schmutzig
169

Bravo Bravko Kuchenwerkstatt
180

We Make It
190

Café am Neuen See
200

Sacrower See
212

Und Gretel Naturkosmetik
172

Goldhahn und Sampson
192

Caligari Bistro
202

Soto Store
214

Lager Lager
181

Candy on Bone
215

Le Petit Royal
206

L'eustache
216

Frank Leder
173

LIV
E & L
EA
RN

PER
FE
CT
DAY

Stella
208

NIG
HT
FA
LL

Hallesches Haus
195

Südblock
231

Paloma Bar
243

Happy Shop Global Alliance
263

Bar Zentral
232

Louis Pretty
254

Standard – Serious Pizza
266

Chrome Store
276

Neu West Berlin
244

Acud Macht Neu
234

Basalt
246

Flatowturm
256

Speiselokal Tulus Lotrek
277

Piñateria – Die Piñata Manufaktur
268

Azzam Lebensmittel
280

Zenkichi
236

Kumpelnest 3000
247

PER
SPE
CTI
VES

Tchoban Foundation – Museum für
Architekturzeichnung
258

Liquid Garden
269

Industry Standard
282

Konzerthaus Berlin
240

Pfaueninsel
260

KAL
EID
OSC
OPE

Bazar Noir
272

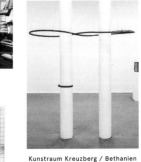

Kunstraum Kreuzberg / Bethanien
283

Zionskirche
249

Aroma
242

Akademie der Künste
252

Bosco
274

INDEX

BORDERLESS

VON PERUANISCHEM
CEVICHE BIS ZU
ISRAELISCHEM
SHAKSHUKA — BERLIN
WIRD JEDEN TAG EIN
WENIG INTERNATIONALER.
WIR NEHMEN GERNE
EINE KOSTPROBE.

BERLIN BECOMES MORE
INTERNATIONAL EVERY
DAY, ESPECIALLY THE FOOD
SCENE. FROM PERUVIAN
CEVICHE TO ISRAELI
SHAKSHUKA — WE'RE UP
FOR TASTING THE WORLD.

KÖNIGINNEN AM KOCHTOPF
QUEENS OF TURKISH CUISINE

Eigentlich gebührt Arzu Bulut und Lale Yanik der Titel Sultans-
königinnen, doch Osmans Töchter, der Name ihres Restaurants, passt
auch. Bei ihnen kommt leckere türkische Hausmannskost mit einem
Touch gehobener mediterraner Cuisine auf den Tisch – bodenständig
und zugleich experimentell, gekocht von „türkischen Mamis" und
internationalen Köchen. Auf diese Mischung legen Arzu und Lale auch
beim Interieur großen Wert: Die Einrichtung ist gemütlich, aber ohne
Orient-Kitsch. Nach dem Genuss köstlicher Vorspeisen wie saftiger
Zucchini-Creme mit Walnüssen oder zarter Lammspieße in hauseigener
Marinade mit geräuchertem Auberginenpüree kommt man gar nicht mehr
aus dem Schwärmen heraus. Mein Lieblingsgericht sind die Garnelen im
Engelshaarmantel mit Portulaksalat oder Babymangold – je nach Saison.
Dazu ein Glas Kyra Terra Öküzgözü aus dem Jahr 2009. Afiyet olsun! You
could call Arzu Bulut and Lale Yanik sultan queens, but actually
their restaurant's name Osmans Töchter, Osman's daughters, suits as
well. They create delicious Turkish home cooking with a touch of Mediterranean haute cuisine; simultaneously down-to-earth yet experimental.
With a menu created by both "Turkish mamas" and international chefs,
these same themes are reflected in their interior, with a blend of comfy
Mediterranean style perfectly placed against Middle Eastern influences.
Their menu reads like pure poetry, with subtle and innovative additions:
delightful starters of juicy zucchini crème with walnuts or tender
lamb skewers in a homemade marinade with smoked eggplant puree. My
favorite is the prawns in angel hair with seasonal baby chard or
purslane salad and served with a glass of Kyra Terra Öküzgözü from
2009. Afiyet olsun!

Text: Deniz Julia Güngör / Photos: Daniel Farò

Osmans Töchter
Pappelallee 15, 10437 Berlin-Prenzlauer Berg
Daily 17:30–24:00
osmanstoechter.de

BORDERLESS

EXTRA TIP

Hausmannskost aus Italien wird auf der anderen
Seite des Helmholtzplatzes aufgetischt: Bei
Pastificio Tosatti, in der Schliemannstraße 14a,
kocht Matteo Tosatti höchstpersönlich. Home
cooking from Italy is served on the other side of
Helmholtzplatz: Matteo Tosatti cooks each dish
himself at Pastificio Tosatti, at Schliemannstraße 14a.

HANDVERLESENE SOUVENIRS
HAND-SELECTED SOUVENIRS

Wen das Fernweh plagt, der sollte bei Bohazel, dem Shop von
Desiree Bühler und Chris Oesterle vorbeischauen. Hier findet
man handgewebte Teppiche und Decken aus Marokko und anderen
Ländern. Aus einigen Stoffen haben die beiden auch Kissen und
Jacken anfertigen lassen. Ergänzt wird die Selektion durch Makra-
mee-Blumenampeln und handgestrickte Mützen, die Desiree als
studierte Modedesignerin selbst herstellt oder produzieren lässt.
Der kleine Laden ist die beste Anlaufstelle, um das Reise-
fieber für einen Moment zu stillen! If you have a craving for
travel, a visit to Bohazel store by Desiree Bühler and Chris
Oesterle will help. Their little space is filled with items the
duo found while traveling in countries like Morocco. The
concept behind their shop is to bring back beautiful handi-
crafts from all over the world to share them with Berliners.
They sell colorful, hand-woven rugs and coverlets as well as
pillows and jackets made from intricately designed fabrics.
Among other unique pieces, you will also find handmade hats
and macramé hanging baskets by Desiree, a trained fashion designer. Bohazel is the perfect place to satisfy your wanderlust.

Text: Nina Trippel / Photos: Daniel Farò, Jacob Pritchard

Bohazel
Kienitzer Straße 111, 12049 Berlin-Neukölln
Thu-Sat 13:00-19:00
bohazel.com

EXTRA TIP

Schöne Kissen und Kelims gibt es auch beim Wild
Heart Free Soul Bazaar, der ab und an in der
Elisabethkirchstraße 13 stattfindet (siehe Facebook).
Find more beautiful pillows and kilims at Wild Heart
Free Soul Bazaar, which takes place irregularly at
Elisabethkirchstraße 13 (see Facebook).

VON PARIS NACH HANOI
FROM PARIS TO HANOI

Im Schaufenster der ehemaligen Apotheke thronen riesige Kochtöpfe und vom alten Schriftzug sind noch ganze drei Buchstaben übrig: PHO. Vietnamesische Phở-Suppen stehen in diesem Restaurant namens Madame Ngo auch auf der Karte, serviert wird aber noch viel mehr. Inhaber Duc Ngo, der Berlin bereits im Kuchi und Cocolo Ramen erfolgreich mit asiatischer Küche versorgt, wagt nämlich ein Crossover: Indochine-French-Cuisine. Im vorderen Teil des Restaurants sieht man den Köchen beim Zubereiten zu, während man selbst an einer langen Tafel Platz nimmt. Im hinteren Teil sitzt man an gemütlichen Holztischen. Von der gebratenen Gänsestopfleber mit Mango in Kalbsjus über ein Phở gà-Suppenhuhn schmeckt alles köstlich und frisch. Besonders die Bouillabaisse ist zu empfehlen. Dazu ein Glas Riesling von Johannes Leitz, und einem perfekten Abend steht nichts mehr im Wege. Big pots decorate the window display and three letters are left from an old sign: PHO. And yes, you will find phở soups here. Yet the restaurant goes by the name Madame Ngo – after the last name of the owner, Duc Ngo, who is an experienced restauranteur and the creator of Kuchi and Cocolo Ramen. In the front section, the chefs prepare meals at long counters in full view of diners, while in the back you can sit comfortably at wooden tables. From fried foie gras with mango in veal juice to a classic phở gà chicken soup, all the dishes are deliciously and freshly prepared. In particular, I recommend the bouillabaisse with a glass of Johannes Leitz's Riesling for the perfect evening.

Text: Helen von der Höden / Photos: Daniel Farò

Madame Ngo
Kantstraße 30, 10623 Berlin-Charlottenburg
Daily 11:30-24:00
madame-ngo.de

ZWEI FÜR ALLE GÄNGE
IT TAKES TWO TO COOK

Kroketten machen mich traurig. Wenn jemand Krokette sagt, muss ich an zu deutsche Vereinslokale in zu deutschen Kleingartensiedlungen denken. Da trifft es sich gut, dass die Krokette in den Niederlanden Bitterballen heißt und solche Assoziationen erst gar nicht möglich sind. Probieren kann man die kleinen, frittierten, mit Rinderrippe gefüllten Bällchen auch in Berlin: Lode van Zuijlen und Stijn Remi, zwei niederländische Köche, haben das Rezept nach Zwischenstopps in Sternerestaurants von Stockholm über Hamburg bis San Francisco mit in die deutsche Hauptstadt gebracht. Wenn die beiden kochen, sind Bitterballen nur das Amuse-Bouche, im Mittelpunkt steht simple, moderne Küche aus saisonalen Zutaten: selbst gebackenes Brot, Lachs in Buttermilchschaum, Lammtatar mit Crème fraîche. Um nun beim Essen mit den Tischnachbarn ins Gespräch zu kommen, liegt ein Thema schon mal auf der Hand: die Ehrenrettung der Krokette. Potato croquettes make me wary. When someone says croquette, I always think of German local clubs in garden colonies, both too German for their own sake. Thankfully, they have quite a different association in the Netherlands, where they are called bitterballen. And now, the small fried meat-stuffed balls have been reinvented for Berlin through the cooking of Lode & Stijn (Lode van Zuijlen and Stijn Remi). After several stints working at high class restaurants around the world, the Dutch chefs brought their Bitterballen recipe to Berlin. Of course, the bitterballen are just an appetizer at their restaurant. What takes the spotlight is a minimalistic, modern, and seasonal kitchen. They offer fresh homemade bread, salmon in buttermilk-foam, and lamb-tartare with crème fraîche. Attending their restaurant means spending the night reclaiming the honor of the croquette.

Text: Laura Storfner / Photos: Daniel Farò

Lode & Stijn
Lausitzer Straße 25, 10999 Berlin-Kreuzberg
Tue-Sat 18:00-22:30
lode-stijn.de

CEE CEE'S GUEST: SARA CHAHRROUR

Nicht jeder, der nach Berlin zieht, schließt mit der Stadt direkt eine Freundschaft fürs Leben. Auch für Sara Chahrrour war der Beziehungsstatus erst mal kompliziert. „Anfangs habe ich Berlin gehasst", sagt die Hessin mit syrischen Wurzeln, die 2008 direkt nach dem Abi zum Studieren kam – und am liebsten wieder umgekehrt wäre. Bis ihr auffiel, dass sie von der Hauptstadt noch gar nichts kannte. Also machte sich die Kulturwissenschaftlerin auf die Suche nach „ihrem" Berlin. Der Beginn einer Reise, die zu einem persönlichen Langzeitprojekt geworden ist, über das sie seit 2010 in ihrem Blog namens FindingBerlin berichtet. Dort erzählt Sara, die heute in Kreuzberg lebt, Geschichten über urbanes Leben und besondere Orte. Inzwischen schätzt sie an der Stadt die starke Community in ihrem Kiez und die zahllosen Möglichkeiten, die Berlin bietet. Und natürlich die kulinarische Vielfalt. Etwa die vielen orientalischen Restaurants wie das Akroum Snack auf der Sonnenallee, wo Kichererbsen-Köstlichkeiten zubereitet werden, die (fast) so gut sind wie bei ihrer Mutter. Not everyone who comes to Berlin falls in love with it at first sight. For Sara Chahrrour, the relationship status was complicated at first. "At the beginning, I hated Berlin," says the Hessian of Syrian roots, who moved here directly after graduation in 2008 – and immediately wanted to turn around. Then she realized that she knew nothing about the capital. So the cultural scientist set out on the search for "her" Berlin. That was the beginning of a journey that developed into a longtime personal project, which she's documented on FindingBerlin since 2010. Through the blog, Sara, who now lives in Kreuzberg, tells tales of urban legends and special places. Meanwhile, she cherishes the strong community of her Kiez and friends and the endless possibilities that Berlin offers. And, naturally, the culinary options! Some of the many oriental restaurants even serve chickpea dishes that are (almost) as good as her mother's, like Akroum Snack on Sonnenallee. →

findingberlin.com
@findingberlin

SARA CHAHRROUR EMPFIEHLT: AKROUM SNACK SARA CHAHRROUR RECOMMENDS: AKROUM SNACK

Vergessen wir für einen Augenblick Döner, Falafel und das zu trockene Schawarma. Wer auf der Suche nach den wahren Aromen des Mittleren Ostens ist, findet sie in den zahlreichen Snack- und Frühstücks-Cafés auf der Sonnenallee. Meinen persönlichen Geschmack trifft Akroum Snack: Hier gibt es traditionelles syrisches und libanesisches Frühstück (auch zur Mittagszeit). Msabaha, eine pikante Hummus-Variation, ist ein Muss, und wer eine weitere arabische Köstlichkeit kennenlernen möchte, bestellt Fatteh oder, wie ich sie nenne, die Middle Eastern Breakfast Lasagna, und verbringt die nächsten Wochen damit, davon zu schwärmen. Fatteh besteht aus Joghurt, getrocknetem Brot, Kichererbsen, gerösteten Pinienkernen sowie viel Knoblauch. Das ist nichts für Leute, die zum Frühstück nur Kaffee und Croissants kennen, aber eine große Sache für alle anderen, die dieses Gericht noch nicht probiert haben! Let's forget for a short moment the sorry sight of a typical döner, falafel, or shawarma. If you really want to enjoy the original flavors of the Middle East, you'll find them at one of the many snack and breakfast cafés on Sonnenallee. My personal tastes always lead me to Akroum Snack. You'll find traditional Syrian and Lebanese breakfast there (even at lunch time): a spicy version of hummus called msabaha is a must-try, and for true Arab delight, order the fatteh, or as I call it, Middle Eastern Breakfast Lasagna. You'll be rhapsodizing about it for weeks. Fatteh is made with yogurt, dried bread, chickpeas, roasted pine nuts, and a lot of garlic. This is not for those who only know the basic coffee-and-croissant breakfast. But it's a big deal for anyone who hasn't tried it yet!

Text: Sara Chahrrour / Photos: Daniel Farò

Akroum Snack
Sonnenallee 45, 12045 Berlin-Neukölln
Daily 08:00–21:00

ESSEN WIE GOTT IN PERU
A REAL TASTE OF PERU

In einem großzügigen Ladenlokal nahe dem Landwehrkanal hat Robert Peveling-Oberhag das Restaurant Chicha eröffnet, wo er diverse Ceviche-Variationen, peruanische Kleinigkeiten und natürlich passend dazu Pisco Sour serviert. Küchenchef Ariel Peralta ist Peruaner und nimmt das Kochen ernst: Die kleinen Teller mit Cuello de Cerdo, gebratener Schweinenacken vom Lavagrill, oder Causa de Pulpo, Oktopus auf einer Art Kartoffelküchlein, sind köstlich. Am meisten Spaß macht es, verschiedene Leckereien zu bestellen, zu teilen und etwas Neues kennenzulernen. Auch das Dessert löffelt man zusammen – denn wer nach Hause geht, ohne das Cacao y Raspadilla probiert zu haben, hat etwas verpasst.

Close to the Landwehr Canal, owner Robert Peveling-Oberhag has transformed a former Spanish restaurant into Chicha, now serving fantastic ceviche dishes, pisco sours, and other specialties of Peruvian cuisine. Chef Ariel Peralta, a native Peruvian, takes his cooking seriously, with highlights being the small plates of cuello de cerdo, pork neck cooked on a lava stone grill, and causa de pulpo, octopus with potato cake. It's the perfect place to go with lots of friends so that you can order as many dishes from the menu as possible and taste all the delights on offer. And leaving without sharing the dessert of cacao y raspadilla means missing out.

Text: Nina Trippel / Photos: Daniel Farò

Chicha
Friedelstraße 34, 12047 Berlin-Neukölln
Wed-Sun 18:00-24:00
chicha-berlin.de

EXTRA TIP

Hervorragendes Ceviche gibt es auch in der Cevicheria in der Dresdener Straße 120 in Kreuzberg. There's also magnificent Ceviche in the Cevicheria, at Dresdener Straße 120 in Kreuzberg.

ERHOLUNG ZWISCHEN DEN GLEISEN RECREATION BETWEEN THE TRAIN TRACKS

Der Park am Gleisdreieck verkörpert modernes Design: Während Sonnenanbeter auf den ausladenden Grünflächen entspannen, können sich Sportbegeisterte auf den vielen Plätzen und Übungsparcours auspowern. Von den streng gepflegten Parks der Stadt unterscheidet sich dieser Ort auch, weil er im Süden an einen kleinen Wald angrenzt, dessen wilde Spuren sich durch die gesamte Anlage ziehen. Dass hier früher einmal ein Güterbahnhof war, merkt man heute noch an den oberirdischen Eisenbahnbrücken und U-Bahn-gleisen. Der Park an sich liegt leicht erhöht – knapp drei Meter über Straßenniveau – und ist auch deswegen ein Platz, an dem sich die Laune hebt. The Park am Gleis-dreieck embodies a sharp contemporary approach in its design. As sprawling fields present sun hunters with generous possibilities to catch rays, the many exercise tracks and sports areas give more active visitors the chance to tire themselves out. The diverse array of plant life echoes the green backdrop of the lush forest, and it's this fluidity that sets Gleisdreieck apart from Berlin's more sedentary parks. The site's history as a freight station survives in the overhead rail bridges and the platform that raises most of the park three meters above the road-side, making it a leisurely and uplifting spot for a day out.

Text: Ben Barlow / Photo: Daniel Farò

Park am Gleisdreieck
Möckernstraße 26, 10965 Berlin-Kreuzberg

EXTRA TIP

Im Café Eule im Gleisdreieck, zu erreichen über den Eingang an der Bülowstraße 68, gibt es Buttercrumble, hausgemachte vegane Kekse und warme Natas. At Café Eule in Gleisdreieck, over the entrance to Bülowstraße 68, you can find butter crumble, home made vegan cookies, and warm natas.

KOREANISCHE KÜCHE FÜR PROS
KOREAN CUISINE FOR PROS

Wer davon träumt, in Berlin authentisch koreanisch essen zu gehen, ist im Arirang Two richtig. Von der Inneneinrichtung, die auf den ersten Blick eher nicht mit der in Berlin mittlerweile allgegenwärtigen Liebe zum Detail zusammengestellt wurde, sollte man sich dabei keineswegs abschrecken lassen – denn hier dreht sich alles ums Essen: Auf den Tisch kommt koreanische Hausmannskost, wie man sie dort in den ländlichen Regionen zubereitet. Bestellt haben wir die So-Bul-Go-Gi-Platte mit koreanischem Grillfleisch für zwei Personen, die durch ihre vielen Beilagen wie Kimchi, süßlich marinierte Kartoffeln und Sojabohnen aber auf jeden Fall auch für drei gereicht hätte. Spätestens wenn man das Fleisch gemeinsam auf dem Tischgrill gart, fühlt es sich ein wenig so an, als säße man in einem kleinen Straßenlokal in Korea. If you dream of authentic Korean food in Berlin, you've come to the right place in Arirang Two. At first glance, the interior does not appear to have been designed with the attention to detail that is now ubiquitous in Berlin. But don't let that deter you – everything revolves around the food here. Typical Korean home cooking is served, just like in Korea's more rural regions. We ordered the So-Bul-Go-Gi plate with Korean grilled meat for two people, although with the many side dishes such as sweet marinated potatoes and soy beans, it could have been for three. By the time you cook the meat together on the griddle it feels a little like sitting in a small street restaurant in Korea.

Text: Sandra Andriani Bitz / Photos: Daniel Faró

Arirang Two
Reichenberger Straße 125, 10999 Berlin-Kreuzberg
Daily 12:00-23:00

PERFEKTION AUF ISLÄNDISCH
ICELANDIC PERFECTION

Meine bisherigen Erfahrungen mit nordischer Küche sind, gelinde gesagt, dürftig – aber nach einem Abend im dóttir denke ich darüber nach, in Zukunft nichts anderes mehr zu essen. Zwischen rohen Wänden konzentriert man sich bei einem Glas Rosé ganz auf das Essen: Warmes, frisch gebackenes Brot mit geschmolzener brauner Butter wird zum Vier-Gänge-Menü gereicht, das bei uns aus einer Auswahl perfekt gekochter und präsentierter Fischgerichte bestand. Wir aßen Forellenkaviar mit Gurke, Makrele mit gerösteten Tomaten und frischen Dorsch mit Birne und hielten uns dabei an die empfohlenen Weine. Zum Nachtisch – gebackener Rhabarber, Erdbeersorbet und krümeliger Marzipankuchen – gesellte sich ein leicht würziger Dessertwein: der perfekte honigdurchtränkte Abschluss! My previous experience of Nordic cuisine has been sparse, to say the least. But after a night at dóttir, I'm considering never eating anything else. Sitting down to a glass of softly sparkling rosé among the high, exposed walls, you can focus all your attention on the food in front of you. The four-course meal, a selection of perfectly cooked and presented fish dishes, was accompanied by warm, freshly baked bread with slow melted brown butter. We ate trout caviar with cucumber, soft and flaking mackerel with slow roasted tomatoes, and fresh cod with pear, all accompanied by expertly chosen wines. For dessert, we had baked rhubarb, strawberry sorbet, and crumbling marzipan cake served with a sweet, slightly spiced dessert wine – the perfect honey-drenched end to the meal!

Text: Antonia Harris / Photos: Daniel Farò, Sven Hausherr

dóttir
Mittelstraße 40-41, 10117 Berlin-Mitte
Tue-Sat from 18:00
dottirberlin.com

DIE GENTLEMEN-BARBER AUS NEUKÖLLN NEUKÖLLN'S GENTLEMEN BARBERS

Echte Spezialisten für die Bartpflege sind in Berlin schwer
zu finden. Gut, dass es die Brüder Hussein und Raed Seif
im Flughafenkiez gibt. Die Renaissance des gepflegten Barts
hat den stets adrett gekleideten Barbiers in den letzten
Jahren einen regen Zulauf beschert. Seit 1996 trimmen,
rasieren und schneiden sie Schnurrbärte, Vollbärte und
deren Verwandte. Ihre Handwerkskunst fußt auf dem Old
School-Konzept, und wenn Chef Hussein die Unterschiede
seiner fünf möglichen Arten der Rasur erklärt, fällt die
Entscheidung schwer. Neben der Kinnpflege sind Frisuren
der Vierziger- und Fünfzigerjahre ein Alleinstellungsmerk-
mal. Nach der Rasur sollte man sich die Bartmassage nicht
entgehen lassen, und für zu Hause empfiehlt sich die Pflege-
serie aus Wachs, Balsam und Öl. It's always a great joy
to find true beard trimming specialists. So if you fancy
being properly taken care of, we suggest heading to
brothers Hussein and Raed Seif's barbershop on Flughafenstraße. Since 1996, not only have they been trimming,
shaving, and cutting hair, but have catered to all beard
styling demands using traditional barbershop methods.
In recent years, the popular renaissance of the beard has
attracted flocks of customers to the master hands of
these sleek and professional barbers. When Hussein explains
their five different shaving styles, it's hard to choose
which sounds best, but it's clear that their 40s and 50s
inspired styles continue to be a unique selling point
of this establishment. You'll receive even more pampering
if you want: they offer a specialized post-shave massage
and have their own beard-care range with wax, balsam, and oil.

Text: Ferdinand Hamsch / Photos: Daniel Faró

Barbershop Kücük Istanbul
Flughafenstraße 15, 12053 Berlin-Neukölln
Mon-Sat 10:00-19:00
kücükistanbul.de

DER ANTI-STRESS-TEMPEL
THE STRESS-RELIEF TEMPLE

Gegen eine gute Massage ist nie etwas einzuwenden. Aber erst an einem kalten, nassen Morgen, an dem man sich völlig erschöpft und überarbeitet fühlt, erkennt man ihren wahren Wert. An solchen Tagen muss man Ryoko Hori anrufen. Schon auf der Schwelle zum Laden lässt man seinen Alltag hinter sich. Dafür sorgen die sanfte Musik und das beruhigende Licht, die im luftigen Vorzimmer auf den Besucher einwirken. Den entspannenden Gesamteindruck komplettiert die Schlichtheit des Massagezimmers, wo unter Ryokos kundigen Händen und dem Einsatz von süßen Ölen der stressgeplagte Körper Linderung erfährt. Auf die eigenen Wünsche und Bedürfnisse abgestimmt, stellt die gelernte Massagetherapeutin ein Treatment zusammen, das sich als rundum heilende Erfahrung erweist. A good massage is always valuable, but it's priceless on a cold, damp morning when you're running on too little sleep and laden with work and stress. On days like that, call Ryoko Hori. When you arrive at Ryoko, you leave your worries at the door with your shoes. The soothing music and light, airy front room are instantly relaxing. The same calming sensation is echoed in the simplicity of the massage room, where Ryoko's experienced hands will smooth away the stress of the outside world with the help of sweet-smelling oils. Ryoko makes sure to ask you about your preferences and stays true to your requests throughout the massage. It truly is a healing experience for every part of you – you will leave feeling lighter in both body and spirit.

Text: Esmé Rocks / Photos: Daniel Kula

Ryoko
Friedelstraße 11, 12047 Berlin-Neukölln
By appointment
ryoko-berlin.com

EXTRA TIP

Ryoko bietet übrigens auch Workshops an, zum Beispiel zur traditionellen japanischen Keramik-Reparaturmethode Kintsugi. Ryoko also offers various workshops, for example on the traditional Japanese art of reparing pottery Kintsugi.

JAPANISCHER FUSION BRUNCH DIREKT AUS WILLIAMSBURG

JAPANESE FUSION BRUNCH FROM WILLIAMSBURG

Eine Wendeltreppe, eingerahmt von viel sattem Grün, führt die Gäste in die erste Etage, die wie eine kleine Oase wirkt. Auf der Speisekarte steht Comfort Food, wobei Frühstück und Lunch den ganzen Tag über serviert werden. Man bestellt die üblichen Verdächtigen wie French Toast – hier als Croissant-Variante – oder japanische Spezialitäten wie Soboro Don und Onigiri. Zu trinken gibt es neben fantastischen japanischen Tees natürlich auch leckeren Matcha Latte. Wer hier gar nicht mehr weg will, geht nach Ladenschluss einfach in den Keller: Die Besitzer Shaul Margulies und Motoko Watanabe haben im Jahr 2015 nicht nur ihr in Brooklyn etabliertes Café nach Berlin gebracht, sondern auch die Izakaya-Bar Zenkichi, die sich im Untergeschoss befindet (s. S. 236). Upon entering the building, you are greeted by potted plants and lush greens as you ascend the stairs into an oasis. Serving breakfast and lunch all day, the comfort food offered here ranges from the delicious croissant French toast to everyday Japanese dishes such as soboro don and onigiri, along with a great selection of teas like the lovely matcha latte. If you want to extend your visit into the night, just head to the basement: in 2015 the owners, Shaul Margulies and Motoko Watanabe, have brought their Brooklyn café to Berlin together with their high-end Izakaya restaurant Zenkichi (s. p. 236).

Text: Rei Matsuoka / Photos: Daniel Farò

House of Small Wonder
Johannisstraße 20, 10117 Berlin-Mitte
Daily 9:00–17:00
houseofsmallwonder.de

EXTRA TIP

**Sehr guten Matcha Latte gibt es noch ein zweites Mal
in Mitte: Bei Mamecha in der Mulackstraße 33.**
There's a second place for an amazing matcha latte
in Mitte: Mamecha at Mulackstraße 33.

HUMMUS, HERZLICHKEIT & BEATS
HUMMUS, HOSPITALITY & BEATS

Wer sich beim Plattenkauf gerne Zeit lässt, ist hier richtig: Die
Besitzer Doron Eisenberg und Nir Ivenizki bieten bei Gordon eine
kleine, feine Auswahl elektronischer Musik auf Vinyl, darunter auch
die des eigenen Labels Legotek Records, das die beiden gebürtigen
Israelis in Tel Aviv gegründet haben. Da ihr Shop auch gleichzeitig
ein Café ist, kann man sich hier auch gerne mal Stunden aufhalten.
Wer am frühen Morgen kommt, trifft mit Rugelach (eine Art jüdisches
Croissant) und Flat White eine gute Wahl. Das leckere Sabich und
die fantastischen Hummus-Teller kann man den ganzen Tag über bestellen und am besten gemeinsam mit Freunden am selbstgebauten
Holztisch drinnen oder im Sommer draußen verspeisen. Ergänzt wird
die kulinarische Auswahl durch Kuchen und Bagels. Schon beim zweiten oder dritten Besuch fühlt man sich als Teil der Stammkundschaft,
und wenn Doron und Nir nicht gerade als DJs irgendwo in der Welt
auflegen, sind die beiden äußerst charmante und herzliche Gastgeber.

If you like to spend your time browsing record stores, you've
come to the right place: at Gordon owners Doron Eisenberg and Nir
Ivenizki offer a small but fine selection of electronic music on
vinyl, some coming from their own label Legotek Records, which the
two Israeli-born musicians founded in Tel Aviv. Their shop doubles
as a café where the hours slip by easily. If you come early in the
morning, a rugelach (a type of Jewish croissant) and a flat white
are always a good combination. You can order the delicious sabich
and the fantastic hummus plates at any time of day, in summer best
consumed outside with friends at one of the homemade wood tables.
These offerings are complemented by the selection of cakes and
bagels. If you come back for a second or a third time, you will
soon feel like a part of the regular clientele, and when Doron
and Nir aren't DJing around the world, they are the most charming
and welcoming hosts.

Text: Nina Trippel / Photos: Daniel Farò

Gordon Café & Recordstore
Allerstraße 11, 12049 Berlin-Neukölln
Mon-Thu 9:00-19:00, Fri 10:00-22:00, Sat 11:00-19:00, Sun 11:00-18:00

EXTRA TIP

Ausgezeichnete israelische und palästinensische
Gerichte werden auch im Kanaan, Kopenhagener
Straße 17, serviert: Hummus isst man hier auf der
Terrasse über dem S-Bahn-Ring. You can also find
excellent Israeli and Palestinian dishes at Kanaan at
Kopenhagener Straße 17: eat hummus on the terrace
overlooking the Ring-Bahn.

HIDDEN GEMS

HINTER GRAUEN FASSADEN UND IN UNSCHEINBAREN HINTERHÖFEN VERSTECKT, WARTEN PERLEN DARAUF, ENTDECKT ZU WERDEN. EINMAL GESUCHT, FÜR IMMER GEFUNDEN. TUCKED BEHIND A BARELY MARKED DOOR OR SECLUDED IN A COURTYARD: ONCE YOU'VE OPENED THESE OYSTERS, YOU'LL TREASURE THE PEARLS YOU FIND FOREVER.

SYMBIOSE AUS TRADITION & EXOTIK THE SYMBIOSIS OF TRADITION & EXOTICISM

Es war nur eine Frage der Zeit, bis die Potsdamer Straße ihr eigenes, vorzeigbares Restaurant bekam: Neben den Galerien zieht nun auch das Panama die Gäste an. Ja, „Oh, wie schön ist Panama" – der Name weckt direkt nostalgische Erinnerungen an das berühmte Kinderbuch. Ludwig Cramer-Klett geht es mit seinem dritten Gastronomieprojekt (nach dem Katz Orange und dem Candy on Bone) um die Symbiose von Exotischem und Traditionellem. So liest sich die Speisekarte wie eine Reise in eine andere Welt: Unterteilt in Blätter & Blüten oder Körner & Gemüse, werden in der Küche unter der Leitung von Sophia Rudolph kleine Wunder kreiert. Mein Favorit: Das Tatar vom Reh mit eingelegtem Shiitake-Pilz, Johannisbeere und Nigella, gefolgt von der gebrannten Auberginencreme mit Ziegenkäse und Wassermelone. Für den perfekten Abschluss an der Bar: ein Basil Smash mit einem Hauch Ingwer. It was only a matter of time before Potsdamer Straße got its own representative restaurant: Panama restaurant and bar has arrived next to all the stylish galleries. The children's book "The Trip to Panama" filled young minds with images of a beautiful and distant land. With his third restaurant (after Katz Orange in Mitte and Candy on Bone in Kreuzberg) Ludwig Cramer-Klett aimed to initiate this symbiosis of exoticism and tradition. The whimsical menu reads like a journey to another world: divided into Leaves & Flowers and Grains & Vegetables, each dish is a tiny miracle prepared under the direction of Sophia Rudolph. My favorite: the venison tartare with shiitake mushrooms, currants, and nigella seeds, followed by roasted eggplant cream with goat cheese and watermelon. For the perfect end to the evening, move on to the bar for a Basil Smash with a marvelous touch of ginger.

Text: Julia Knolle / Photos: Anna Küfner, Philipp Langenheim, Corina Schadendorf

Panama Restaurant & Bar
Potsdamer Straße 91, 10785 Berlin-Tiergarten
Tue-Sat: bar from 17:00, restaurant from 18:00
oh-panama.com

EXTRA TIP

Wer tagsüber in der Gegend um das Panama
unterwegs ist, findet im Oliv Eat in der
Potsdamer Straße 91 einen Ort für exzellentes
Mittagessen. If you're in the area for lunch-
time, Oliv Eat at Potsdamer Straße 91 offers
excellent lunch.

ZEITGENÖSSISCHE POSITIONEN IM HINTERHOF CONTEMPORARY ART IN A HIDDEN BACKYARD

Mitten in Mitte, in einem kleinen Hinterhof, fördern die Macher des Projektraums Smac, Matthias Birkholz und Stephanie Hundertmark, Berliner Künstler. Die Ausstellungen spiegeln hier oft persönliche Vorlieben und Sammlungsschwerpunkte der beiden Initiatoren wider. Jeder ausstellende Künstler konzipiert zusätzlich zu seiner Schau eine Arbeit in einer Auflage von mehreren Exemplaren, die online zu einem niedrigeren Preis als Unikate erhältlich sind. Dadurch wird die Schwelle zum Erwerb eines Kunstwerks herabgesetzt und Kunst ein kleines Stückchen demokratisiert. Kunstbegeisterte verschaffen sich am besten selbst bei einer Vernissage mit einem Glas Wein einen Eindruck. In the middle of Mitte, in a small courtyard, the founders of Smac, Matthias Birkholz and Stephanie Hundertmark, support Berlin artists. The exhibitions here often reflect the personal preferences and focus of the founders within each exhibition. In addition, each featured artist designs smaller versions of his or her pieces to be sold online at lower prices. Thus, the threshold for the acquisition of artwork is lowered and a small piece of the art world is democratized. Art enthusiasts should head to an exhibition, sip a glass of wine and take everything in.

Text: Leonie Haenchen / Photos: Sven Hausherr

Smac
Linienstraße 57, 10119 Berlin-Mitte
smac-berlin.de

CRAFT BEER IM ROLLBERGKIEZ
CRAFT BEER AT ROLLBERGKIEZ

Der Rollbergkiez war einst Zentrum der Berliner Brauwirtschaft. An diese Tradition knüpfen die drei Gründer Uli Erxleben, Finn Age Hänsel und Robin Weber mit ihrer Brauerei Berliner Berg an und eröffneten 2015 das Bergschloss – einen liebevoll restaurierten Schankraum, der sich im Gebäudekomplex einer alten Schmalzfabrik befindet. Auf der eigenen Brauanlage werden nun Biere wie Pale Ale und Lager kreiert. Neben diesen Craft Beer-Klassikern planen die drei Experten auch die Berliner Weiße wieder zum Leben zu erwecken. Ein Prosit dem Lokalpatriotismus! The Rollberg neighborhood was once the center of the Berlin brewing industry. Uli Erxleben, Finn Age Hänsel, and Robin Weber decided to continue this tradition with the opening of their brewery Berliner Berg and their Bergschloss bar in 2015. The lovingly restored taproom is built inside the premises of an old lard factory, an impressive building serving equally impressive drinks. However, the highlight has to be the Berliner Berg brewing facility, where delicious beers, pale ales, and lagers are created. Besides these signature craft beers, the Berliner Berg experts will also bring back a classic: genuine Berliner Weisse beer. Cheers to local patriotism!

Text: Helen von der Höden / Photos: Daniel Farò

Bergschloss
Kopfstraße 59, 12053 Berlin-Neukölln
Thu-Sat 18:00-2:00
berlinerberg.com

EXTRA TIP

Auch am anderen Ende der Stadt, im Wedding, braut sich etwas zusammen: In der Vagabund Brauerei, Antwerpener Straße 3, trinkt man Pale Ale im US-Style. On the other side of the city, in Wedding, something is brewing, too. In the Vagabund Brauerei on Antwerpener Straße 3, you can drink US-style Pale Ale.

EXTRA TIP

Geröstet wird auch ein paar Hausnummern weiter, in der Adalbertstraße 23: Das Team der Kaffee-kirsche bietet hauseigene Röstungen zum Genuss vor Ort oder für zuhause. Find even more coffee beans a few houses down, at Adalbertstraße 23: the team from the Kaffeekirsche offer their own roasts, too. Enjoy your coffee on site or take your favorite roast home.

BONANZA COFFEE ROASTERS: EIN BLICK HINTER DIE KULISSEN A PEEK BEHIND THE SCENES: BONANZA COFFEE'S TRANSPARENT ROASTERY

Das kleine Café auf der Oderberger Straße kennen wir schon lange. Schließlich ist Bonanza Coffee von Kiduk Reus und Yumi Choi maßgeblich an der Kaffee-Hysterie in der Stadt beteiligt. Da macht es Sinn, dass sie sich zu ihrem zehnjährigen Bestehen selbst das größte Geschenk gemacht haben: eine weitere Niederlassung mit eigener Rösterei in einem Kreuzberger Innenhof. Als ehemalige Tischlerei und Schlosserei beherbergt das denkmalgeschützte Gebäude heute einen kleinen Shop, eine Barista-Bar für die Kaffeekreationen und natürlich die Rösterei selbst. Das Raumkonzept stammt von Marick Baars: Eine getäfelte Glaswand teilt den hellen Raum und ermöglicht einen Blick hinter die Kulissen der Rösterei. Priorität hat die Kaffeebohne und ihre Beschaffung, basierend auf einem großen Netzwerk an Lieferanten aus Ländern wie Äthiopien, Kolumbien und Honduras. Die Bohnen werden in einer Probat UG22 von 1965 geröstet und mit einer abgestimmten Biomilch aus Brandenburg serviert – für den perfekten Flat White. Anyone who has lived in Berlin is sure to know the little café at Oderberger Straße: Bonanza Coffee by Kiduk Reus and Yumi Choi was partially responsible for igniting the third wave coffee hysteria here. It's understandable, therefore, that for their 10th anniversary, the guys from Bonanza treated themselves to a shiny present: a new roastery and coffee shop located in a Kreuzberg courtyard. With an interior designed by Marick Baars, the listed metalwork and carpentry building now hosts a small shop area, a counter for ordering drinks and, needless to say, the roastery. Their priority remains the coffee itself, as they work with beans from a network of suppliers in countries such as Ethiopia, Colombia, and Honduras. After carefully roasting their beans in a rebuilt 1965 Probat UG22, they serve it with specially sourced organic milk from Brandenburg to make that perfect flat white.

Text & Photos: Daniel Farò

Bonanza Roastery Café
Adalbertstraße 70, 10997 Berlin-Kreuzberg
Wed-Fri 9:00-17:00, Sat & Sun 10:00-17:00
bonanzacoffee.de

HIDDEN GEMS

VOM KREMATORIUM ZUM KUNST-GELÄNDE THE CREMATORIUM TURNED ART SPACE

Als Kurator verschiedener Institutionen wurde der gebürtige Kameruner und studierte Biotechnologe Bonaventure Ndikung schnell Teil der Berliner Kunstszene – doch der Eurozentrismus der Berliner machte ihm von Anfang an zu schaffen. Mit seinem eigenen, unabhängigen Projektraum Savvy Contemporary wollte er dazu betragen, den Blick zu schärfen. Sein Ansatz: westliche und nichtwestliche Diskurse, vor allem aus Afrika, Südamerika und Asien, sollten gefördert werden, ohne dabei naiven oder exotischen Klischeevorstellungen zu folgen. 2012 wurde sein Projekt dafür mit dem Preis des Berliner Senats für künstlerische Projekträume ausgezeichnet, und mittlerweile setzt er sein Vorhaben auch im Wedding um. Auf dem Gelände des silent green Kulturquartiers, einem ehemaligen Krematorium mit eindrucksvoller Trauerhalle, zeigt er Ausstellungen und Performances, organisiert Lesungen und realisiert gemeinsam mit dem Goethe-Institut Projekte. Cameroon-born Bonaventure Ndikung, who studied biotechnology, quickly became part of the Berlin art scene when he worked as a curator for some of the major institutions here. However, something bothered him from the start: the eurocentricity of the art world in Berlin. To help fill this gap, he opened his own independent project space. His approach was to try and encourage a dialogue without native or exotic stereotypes regarding Western and non-Western discourses, especially from Africa, South America, and Asia. In 2012, Savvy Contemporary was awarded the Berlin Senate Prize for Artistic Project Spaces. After establishing the project in Neukölln, Ndikung moved to Wedding, where he re-opened his space. On the grounds of the silent green Kulturquartier, a former crematorium with an impressive ceremonial hall, he now shows exhibitions and performances, organizes readings, and directs local projects in collaboration with the Goethe-Institut.

Text: Laura Storfner / Photos: Lee Edward, India Roper-Evans

Savvy Contemporary
c/o silent green, Plantagenstraße 31, 13347 Berlin-Wedding
Variable opening hours
savvy-contemporary.com

EXTRA TIP

Auf dem Areal des silent green Kulturquartiers kann man auch hervorragend frühstücken (im Moos Restaurant, Gerichtstraße 35) und noch mehr Kunst sehen (in der Galerie Patrick Ebensperger, Plantagenstraße 30). The silent green Kulturquartier also has excellent breakfast (Moos Restaurant, Gerichtstraße 35) and even more art to see (Galerie Patrick Ebensperger, Plantagenstraße 30).

„Brandenburg", prangt in Frakturschrift unter seinem Namen. Aber Christian Metzner setzt den Assoziationen, die dieser rustikale Schrifttyp mit sich bringt, etwas ganz anderes entgegen: Fragilität. Deutlich wird das beispielsweise am hauchdünnen Trinkglas seiner erfolgreichen „Rien"-Serie, die er für das Berliner Studio New Tendency entworfen hat. Studiert hat der 1983 geborene Produktgestalter an der FH Potsdam, seine Diplomarbeit schrieb er in Kooperation mit dem Label Bree. Philipp Bree holte ihn in Folge ins Designteam für die Taschenmarke PB0110. Ob Portemonnaies oder Porzellanobjekte, die perfekt proportionierten Objekte wirken fast ätherisch. Die Bodenhaftung verliert der – natürlich – gebürtige Brandenburger jedoch nie. Das mag an seinem Wohnort liegen: Er lebt in Potsdam, wo er sich gerne auf seine kleine Segeljolle flüchtet. Denn ab und an braucht er das Gefühl von Freiheit und etwas Himmel, um sich von den engen Rastern des Designs zu befreien. Eine kleine Alltagsflucht ist auch die Fahrt mit der Woltersdorfer Straßenbahn – natürlich Richtung Wasser, zum Flakensee. Gothic letters below his name read "Brandenburg." But Christian Metzner knows how to advance an alternative to the associations one might have with this rustic font: fragility. The best example is the ultrathin drinking glass series called "Rien" he created for product design studio New Tendency. Born in 1983, he trained as a product designer at the School for Applied Sciences Potsdam and completed his diploma in cooperation with the bag brand Bree. Afterwards, Philipp Bree added him to the design team behind his new line PB0110. Whether purses or porcelain, his perfectly-proportioned creations appear almost ethereal. However, he's quite down-to-earth and, of course, is a Brandenburg native. Maybe that's thanks to the location of his home base in Potsdam, where he enjoys taking his quaint little boat out on the water. Once in a while he simply needs the feeling of freedom and open sky to free himself from the design world's tight grid. Another little escape from everyday life is a trip with the Woltersdorf tram, of course in the direction of water, towards Flakensee. →

christian-metzner.com
@christianmetznerbrandenburg

CHRISTIAN METZNER EMPFIEHLT: DIE WOLTERSDORFER STRASSENBAHN
CHRISTIAN METZNER RECOMMENDS: WOLTERSDORF TRAM

Nur ein paar Schritte trennen den S-Bahnhof Rahnsdorf von einer Halte-stelle am Wald. Dort wartet auch schon eine kleine, schmale Straßenbahn aus den Sechzigerjahren. Gerade eingestiegen, fragt der Fahrer bereits in die Runde: „Tachchen, noch jemand ohne Fahrschein?" Zwei hölzerne Schiebetüren schließen mit lautem Gebimmel. Ein Ruck nach vorn, und die Tram rattert in Richtung Woltersdorf. Die Fahrt führt durch einen lichtdurchfluteten Wald bis hinunter an die Schleuse und den Flakensee. Am Ende der kurzen Strecke warten eine Handvoll gediegener Cafés, zwei schöne Badeseen, ein kleiner Aussichtsturm und ein Tretbootverleih. Es scheint, als wäre nicht nur die Bahn, die sich für immer auf der nicht enden wollenden Reise von Berlin nach Brandenburg befindet, ein Relikt aus einer anderen Zeit. Wie ein Uhrwerk fährt sie ihre Strecke ab und bietet allen, die es in die nahe Ferne und zurück zieht, einen freien Platz. The sign of the Rahnsdorf train station stands just a few steps outside the forest. The tiny, rickety, 60s-era street tram is there already, having been waiting for some time. The driver has already made his rounds: "Morning all, anyone without a ticket?" Two wooden doors close with a loud thunk. A jerk forward, and the train begins to rattle its way to Woltersdorf. The journey passes through a light-dappled forest, on to the Schleuse and then – the Flakensee. At the journey's end wait a handful of quaint cafés, two gorgeous lakes, a small observation tower, and a paddle-boat rental shop. The tram seems like a piece of a bygone era, forever on an endless path between Berlin and Brandenburg and back. Like clockwork, it makes its journey over and over, always offering an empty space to those who long for the nearby distant lands.

Text: Christian Metzner / Photos: Daniel Farò

Woltersdorfer Straßenbahn
Between Rahnsdorf Bahnhof and Woltersdorfer Schleuse
Journey times Mon-Fri 4:37-24:18, Sat & Sun 5:43-24:18

ERSTKLASSIGE KÜCHE IM ZWEITEN HINTERHOF FIRST CLASS DINING IN THE SECOND BACKYARD

EXTRA TIP

Vor dem Heimweg trinkt man um die Ecke im Mendy & Edeltraut, Weserstraße 43, noch einen Mint Julep. Rauchen darf man hier übrigens auch! Before going home, drink one more mint julep on the corner at Mendy & Edeltraut, at Weserstraße 43. A side note: Incidentally, you can smoke there, too!

Zufällig hätte ich das eins44 vermutlich nicht entdeckt – im Flüsseviertel Neuköllns, versteckt im zweiten Hinterhof, erwartet man ein Restaurant dieser Liga nicht unbedingt. Hat man den Weg aber gefunden, lässt es sich hier vorzüglich speisen, und zwar in einem sorgsam renovierten Loft mit Industrie-Charme und internationaler Cuisine. Bevor der Gaumen entzückt wird, ist das Auge begeistert: alles ist ansprechend angerichtet, in meinem Fall besonders die Vorspeise, eine Variation von Kürbis und Ziegenkäse. Die Gazpacho überrascht durch ihre intensive, scharfe Erdbeer-Süße. Auf den Punkt ist das argentinische Steak. „Perfekt", sagt mein Vater dazu. Und er muss es wissen, hat er doch schon in den besten Restaurants auf der ganzen Welt Steaks gegessen. Im Sommer unbedingt auf der Terrasse reservieren – es ist so angenehm ruhig in diesem Hinterhof. Without knowing it was there, I probably never would have stumbled upon this gem tucked in among the back courtyards of canal-side Neukölln. It's not the kind of place you'd expect to find a restaurant like eins44. However, dining in this carefully renovated loft, all its industrial charm kept intact, be prepared to be seduced by the surroundings before you even sample the international cuisine. A taste of my pumpkin and goat cheese starter quickly confirmed that the food lives up to the ambience. The strawberry-laced gazpacho was refreshingly spicy, sweet and cold, and the only thing my father could say about his Argentinian steak was a reverent "perfect," and he has probably tried some of the best steaks in the world. During summer, be sure to make a reservation for a table on the terrace – it's oh so quiet there.

Text: Nina Trippel / Photo: Daniel Farò

eins44
Elbestraße 28-29, 12045 Berlin-Neukölln
Lunch: Tue-Fri 12:30-14:30, Dinner: Tue-Sat 19:00-24:00
eins44.com

KLASSISCHE MUSIK & KULTUR IM PRIVATEN LOFT A LOFT FOR CLASSICAL MUSIC & CULTURE

Von außen ahnt man nichts von der Existenz des Studio Niculescu, der privaten Location für Musikliebhaber mitten in Kreuzberg. Der Raum strahlt eine warme, intime Atmosphäre aus und gehört dem Klavier-Virtuosen Cristian Niculescu (s. S. 238). Normalerweise hört man den Pianisten in der Berliner Philharmonie, in seinem eigenen Studio performt er in kleiner Runde – ein unvergessliches Erlebnis. Aber nicht nur er selbst sitzt am Flügel, der gebürtige Rumäne lädt auch immer wieder Gastmusiker in sein Loft ein – Freunde, junge Talente, Tango-Komponisten – und beschert so jedes Mal aufs Neue einen einzigartigen Abend.

Nestled in an unlikely location in the heart of Kreuzberg, Studio Niculescu is a sanctuary for lovers of music. This warm, intimate, and unpretentious space belongs to the piano maestro Cristian Niculescu (s. p. 238). Needless to say, watching him perform at the Berlin Philharmonie is fantastic, but imagine sitting in a small room with just him, his piano and a tiny crowd, experiencing some of his most unforgettable performances up close and personal. The Romanian native regularly invites other talented artists to join him, ranging from young musicians to internationally renowned tango composers, offering unique and magical evenings to the public.

Text: Rei Matsuoka / Photo: Anton Roland Laub

Studio Niculescu
Oranienstraße 163, 10969 Berlin-Kreuzberg
By appointment
studioniculescu.com

ALTE HALLE FÜR JUNGE KUNST
AN OLD FACTORY FOR YOUNG ART

„Was wollen Sie denn da?", fragt der Taxifahrer auf dem Weg zur Sexauer Gallery. Eigentlich hätte er die Adresse schon des Öfteren anfahren müssen, findet man in dieser wenig beachteten Ecke von Weißensee doch eine Galerie, deren Vernissagen zu den bestbesuchten der Stadt gehören. Jan-Philipp Sexauer, Rechtsanwalt, Kunstsammler und Kulturförderer, hat sich hier zwischen KFZ-Werkstätten und Boxstudios niedergelassen. In einer alten Industriehalle, wo im 20. Jahrhundert die „Erste Glimmer-Waren-Fabrik in Berlin" Kondensatoren herstellte, zeigt er junge Künstler: Jay Gard ließ zur Eröffnung selbstgebaute Sideboards schweben und Alexander Iskin stellte hier seine neue Kunstrichtung, den sogenannten Interrealismus, vor. Nach den Openings bleibt man oft noch ein wenig länger. Dicht gedrängt sitzt man im Sommer auf Bierbänken mit Blick auf den Beton-Swimmingpool und kann die Frage des Taxifahrers auf einmal ganz einfach beantworten: Wenn die Kunst so sehenswert und die Atmosphäre so ungezwungen ist, kommt man einfach gerne hierher. "What are you going there for?" asks the taxi driver on the way to Sexauer Gallery. In fact, this address in a neglected corner of Weißensee could have been on his route more frequently in the past couple of years, as this part of the city houses a gallery whose openings are popular not only because of the artists they feature. Jan-Philipp Sexauer, lawyer, art collector, and cultural patron, has settled himself here between the garages and boxing gyms. In an old industrial hall where electrical products were once manufactured by the "First Mica-Products-Factory in Berlin," Sexauer shows young artists. Jay Gard created hand-made hovering sideboards and Alexander Iskin presented his new art movement Interrealism. After the openings, people often stay a little longer. Crowded together on the beer benches in the summer with a view of the concrete swimming pool, it's easy to explain to the taxi driver that when the art is worth seeing and the atmosphere is so informal, it's easy to enjoy coming here.

Text: Laura Storfner / Photo: Marcus Schneider

Sexauer Gallery
Streustraße 90, 13086 Berlin-Weißensee
Tue-Sat 13:00-18:00
sexauer.eu

EXTRA TIP

Ein paar Schritte weiter, in der Gustav-Adolf-Straße 2, werden im ehemaligen Stummfilmkino Delphi heute zwar keine Filme mehr gezeigt, dafür aber Ausstellungen, Konzerte und Theaterstücke. A few steps away, at Gustav-Adolf-Straße 2, the former silent movie theater Delphi shows exhibitions, concerts, and plays.

DAS KLEINE VERSTECKTE KINO
THE LITTLE HIDDEN CINEMA

Il Kino, nennt sich das sympathische Lichtspielhaus, versteckt in einer kleinen Seitenstraße unweit des Maybachufers. Die Besitzer sind ein kosmopolitisches Trio: Daniel Wuschansky ist aus Deutschland, Carla Molino kommt aus Italien und Kristian S. Pålshaugen aus Norwegen. Gemeinsam haben sie sich einen Traum erfüllt und im Seitenflügel eines Altbaus einen gemütlichen Saal mit 52 Plätzen installiert. Gezeigt werden hier Dokumentar- und Spielfilme aus allen Teilen der Welt und abseits des Mainstreams – natürlich im Original mit deutschen oder englischen Untertiteln. Eine willkommene Abwechslung zur Yorck-Gruppe, die Kreuzberg und Neukölln dominiert. Was Il Kino zu meinem neuen Lieblingslichtspielhaus macht? Die Tatsache, dass man im angeschlossenen Café – im Gegensatz zum Gros der meisten Foyer-Bars – gerne verweilt. Vor oder nach dem Film. Hidden in a small side street off Maybachufer, there is a little cinema called Il Kino. Carla Molino, an Italian, Daniel Wuschansky, a German, and Kristian S. Pålshaugen, a Norwegian, created it to fulfill their dream of owning a cinema together. The small hall, which boasts 52 seats, was installed in the side wing of a residential building. This place is a welcome expansion from the Yorck-Gruppe, which dominates the cinema scene in Kreuzberg and Neukölln, showing documentaries and little-known films from all over the world in their original languages with German or English subtitles. Il Kino has already won my heart, thanks to its adjacent café-bar, which will keep you entertained before and after the film.

Text: Nina Trippel / Photos: Malene Korsgaard Lauritsen

Il Kino
Nansenstraße 22, 12047 Berlin-Neukölln
Mon-Fri from 15:30, Sat & Sun from 11:30
ilkino.de

EXTRA TIP

Klassiker und Arthouse-Filme zeigt auch das City Kino Wedding im Innenhof des Centre Français in der Müllerstraße 74: Die Innenarchitektur stammt aus den Sechzigerjahren. The City Kino Wedding shows classics as well as Arthouse films in the courtyard of the Centre Français at Müllerstraße 74: the interior design dates to the 60s.

IN 10 GÄNGEN DURCH DIE REGION
THE LOCAL REGION IN 10 COURSES

Im einsunternull findet der Betrieb nur mittags im ebenerdigen Lokal statt – am Abend befindet sich der Gastraum im Untergeschoss. Die Macher haben den Laden aufwendig renoviert, den Kellerboden ausgehoben und einen Garten im Atrium angelegt. Im Untergeschoss, das man nun über einen Fahrstuhl erreicht, widmet sich das Küchenteam in unaufgeregter Atmosphäre voll und ganz den hochwertigen Zutaten; ein halbes Jahr dauerte allein die Suche nach den perfekten Haselnüssen. Der Spargel wird wie Sauerkraut eingemacht, damit er butterzart ist. Los geht es ab einem Menü mit sechs Gängen; wer mehr will, bestellt bis zu zehn. Und da Betreiber Ivo Ebert Sommelier ist, ist die passende Weinbegleitung für mich obligatorisch. The more casual upper floor of einsunternull is open for lunch only, while dinner takes place in the basement. If the word basement is off-putting, don't worry – the property was renovated with a huge amount of care and attention, with the subterranean floor dug out to create a high ceiling and an adjoining garden atrium. The lower dining area has a calm and peaceful atmosphere, which intensifies as you descend in the elevator and take a seat. Every ingredient listed on the menu has been scrutinized, tested, and locally sourced – it took them half a year to find the perfect hazelnuts, and the asparagus is pickled and preserved like sauerkraut, leaving it as soft and tender as butter. Start off with the six-course menu; if you want more, you can order up to ten. Owner Ivo Ebert is also a sommelier, so the suggested paired wine list is a must for me.

Text & Photos: Sven Hausherr

einsunternull
Hannoversche Straße 1, 10115 Berlin-Mitte
Lunch: Tue-Sat 12:00-14:00, Dinner: Mon-Sat 19:00-22:30
einsunternull.com

EXTRA TIP

Wer das Gängemenü vom einsunternull wieder
abtrainieren will, tanzt in der Bravo Bar, Torstraße
230, durch die Nacht. If you want to work off the
food from einsunternull, dance all night in Bravo Bar
at Torstraße 230.

Sucht man nach Angie Ziehmann – etwa in einem vollen Café –, kann man sich von ihrem herzlichen Lachen leiten lassen. Angie steckt voller positiver Energie, und das wirkt auch auf ihre Gesprächspartner ansteckend. Langweilig wird es aber auch auf inhaltlicher Ebene nie, arbeitet Angie doch mindestens an zwei Projekten gleichzeitig und hat stets viel zu erzählen. Nach ihrem Abschluss in Architektur an der Hochschule in Kiel und einem Master in Performance Design & Scenography vom Central Saint Martins College of Art und Design in London spezialisierte sie sich auf die Gestaltung von Innenräumen. Eine zentrale Farbe steht bei ihren im Ganzen betrachtet eher minimalistischen Konzepten meistens im Fokus – und auch in ihrem Namen: Pink Action, heißt ihr Design-Studio. Zuletzt hat sie dem Kreuzberger Diner Mister T, Möckernstraße 91, einen rosafarbenen Touch verpasst und auch das Interieur vom Wallyard Hostel (s. S. 125) sowie vom Restaurant Klub Kitchen (s. S. 156) erdacht. Das Bootshaus Köpenick gehört noch nicht dazu – aber wer weiß … Angie hat diese charmante Location fest im Blick. If you're looking for Angie Ziehmann – perhaps in a crowded café – you can just follow the sound of her hearty laugh. Angie is full of positive energy that is contagious to anyone she speaks to. And the content of what she has to say is never boring – she's always working on at least two projects and always has lots to say about them. After graduating with a degree in architecture in Kiel and a Master in Performance Design & Scenography from Central Saint Martins College of Art and Design in London, she specialized in interior design. Her minimalistic design concept centers on a single color – just like the name of her design studio, Pink Action. Most recently, she's designed the Kreuzberger diner Mister T, Möckernstraße 91, giving it a bold rosy touch, as well as the interior of the Wallyard Hostel (s. p. 125) and the restaurant Klub Kitchen (s. p. 156). The Boothaus Köpenick isn't in her portfolio yet – but who knows … Angie has her eye on this charming location as well. →

pinkaction.co.uk
@pinkaction

ANGIE ZIEHMANN EMPFIEHLT: BOOTSBAU KÖPENICK ANGIE ZIEHMANN RECOMMENDS: BOOTSBAU KÖPENICK

Als ich im Köpenicker Wassersportzentrum ein Boot ausleihen wollte, bin ich auf dieses verlassene Gebäude gestoßen – ein wahrer Schatz. Ich liebe Orte, die eine Geschichte erzählen: abgeplatzte Wandfarbe, Holz, das mit der Zeit silbrig geworden ist, zurückgelassene Möbel … Wer solche Lost Places genauso inspirierend findet wie ich, der sollte sich dringend den leerstehenden Bootsbau Köpenick ansehen, dessen riesige Halle einen bereits von außen magisch anzieht, wobei der Wahnsinnsblick auf die anliegenden Häuser, die zur Versorgung und als Werkstätten dienten, fast noch mehr beeindruckt. Das Dach der monumentalen Halle besteht aus einem leichten Holzgerüst und entfaltet, nach oben strebend, seine majestätische Wirkung. Heute wuchern Pflanzen in das Gebäude hinein und die Wände sind eingebrochen, sodass die Stockwerke sichtbar werden. Beeindruckende Architektur, von der sich Bootsbaugeschichte ablesen lässt – und noch viel mehr. Once I wanted to rent a boat in the Köpenick water sports center and came across this house – a true gem. I love places that have traces of what they once were. Paint peeling off the walls, wood that's gone silver over time, and pieces of furniture that tell a story. If you find such places as inspiring as I do, take a closer look at the empty Bootsbau Köpenick. As you step inside, you almost feel sucked in by the giant hall, offering a stunning view of the adjoining houses that once acted as service stations and workshops. The roof was timbered from fine wood and has a majestic feel. Nowadays plants are finding their way into the house and the walls are coming down, so you see the different levels. It's architecture in which you can read the history of this shiphouse – and so much more.

Text: Angie Ziehmann / Photos: Daniel Farò

Bootsbau Köpenick
Müggelseedamm 70 (Wassersportzentrum Berlin)
12587 Berlin-Friedrichshagen

DAS KLEINOD FÜR KAFFEEFANS
A COFFEE FRIEND'S PARADISE

Als in Berlin die Third Wave-Bewegung ausbrach, bin auch ich zum Kaffee-Snob mutiert. Bei Father Carpenter war es der Cappuccino, der mich von Anfang an umgehauen hat: cremig, süß, frisch – eine runde Sache. Karl-Heinz Müller und Krésten Thøgersen, der jede Menge Erfahrung im Bereich der Kaffeeherstellung mitbringt, servieren ihn in einem wunderschönen Innenhof am Hackeschen Markt. Hier kommen nur selbst geröstete Bohnen in die Maschine: Verarbeitet werden sie bei den Fjord Coffee Roasters – einer Rösterei, die Father Carpenter gemeinsam mit dem Silo Coffee betreibt. Das Café bietet auch leckere Snacks an. Mein Favorit: Eggs Benedict mit geschmorter Schweineschulter. Kein Zweifel also, dass diese versteckte Kaffee-Oase im touristischen Zentrum von Mitte ein beliebter Treffpunkt geworden ist. I've become a bit of a coffee snob living in Berlin through its third wave of coffee. When I first made it to Father Carpenter, I was blown away by their cappuccino. It was simply perfect: creamy, sweet, clean, and round. The café opened in January 2015 in the beautiful courtyard of an old building in Hackescher Markt. Krésten Thøgersen, who has over a decade of experience in making coffee, made his way to Berlin to spread the love and teamed up with Karl-Heinz Müller to open their first coffee shop here. Their high quality beans are roasted at their own Fjord Coffee Roasters, a roastery collaboratively run with Silo Coffee. The café offers delicious snacks too: my favorite is the chipotle-braised pork shoulder with eggs Benedict. Needless to say, this hidden coffee haven in the center of touristy Mitte has become a destination in its own right.

Text: Rei Matsuoka / Photos: Daniel Farò

Father Carpenter Coffee Brewers
Münzstraße 21, 1st backyard, 10178 Berlin-Mitte
Mon-Fri 9:00-18:00, Sat 10:00-18:00
fathercarpenter.com

ERÖFFNUNG WIRD IN BERLIN JEDEN TAG GEFEIERT. ZEITGLEICH VERSCHWINDET LEISE ETWAS. ANDERES ÜBERDAUERT DIE ZEIT. HIERHER KEHREN WIR IMMER WIEDER ZURÜCK. BERLIN SEES NEW PLACES OPENING ON A DAILY BASIS WHILE OTHERS BITE THE DUST. SOME LOCATIONS STAND THE TEST OF TIME. HERE ARE THE PLACES WE KEEP COMING BACK TO.

TROTZT DEM WANDEL: DAS BELLMAN
AMIDST CHANGE, BELLMAN REMAINS

In einer im steten Wandel begriffenen Stadt ist es manchmal schön, an
Orte zurückzukehren, wo alles wie immer ist. Das Bellman ist ein
solcher. Die Musik spielt, die Kerzen brennen. Man sitzt an alten Holztischen, die hier schon standen, bevor das in Berlin en vogue war.
Vielleicht trinkt man ein Bier oder ein Glas Rotwein. Man bestellt einen
Snack dazu oder auch nicht – das alles ist im Einzelnen unwesentlich.
Ins Bellman geht man für die Summe der Teile. Um die Köpfe zusammen-
zustecken mit Menschen, die eben auch die Zeit überdauern, guten
Freunden also. Wenn man dann gemeinsam aus der Bar stolpert und sich
alle in unterschiedliche Richtungen verstreuen, fühlt man sich
meistens ein bisschen beseelt. Was könnte man mehr von einer Bar an
einer unscheinbaren Kreuzberger Straßenecke erwarten? In a city
of constant change, sometimes it's nice to go back to a place that
remains the same, and Bellman is just such a place. The music
plays, the candles flicker. You sit at the wooden tables, which have
stood here long before they were en vogue in Berlin. Maybe you
drink a beer or a glass of red wine, or perhaps order a snack to go
with your drink, or don't – but these small details are trivial.
You go to Bellman for the sum of these things. You put your head together
with old friends who have stood the test of time. When you finally
stumble out of the bar together and meander in different directions
towards home, you feel animated and satisfied. What more could you
ask for from a bar on a nondescript Kreuzberg street corner?

Text: Nina Trippel / Photos: Daniel Farò

Bellman Bar
Reichenberger Straße 103, 10999 Berlin-Kreuzberg
Daily 18:00-4:00

WO MARLENE DIETRICH IHREN DUFT FAND WHERE MARLENE DIETRICH FOUND HER SCENT

Selten hat mich ein Geschäft so verzaubert wie Harry Lehmann, wo seit 1926 Parfum nach Gewicht verkauft wird. Wenn man auf der Kantstraße stadtauswärts fährt, kommt es einem fast vor, als verließe man Berlin, aber nein … auf der linken Seite, etwas versteckt, taucht auf einmal dieser besondere Laden mit seiner ausgefallenen Schaufensterdekoration aus getrockneten Blumen auf. Meinen persönlichen Lieblingsduft habe ich hier schnell gefunden: Châtelaine entspricht genau meinem Geschmack – schwer, süß, feminin und kraftvoll. Wenn ich ein Mann wäre, würde ich den dezenten Duft Vamos mit seiner holzigen Note wählen, oder den sportlicheren Duft Valeria. Über 50 Duftnoten stehen zur Auswahl, wobei man die Parfums auch individuell zusammenstellen kann, sodass eine ganz persönliche Komposition entsteht. **Das wusste bereits Marlene Dietrich, die sich hier ihr Parfum kreieren ließ!** Rarely has a shop charmed me as much as Harry Lehmann Parfums nach Gewicht (Perfume by Weight), opened in 1926. When you head down Kantstraße away from the city center, it almost feels like you're leaving Berlin until hidden on the left, a perfume store suddenly emerges, complete with an outrageous dried-flower décor. I quickly found my personal favorite scent. It's called Châtelaine and corresponds exactly to my tastes: heavy, sweet, feminine, and powerful. If I were a man, I'd opt for Vamos, an understated scent with a slightly woody note, or, for something more sporty, Valeria. There are more than 50 fragrances to choose from, and you can even mix and match to create your own unique concoction. Marlene Dietrich certainly appreciated that – she had her perfumes made here back in the day!

Text: Brigitta Horvat / Photos: Daniel Farò

Harry Lehmann
Kantstraße 106, 10627 Berlin-Charlottenburg
Mon-Fri 9:00-18:30, Sat 9:00-14:00
parfum-individual.de

APFELSTRUDEL FÜR DIE AVANTGARDE
APPLE STRUDEL FOR THE AVANTGARDE

Vom Frühstück, serviert auf Etageren, über österreichische Klassiker wie Tafelspitz zum Mittag bis hin zu den süßen Spezereien zum Kaffee: im Einstein Stammhaus lässt es sich den ganzen Tag fürstlich speisen. In der Nacht glänzt die Bar Lebensstern im oberen Stockwerk der Villa und nimmt die Besucher mit in die Zwanzigerjahre. Für das besondere Ambiente sorgt neben dem imposanten Haus vor allem dessen bewegte Geschichte: Die 1878 im Stil der Neorenaissance erbaute Villa war in den goldenen Zwanzigern ein illegales Casino, bevor es zehn Jahre später zur SS-Behörde umfunktioniert wurde. 1978 kreierte die Exil-Österreicherin Uschi Bachauer in der Küche des Einsteins schließlich die „perfekte Symbiose aus Apfelstrudel und Avantgarde". Kein Zufall, dass Quentin Tarantino seinen Schauspieler Christoph Waltz in „Inglourious Basterds" hier Kaffee trinken ließ. Heute geben sich Künstler, Stammgäste und neugierige Touristen die Klinke in die Hand. From breakfast, served on picturesque platters, to Austrian classics like Tafelspitz for lunch or dinner, and of course coffee and cake, you can dine like royalty at Einstein Stammhaus all day. At night, the Lebensstern Bar shines from the upper floor of the villa, taking guests back to the 20s. The colorful history of the impressive neo-Renaissance style villa creates a special ambiance: built in 1878, it was an illegal casino in the golden twenties and an SS agency in the 30s. In 1979, Austrian exile Uschi Bachauer created "the perfect mixture of apple strudel and avant-garde." It is no coincidence that Christoph Waltz drank coffee here in Tarantino's "Inglourious Basterds." Today, the Einstein is the favorite haunt of artists, regulars, and curious tourists.

Text: Ferdinand Hamsch / Photos: Daniel Faró

Café Einstein Stammhaus
Kurfürstenstraße 58, 10785 Berlin-Tiergarten
Daily 8:00-24:00
cafeeinstein.com

CLASSICS

Friedrichshain, Mitte, Schöneberg: Vladimir Karaleev hat schon in vielen Ecken der Stadt gewohnt. Am besten mit einer Verkehrsader vor der Tür, denn dafür hat der Modedesigner eine Schwäche. „Weil sie der Inbegriff von Großstadt ist" – und damit der Hauptgrund, warum es den Bulgaren 2001 zum Studium nach Berlin zog. Mal abgesehen von der Partyszene natürlich! Die damaligen Clubs der Stunde hießen WMF und Rio – und Vladimir zog von Bar zu Bar. „In Berlin war alles vage, positiv und grenzenlos. Jeder hat etwas Kreatives auf die Beine gestellt." Genau wie er selbst, der 2010 sein eigenes Modelabel gründete. Ein Stück jenes berüchtigten Berlins findet sich auch in seinen Kollektionen: der Raum zum Experimentieren in dekonstruierten Formen und das Unfertige an offenen Säumen, was zu seinen Markenzeichen wurde. Die hiesige Modeszene hat Vladimir mit seinem prägnanten Stil maßgeblich mitgeprägt; heute gehört er schon zu den alten Hasen. Da passt es irgendwie, dass das Rave-Kid der Nullerjahre, ohnehin von Haus aus ein bedächtiger Typ, ruhiger geworden ist und freie Nachmittage gerne im Teehaus im Tiergarten verbringt. Friedrichshain, Mitte, Schöneberg: Vladimir Karaleev has already lived in most corners of this city. Ideally, he likes to live on a busy street, because that's the fashion designer's weakness. "It's the epitome of the big city," he says, and it's what attracted the Bulgarian to Berlin back in 2001, when he moved here for his studies. Aside from the party scene, of course! The clubs of the moment at that time were WMF and Rio – and Vladimir moved from one bar to the next. "In Berlin everything was vague, positive, and borderless. Everyone had something creative going on." He's no different: in 2010 he founded his own fashion label. A piece of the infamous Berlin of his early years can be found in his collections today: the space to experiment with deconstructed shapes and the unfinished look of open hems have become his trademark. The pragmatic style of the local fashion scene has been a fundamental influence in Vladimir's work, although today he is an old hand himself. It seems somehow appropriate that the rave kid from the noughties, an innately thoughtful type anyway, has mellowed and now happily spends free afternoons in the Tiergarten's Teehaus. →

vladimirkaraleev.com
@vladimirkaraleev

VLADIMIR KARALEEV EMPFIEHLT: DAS TEEHAUS IM ENGLISCHEN GARTEN VLADIMIR KARALEEV RECOMMENDS: THE TEAHOUSE IN THE ENGLISH GARDEN

Ein Teehaus inmitten des Englischen Gartens, welcher am nordwestlichen Rand des Großen Tiergartens liegt. Schon die Lage verrät: Hier handelt es sich um einen verborgenen Ort, den es zu entdecken gilt. Umso mehr, wenn bereits der Name Tee verspricht – den man in der von Kaffee geprägten Stadt bisweilen vermisst. Wie so oft in Berlin bietet das Haus aber auch ein Stück Geschichte: Seit Mai 1952 steht das Anwesen, das auf Betreiben des damaligen Stadtkommandanten der britischen Besatzungszone realisiert wurde, für Besucher offen. Um die im Tiergarten augenfälligen Kriegsfolgen – von ehemals 200.000 Bäumen standen noch etwa 700 Exemplare – durch eine Geste der Freundschaft zu mildern, hatten die Briten mehr als 5000 Gehölze gespendet. Auf den Grundmauern des Wohnhauses von Schauspieler Gustaf Gründgens errichtet, bietet das Teehaus heute genau das, was man sich von einem Ausflug in Berlin erwartet: die richtige Mischung aus Tradition und Kuriosität. In the middle of the Englischer Garten, which in turn is located on the northwestern edge of the Tiergarten, sits a tea house. The location itself indicates that this is a secret place waiting to be discovered. As the name already implies, it offers a fine selection of teas, which you might miss sometimes in a coffee-centered city like Berlin nowadays. As with many other Berlin landmarks, there's also history alive in the Teehaus: since May 1952 the guest house and the garden have been open to the public thanks to the initiative of the Commandant of the British occupation zone. Again like so much else in Berlin, the Tiergarten did not escape the effects of the war – only 700 of the 200,000 trees that covered the park survived. As a gesture of friendship, the British donated more than 5000 trees. Built on the foundations of actor Gustaf Gründgens' home, the Teehaus offers exactly what you'd expect from a day trip in Berlin: a mixture of tradition and curiosity.

Text: Vladimir Karaleev / Photos: Daniel Farò

Teehaus im Englischen Garten
Altonaer Straße 2, 10557 Berlin-Tiergarten
Mon-Fri from 12:00, Sat & Sun from 10:00
teehaus-tiergarten.com

CAPONATA IM KERZENSCHEIN
CANDLELIGHT & CAPONATA

Der Goldene Hahn ist der Kreuzberg-Klassiker schlechthin,
wenn es um einfache, aber köstliche italienische Küche
geht. Die Karte – stilecht auf einer schwarzen Kreidetafel,
die der Kellner an den Tisch bringt - wechselt täglich.
Die Caponata Siciliana: einfach großartig, sie gehört zur
Spezialität des Hauses. Bei unserem Besuch erspähen wir
eine ältere italienische Nonna in der Küche, die Pasta und
Brot, natürlich hausgemacht, anrichtet – ein Traum! Das
Interieur schwankt zwischen einfach und anheimelnd bis hin
zu leicht abgewrackt, aber das Ambiente ist mit Kerzenschein, rot-karierten Tischdecken und Backsteinwänden
unschlagbar charmant! This Kreuzberg classic is any
local's go-to for simple but delicious Italian cuisine.
The seasonal menu, scrawled on a blackboard that the
waiter rings to the table, changes daily. The Caponata
Siciliana: simply magnificent, the house specialty. During
our visit we spotted an old Italian nonna in the kitchen,
dishing out pasta and bread, made from scratch, of course –
a dream come true. The interior ranges from simple and quaint
to somewhat cracked, but the ambience, candlelight, red-
checked tablecloth, and brick walls included, is charming!

Text: Nella Beljan / Photos: Daniel Faró

Der Goldene Hahn
Pücklerstraße 20, 10997 Berlin-Kreuzberg
Daily from 19:00
goldenerhahn.de

EXTRA TIP

Wer stattdessen Lust auf jamaikanische Küche hat,
schaut um die Ecke bei Rosa Caleta in der
Muskauer Straße 9 vorbei und bestellt das Jerk
Chicken. If you're more in the mood for Jamaican
cuisine, look around the corner for Rosa Caleta in
Muskauer Straße 9 and order the jerk chicken.

SOMMERNACHTSTRÄUME BEGINNEN HIER ... WHERE A MIDSUMMER NIGHT'S DREAM BEGINS ...

Lichterketten über dem Eingangsbereich leuchten den Weg zu zwei
kleinen, hölzernen Kassenhäuschen. Sobald man sein Ticket
gekauft hat, führt der Weg unter dichten Bäumen zu einer Tribüne,
die an ein Amphitheater erinnert. Seit 1954 gehört das ehemalige
Sommertheater neben einem Streichelzoo und einer Minigolfanlage
zum Volkspark Hasenheide, der Mitte der Zwanzigerjahre eröffnet
wurde. Ursprünglich für Theateraufführungen und Konzerte genutzt,
ist es seit den Achtzigern ein Freiluftkino. Und weil in dem
kleinen, noch originalen Vorführkasten nur Platz für einen Projektor
ohne Tellersystem ist, gibt es bei jeder Vorführung eine 10-
minütige Pause. Während man sich auf den zweiten Teil des Films
freut, bietet eine kleine Snackbar Ablenkung. Arthaus-Produkti-
onen werden hier genauso gezeigt wie oscarprämierte Blockbuster.

Lights hang over the entrance and illuminate the path to two
small wooden ticket booths. Once you've bought your ticket, go
through the metal gate, guarded by dense trees, and emerge into
an amphitheater with a huge screen. Since 1945, the former summer
theater has stood next to a petting zoo and a mini-golf course
in the Volkspark Hasenheide in Neukölln, which opened in the mid-
twenties. While originally used for theatrical performances
and concerts, the amphitheater became an open-air cinema in
the 80s. As there is only room for a projector without a teller
system, a 10-minute break in each show means that you can visit
the small snack bar to pass the time while you look forward to
the second half of the film. Arthaus productions rub elbows with
Oscar winning blockbusters in the diverse selection of films.

Text: Stephanie Johne / Photos: Daniel Farò

Freiluftkino Hasenheide
At Volkspark Hasenheide, 10967 Berlin-Neukölln
May-September, check online for program and film times
freiluftkino-hasenheide.de

DER GARTEN VON VERSAILLES, MITTEN IN NEUKÖLLN A TOUCH OF VERSAILLES IN NEUKÖLLN

2016 wurde der Körnerpark 100 Jahre alt – im letzten Jahrhundert hat er Generationen von Berlinern beim Spazierengehen, Laufen, Picknicken, Entspannen und Wandern erlebt. Der Park gleicht einem großen, prunkvollen Garten mit Blumenareal, Brunnen und Orangerie, in der sich die Galerie am Körnerpark befindet. Eine Oase inmitten des hektischen Neuköllns! In 2016, the Körnerpark turned 100 years old – it has seen generations of Berliners walking, running, picnicking, relaxing, and wandering through its grounds over the last century. The park resembles a large, palatial garden with a sprawling flower garden, fountains, and an orangery in which the Galerie am Körnerpark resides. It's an oasis in the midst of hectic Neukölln.

Text: Antonia Harris / Photos: Daniel Faró

Körnerpark
Schierker Straße 8, 12051 Berlin-Neukölln

BEGEGNUNGEN MIT MEISTER-
WERKEN DES SURREALISMUS
INTIMATE ENCOUNTERS WITH
SURREALIST MASTERS

Seit Sommer 2008 der Öffentlichkeit zugänglich, zeigt die Sammlung Scharf-Gerstenberg eine Vielzahl beeindruckender Kunstwerke, darunter Gemälde Alter und Neuer Meister wie Francisco de Goya, Max Ernst und René Magritte. Im Westen Berlins gelegen, mit Blick auf das eindrucksvolle Anwesen Schloss Charlottenburg, präsentiert das Museum 250 Werke auf drei Etagen, darunter Gemälde, Skulpturen und Arbeiten auf Papier. Zusätzlich zählt eine umfangreiche Sammlung klassischer Filme von Luis Buñuel, Salvador Dalí und zeitgenössischen Surrealisten zum Programm. Auf der gegenüberliegenden Straßenseite präsentiert das Museum Berggruen Meisterwerke der klassischen Moderne, die dank einer kombinierten Eintrittskarte ebenfalls besichtigt werden können. Opened to the public in summer 2008, the Sammlung Scharf-Gerstenberg features an impressive collection of art, including eminent works from old and recent masters such as Francisco de Goya, Max Ernst, and René Magritte. Located in West Berlin's Charlottenburg neighborhood, opposite the Charlottenburg Palace, the museum holds 250 works ranging from paintings to sculptures and works on paper across three floors. In addition to this, the gallery offers a film program of classical movies by Luis Buñuel, Salvador Dalí, and contemporary Surrealist artists. Opposite the Sammlung Scharf-Gerstenberg, the Berggruen Museum presents classical modernist masterpieces, which can be viewed with the combined entrance ticket.

Text: Victoria Pease / Photos: Nina Straßgütl, David von Becker

Sammlung Scharf-Gerstenberg
Schloßstraße 70, 14059 Berlin-Charlottenburg
Tue-Fri 10:00-18:00, Sat & Sun 11:00-18:00

EXTRA TIP

Fantastische Vintage-Designmöbel gibt es fünf Gehminuten entfernt bei Spezialschön in der Nehringstraße 34. Fantastic vintage-design furniture is just a 5-minute walk away at Spezialschön at Nehringstraße 34.

AUF EIN BIER MIT JOSEPH ROTH
FOR A BEER WITH JOSEPH ROTH

Joseph Roth wurde mit Berlin nie richtig warm. 1920 zog der Journalist und Schriftsteller von Galizien über Wien in die Potsdamer Straße. Zwei Romane und unzählige Miniaturen zum Berliner Alltag, die heute noch genauso in der Zeitung stehen könnten, entstanden während dieser Zeit – Nachtschwärmer, Bohemiens und leichte Mädchen bevölkerten seine Seiten. Knapp 100 Jahre später scheinen sich Roths Helden in einem Lokal wiederzutreffen, das seinen Namen trägt. Unter der Markise der Joseph Roth Diele beobachtet man bei einem Kölsch das Stammpublikum aus Galeristen, Alkoholikern, Obstverkäufern und Modedesignern. Innen sitzt man auf Thonet-Stühlen, liest an Tischen mit rot-weiß-karierten Decken Zeitung oder Roths Zitate, die die Wände zieren. Während man Rinderroulade oder hausgemachte Spätzle bestellt, meint man fast, Roth selbst im nächsten Moment zur Tür hereinkommen zu sehen. Stattdessen kommt einem nur ein Satz in den Sinn, den er 1930 notierte: „Berlin ist eine junge, unglückliche und zukünftige Stadt." Viel scheint sich bis heute nicht geändert zu haben. Joseph Roth never really warmed up to Berlin. In 1920, the journalist and author moved from Galicia to Vienna and from there to Potsdamer Straße. Two novels and countless feuilletons – which seem just as current today as they did a century ago – emerged during this time, with nighthawks, bohemians, and harlots populating the pages. Nearly 100 years later, Roth's heroes seem to meet in a restaurant that bears his name: the Joseph Roth Diele. Sitting under the awning, Kölsch beer in hand, you can watch as gallery owners, alcoholics, fruit vendors, and fashion designers drift in and out. Inside, Roth's quotes adorn the walls and you will find yourself reading the newspaper in a Thonet chair at a table with a red-and-white-checkered tablecloth. Even as you order beef roulade or homemade spätzle you feel as if Roth himself may stroll through the door. Instead, only one of Roth's quotes, written in 1930, jumps out at you: "Berlin is a young and unhappy city-in-waiting." Today, not much seems to have changed.

Text: Laura Storfner / Photo: Steffen Roth

Joseph Roth Diele
Potsdamer Straße 75, 10785 Berlin-Tiergarten
Mon-Fri 10:00-24:00
joseph-roth-diele.de

CLASSICS

EXTRA TIP

Nach dem Gallery-Hopping von Blain|Southern zur Galerie Thomas Fischer geht man auf ein Glas Crémant in die Weinbar Les Climats in der Pohlstraße 75. After gallery hopping from Blain|Southern to Galerie Thomas Fischer, go for a glass of crémant in the Les Climats wine bar at Pohlstraße 75.

EXTRA TIP

Hervorragendes Dinner bekommt man vorher bei Ojo de Agua in der Ludwigkirchstraße 10A, einem Restaurant des Aktionskünstlers und Yello-Musikers Dieter Meier. Oh Yeah! Beforehand, head to Ludwigkirchstraße 10A for a delicious meal at Ojo de Agua, the restaurant by action artist and Yello-musician Dieter Meier. Oh Yeah!

CLASSICS

DIE WESTBERLINER BÜHNE FÜR THEATER, DISCO & ZEITGEIST THE WESTERN STAGE FOR THEATER, DISCO & ZEITGEIST

Ich bin - man kann das so sagen - Stammgast in der Schaubühne und habe somit fast das ganze Programm der letzten 10 Jahre gesehen. Und ich liebe es! Intelligent, sprachlich stark, intensiv, laut und mit Humor, ist es einfach am Puls der Zeit. Eines meiner ersten Stücke, das mir bis heute in Erinnerung geblieben ist und mich nachhaltig beeindruckt hat, war „Unter Eis" von Falk Richter. Rund 90 Minuten klirrende Kälte. Großartig. Nicht zuletzt durch die Auftritte von Lars Eidinger, der meinen Blick auf das Theater mit dem „Sommernachtstraum" komplett verändert hat: Er belehrte mich eines Besseren, indem er mir zeigte, dass Theater auch berühren kann. Umso schöner, im Anschluss seiner Auftritte seine Musikwahl bei der Partyreihe Autistic Disco zu hören, wo man zu unvergessenen Songs aus Jugendzeiten das Foyer der Schaubühne als Tanzfläche nutzt. Einfach der perfekte Abend in diesem Haus: Bildung, Genuss und Amüsement! I am a regular at Schaubühne, so I've seen nearly the entire program over the past 10 years. I love it. It's intelligent, linguistically clever, intense, loud, and humorous, sharply tapping into the pulse of our modern times. To this day, I still remember one of my first experiences there: "Unter Eis" by Falk Richter. It really got under my skin, with 90 minutes of magnificent, bone-chilling cold. The appearance of Lars Eidinger completely washed away everything I thought I knew about theater. His "A Midsummer Night's Dream" taught me that theater can be a moving experience. Just as good, if not better, were the musical choices following the performance - the party Autistic Disco used the foyer of the theater as a dance floor for the unforgettable songs of youth. Simply the perfect evening: educational and fun!

Text: Milena Kalojanov / Photos: Thomas Aurin, Arno Declair

Schaubühne am Lehniner Platz
Kurfürstendamm 153, 10709 Berlin-Charlottenburg
Mon-Sat 11:00-18:30, Sun & holidays from 15:00
schaubuehne.de

MAUERPARK, PRENZLAUER BERG

BÄRENQUELL BRAUEREI, TREPTOW-KÖPENICK

HUMBOLDTHAIN, WEDDING

ADMIRALBRÜCKE, KREUZBERG

POSTBAHNHOF / FRANKFURTER TOR, FRIEDRICHSHAIN

TREPTOWER PARK, ALT-TREPTOW

NEW CLASSICS

FÜR ALTBERLINER SIND
SIE JUNGE HÜPFER. FÜR
ZUGEZOGENE SCHON
FESTE INSTITUTIONEN DER
STADTLANDSCHAFT – DIE
KLASSIKER VON MORGEN.
THEY MAY NOT HAVE THE
PEDIGREE OF BERLIN'S MANY
HISTORIC INSTITUTIONS,
BUT THESE NEW PLACES
ARE SIMPLY ICONIC. TRUST
US, THESE ARE THE FUTURE
CLASSICS OF BERLIN.

LUXUS FÜR ALLE LEBENSLAGEN
LUXURY FOR ALL LIFE'S NEEDS

Wenn man The Store im Soho House betritt, fällt als erstes auf, wie unglaublich schön hier alles ist: Marmor trifft auf raue Betonsäulen, gepolsterte Sofas auf eine Fülle von Pflanzen. Unter dem kritischen Blick von Designerin Alex Eagle wurde jede Tischplatte, jede Kleiderstange und jede noch so versteckte Ecke des Raums in eine perfekt arrangierte Warenwelt verwandelt. Trotz aller Makellosigkeit ist es ihr gelungen, einen Raum zu kreieren, in dem man sich wohlfühlt. Der Übergang zwischen den verschiedenen Angeboten des Stores ist spielerisch: Mode, Kosmetik, Design, Literatur, Möbel, Musik und Essen aus der hauseigenen Store Kitchen passen einfach zusammen. Während der Resident-DJ Platten auflegt, nimmt man selbst an einem der vielen Tische Platz, bestellt einen frisch gepressten Saft, blättert durch die Auswahl an Büchern und Zeitschriften oder stöbert durch die Kollektionen internationaler Designer wie Balenciaga und Comme des Garçons. So könnte man den ganzen Tag verbringen. The first thing you notice when you enter The Store at Soho House is the overwhelming beauty of the place. Marble surfaces collide with stark concrete pillars, while enormous upholstered sofas and an abundance of plant life lend a softer touch. Under the discerning eye of creative director Alex Eagle, every tabletop, every clothing rail, every hidden corner is a perfectly curated showcase of items. And yet despite the flawless composition, this is a space in which to feel at ease. Visitors seamlessly transition between The Store's many offerings: fashion, beauty, design, literature, furniture, music, and food, thanks to the in-house restaurant, The Store Kitchen. As the resident DJ spins a musical backdrop, take a seat at one of the many tables to enjoy a freshly pressed juice, flick through the wonderful assortment of books and magazines, or explore the capsule collections of international and local fashion designers. Expect to find labels from the likes of Balenciaga, Vetements and Comme des Garçons among others. Be warned! You could easily lose a day to this place.

Text: Chloë Galea / Photos: Daniel Farò

The Store x Soho House Berlin
Torstraße 1, 10119 Berlin-Mitte
Mon–Sat 10:00–19:00
thestore-berlin.com

NEW CLASSICS

EXTRA TIP

Wer raus aus der Mitte-Blase möchte und trotzdem
nur ein paar Schritte weitergehen will, bestellt
beim Thai Window Asia in der Torstraße 22 hervorragendes grünes Curry. If you want to escape Mitte,
but don't want to go too far, order the magnificent
green curry from Thai Window Asia on Torstraße 22.

EXTRA TIP

Nebenan, bei 3 minutes sur mer (Torstraße 167),
wird am Wochenende immer ausgezeichnetes fran-
zösisches Frühstück serviert: unbedingt Croque
Madame bestellen. Next door, at 3 minutes sur mer
(Torstraße 167), an excellent French breakfast is
always served at the weekend: absolutely order the
Croque Madame.

HIER WARTEN ZUKÜNFTIGE LIEBLINGSSTÜCKE YOUR FUTURE WARDROBE AWAITS

Nachdem Nicole Hogerzeil über Jahre hinweg zwei Geschäfte in der Mulackstraße betrieben hatte, beschloss sie 2015, ihre beiden bisherigen Shops zusammenzuführen. Mitte ist sie treu geblieben und ihrem einzigartigen Geschmack auch. Auf den Kleiderstangen findet man das Beste der beiden bisherigen Läden, zum Beispiel das Berliner Label Perret Schaad oder Entwürfe internationaler Designer wie Dries Van Noten, Carven und Isabel Marant. Kurz gesagt: Bei Schwarzhogerzeil gibt es genau jene Marken, die man haben möchte, weil sie nicht nur gut im Geschäft aussehen, sondern vor allem angezogen, weil sie zu Lieblingsteilen werden und über Jahre bleiben. For many years Nicole Hogerzeil ran two stores on Mulackstraße, but in 2015 she merged them and opened a new, bigger shop. Yet she stayed true to her home, Mitte, and her excellent selection remains unchanged. The racks now feature the owner's favorite brands from both former shops, including international designers such as Dries Van Noten, Carven, and Isabel Marant as well as Berlin-based labels like Perret Schaad. In short: this store stocks clothing we'd love to call our own. It looks good on, not just in the store – anything from here is sure to become one of your favorite pieces over the years.

Text: Nina Trippel / Photo: Ludger Paffrath

Schwarzhogerzeil
Torstraße 173, 10115 Berlin-Mitte
Mon–Fri 12:00–20:00, Sat 12:00–18:00
schwarzhogerzeil.de

NEW CLASSICS

RUND UM DIE UHR VOM GUTEN DAS BESTE A TASTE OF THE BEST ROUND THE CLOCK

In Johanna Schellenbergers Kaffeebar ergänzt exzellenter Cappuccino hervorragende Kuchen, Sandwiches und Salate. „Du bist tagsüber unser Wohnzimmer. Jetzt brauchen wir noch etwas für abends", sagten die Gäste. Also eröffnete sie 2013 ein Restaurant, minimalistisch aber anheimelnd eingerichtet und jüngst von Designer Jonas Klock von Accidental Concrete umgestaltet: Im vorderen Raum dominieren schwarze Wände, Holz und Beton, weiter hinten lädt der neue Tresen zum Verweilen ein. Barchefin Alana stellt bei den Drinks mit saisonalen Zutaten ihr Können unter Beweis, Küchenchef Luka lockt Fleisch- und Fischliebhaber, aber auch Vegetarier. Lachs wird mit Vanille gebeizt und an medischem Apfel sowie Kokoscreme serviert, der Baby Leaf-Salat aus Wildkräutern, Erd- beeren und Mozzarella mit Popcorn (!) verfeinert. Besonders, simpel, superlecker. Bon, le bon! In Johanna Schellenberger's coffee bar you'll find excellent cappuccino to complement superb cakes, sandwiches, and salads. "You're our favorite living room all day long. Now we need something for the evenings," the guests told her. So in 2013 she opened a minimalist but cosily furnished restaurant. Jonas Klock of Accidental Concrete recently redesigned the space: black walls, wood, and concrete dominate the front room. The bar, also a new addition, invites you to linger. Head bartender Alana brings a masterful touch to her drinks, made with seasonal ingredients. Chef Luka attracts meat and fish lovers and vegetarians alike to the premises. Vanilla-smoked salmon is served with citron and coconut cream. The baby leaf salad with wild herbs, strawberries, and mozzarella is refined with popcorn (!). Simple and delicious. Bon, le bon!

Text: Nella Beljan / Photos: Robbie Lawrence

Le Bon
Boppstraße 1, 10967 Berlin-Kreuzberg
Tue-Sat 9:00-23:30, Sun 9:30-16:00
lebon-berlin.com

NEW CLASSICS

EXTRA TIP

In Schellenbergers Kaffeebar in der Graefestraße 8 bestellt man neben Kaffee und Kuchen auch die Buddha Bowl mit Quinoa, Süßkartoffel und Avocado.
In Schellenberger's coffee bar at Graefestraße 8, order coffee and cake or a Buddha Bowl, filled with quinoa, sweet potato, and avocado.

MAILAND LIEGT IN MITTE!
MILAN IS IN MITTE!

Es gibt nichts Schöneres als Orte, die von Menschen geführt werden, die genau wissen, was sie wollen! Eva und Kappas Bar Milano ist ein solcher Ort. Die beiden haben sich beim Studium in Mailand kennengelernt und teilen eine Vision: Sie wollen den Aperitivo nach Berlin bringen und leckeres Essen in schönem Interieur servieren. Die über sechs Meter lange Bar aus italienischem Marmor thront mitten im Lokal; man bestellt einen der fein abgestimmten Drinks, die mit kleinen Leckereien angeboten werden, und lässt den Tag ausklingen. Diese wunderbaren Köstlichkeiten gehören zum Service und sind somit im Preis inbegriffen. Wer mehr Hunger hat, bestellt zum Beispiel frisch zubereitete Panini mit Bresaola oder Affettato Misto dazu. Und wer wissen will, wo die einzelnen Zutaten herkommen, sollte unbedingt nachfragen - die Antworten verraten, wie viel Liebe und Entschlossenheit in der Bar Milano stecken. There's nothing better than a place run by people who know exactly what they want, and Bar Milano is just that. Eva and Kappa hail from south of the Alps and got to know each other while studying in Milan. They share a vision: bringing aperitivo culture to Berlin. The Italian marble bar, over six meters in length, is the focal point at this tasteful venue. Stop by after work to unwind and order one of their delicious drinks that come with small yummy surprise bites. If you have a bigger appetite, opt for the creative selection of panini with bresaola or affettato misto, all freshly prepared. If you'd like to know where the ingredients come from, feel free to ask: the answers are always given in stories peppered with the love and dedication of the owners.

Text: Claudia Maria Zenk / Photos: Sven Hausherr

Bar Milano
Brunnenstraße 11, 10119 Berlin-Mitte
Mon & Tue 18:00-24:00, Wed & Thu 18:00-1:00, Fri & Sat 18:00-2:00
bar-milano.de

Blätternder Putz, knarrende Dielen, marode Fassade: Victoria Eliasdóttir liebt das runtergerockt Lässige an ihrem Restaurant dóttir (s. S. 33) in Berlin-Mitte. So herrlich typisch für die Stadt! Inspirierende Räume für die feinsinnige und herzliche Isländerin, die aus einer Künstlerfamilie kommt. Sie selbst wollte Modedesignerin werden, ihr Vater war Koch und Kreativer, ihr Halbbruder ist der Künstler Olafur Eliasson. 2014 zog es die aufstrebende Köchin nach Berlin, um die Studio-Küche ihres Bruders auf Vordermann zu bringen. Die modernen isländischen Speisen, die Victoria seit einem Jahr im dóttir ästhetisch anrichtet? Eine Kunst für sich. Victoria ist eben Perfektionistin und macht nur, was ihren hohen Ansprüchen genügt. Die Berliner wissen es zu schätzen. Wenn sie gerade nicht in ihrer dóttir-Küche steht, trifft man sie in ihrem Kiez, in Prenzlauer Berg – oder in einem anderen Restaurant in Mitte: dem Koreaner YamYam. Der wird übrigens auch von einer Frau geleitet, die Mode-Bezug hat, aber, viel wichtiger: fantastische Küche kreiert.

The paint is flaking off the wall, the old floorboards creak, the façade is washed-out: but that kind of run-down, casual beauty is what Victoria Eliasdóttir loves about her Mitte restaurant, dóttir (s. p. 33). It's so typical of this city! It's an inspiring room for the sophisticated Iceland-native, who comes from a family of artists and once dreamt of being a fashion designer; her father was a chef and creative, and her half-brother is Olafur Eliasson, the well-known contemporary artist. In 2014 the then-aspiring chef moved to Berlin to brush up her brother's studio kitchen. And the modern Icelandic dishes Victoria has served since 2015? An art form of their own. Victoria is a perfectionist and all her creations must match her own high expectations. Berliners appreciate it. When she's not in the dóttir kitchen, you can find her in Prenzlauer Berg, where she lives, or in another Mitte restaurant: the Korean YamYam. This also suits her aesthetic image: the owner, Sumi Ha, used to run a fashion boutique. But much more importantly, she serves fantastic cooking. →

VICTORIA ELIASDÓTTIR EMPFIEHLT: YAMYAM VICTORIA ELIASDÓTTIR RECOMMENDS: YAMYAM

Als ich noch in Island wohnte und zu Besuch in Berlin war, brachte mich mein Bruder Olafur an einem sonnigen Spätnachmittag ins YamYam. Beim Anblick des kühlen, weißen Raums war ich zuerst nicht gerade angetan – das Gefühl schwand aber direkt bei dem Geruch von hausgemachtem Kimchi und brutzelndem Bibimbap. Fortan war ich süchtig und gehe seither regelmäßig ins YamYam, um mich mit großartigen, perfekt ausbalancierten, hocharomatischen Gerichten zu stärken. Sumi Ha – eine Deutsche mit koreanischen Wurzeln – ist die Chefin dieses authentischen Lokals. Für mich wäre Berlin ohne ihre Dumplings, das Bulgogi und die Glasnudeln nicht dasselbe. Ein charmantes Merkmal des gut besuchten Lokals ist die Vielfalt der Kundschaft: Egal, ob man die teuerste Handtasche trägt oder als Backpacker in abgenutzten Shorts vorbeikommt, hier wird man gleichermaßen bodenständig bedient! Ich schätze auch die Kraft des (gemeinsamen) Essens. Alle sind aus demselben Grund hier: um die gute Küche zu genießen und sich mit Kollegen, Freunden oder der Familie auszutauschen. Im YamYam vermittelt der Essbereich das schöne Gefühl, den Raum mit dem Paar neben sich zu teilen, während man bisweilen unbeholfen an die Ellenbogen der Sitznachbarn stößt oder zufällig den neuesten Klatsch des Start-ups am Nebentisch hört. Und wo Einfachheit in seiner besten Form regiert, braucht das Auge weder Dekoration noch Blumen. Kurz: Das YamYam gehört einfach zu meinem Best of Berlin! During one of my first visits to Berlin, back when I was still living in Iceland, my brother Olafur brought me to YamYam late on a sunny afternoon. I will admit that at first I wasn't all that excited about this white, cold room – but the feeling disappeared in a split second with the warm scent of the homemade kimchi and sizzling bowls of bibimbap. It only took one taste and I was addicted. Ever since, I've gone to YamYam for fantastic, perfectly balanced, deliciously aromatic dishes. Sumi Ha, a German born of Korean heritage, runs this authentic spot. For me Berlin would not be the same without the steamed dumplings, the bulgogy, and the glass noodle bowl. One of the charming features of this modest but ever so lively restaurant is the variety of customers. Bring your most expensive handbag and you will still get the same down to earth, straightforward service as the backpacker in the worn-out shorts. I truly appreciate the power of food in the sense of equalizing people – we are all here for the same purpose: enjoying the honest cooking while sharing thoughts and ideas with colleagues, friends, or family. The dining area at YamYam brings a positive feeling of sharing space with the couple next door, awkwardly bumping elbows or accidentally overhearing the start-up business' latest gossip. It is simplicity in its truest form – there is no need for seducing the eye with decorations and flowers. In short: YamYam is definitely on my "Best of Berlin" list!

Text: Victoria Eliasdóttir / Photos: Daniel Farò

YamYam
Alte Schönhauser Straße 6, 10119 Berlin-Mitte
Mon-Sat 12:00-24:00, Sun 13:00-23:00
yamyam-berlin.de

MÖBEL FÜR MINIMALISTEN
FURNITURE FOR MINIMALISTS

NEW CLASSICS

„Es geht nicht ums Verkaufen, sondern darum, etwas zu zeigen, zu diskutieren und weiterzuentwickeln – es geht uns um das, was Andreas Murkudis ausmacht", sagt der Berliner Künstler Raphael Danke. Er arbeitet bei AM Möbel + Architektur, dem neuesten Zuwachs des Murkudis'schen Imperiums der schönen Dinge. Der neue, auf Möbel spezialisierte Laden befindet sich ganz in der Nähe seines großen Bruders, dem bekannten Concept Store namens Andreas Murkudis. Man fühlt sich wie in einer Galerie: Alles ist sorgsam arrangiert, jedes Stück hat seinen Platz verdient und ist fast zu schön und perfekt, um fürs reale Leben gedacht zu sein. Der Blick wandert von einem Marmortisch des Designers Jerszy Seymour zu einer geradlinigen Lampe von E15 und findet viele wunderbar gestaltete Elemente, über die man sich mit den Mitarbeitern austauschen kann. "It's not just about selling, it's about showcasing, discussing, and developing our design; the idea that is Andreas Murkudis," explains Raphael Danke. He works at AM Möbel + Architektur, a new sister store located just a few doors down from their flagship fashion branch called Andreas Murkudis. It is clear that impeccable style runs in the family. The store is reminiscent of a gallery: looking around, the quality and exclusivity of each piece proves that it has earned its spot on display. The dramatic design of Jerszy Seymour's marble table or the clean-cut lamp by E15 – each item is remarkably special and unique. Whether you wish to browse, purchase, or simply chat about design with the sales staff, this new store is definitely worth your time.

Text: Isabelle Kagelius / Photos: Ana Santl

Andreas Murkudis Möbel + Architektur
Potsdamer Straße 77, 10785 Berlin-Tiergarten
Mon-Fri 12:00-20:00, Sat 12:00-18:00
andreasmurkudis.com

EXTRA TIP

**Wunderbare Ausstellungen zeigen 401contemporary
und die Galerie Jarmuschek + Partner im Hinterhof
der Potsdamer Straße 81b.** Inspiring exhibitions are
shown in the courtyard of Potsdamer Straße 81b that
houses 401contemporary and Jarmuschek + Partner.

FRANZÖSISCHES FLAIR IM WESERKIEZ A TASTE OF FRENCH PANACHE IN WESERKIEZ

Vorsicht, glückliche Menschen! In die Beuster Bar pilgern nicht nur Liebhaber der gepflegten Trinkkultur. Diesen gastronomischen Sehnsuchtsort habe ich auf einem Streifzug entdeckt. „Bar" ist nämlich wirklich Understatement: Verantwortlich dafür ist die moderne Bistro-Küche. Die strahlt französische Noblesse mit großer Lässigkeit aus. Darf es ein Glas Riesling zum perfekt gebratenen Pulpo sein? Oder ein Steak Tartar, kurz angebraten, die Matchstick-Pommes kross mit einem Glas Sancerre als echten Gaumenschmeichler? Der Gastraum ist gemütlich, die Karte klein und raffiniert, der Service flink und freundlich. Beim Cheesecake verfalle ich in ein zufriedenes Jauchzen, dazu einen Espresso-Martini, dann weiter an die Bar. Spätestens ab hier ist der Abend eine Spielart von Glück. A warning to the cynics: there are only happy people here. Despite the name, Beuster Bar is not only a destination for lovers of immaculately tended drinks. Indeed, during my pilgrimage there, I discovered a true dedication to food and flavor, and realized that calling Beuster a "bar" truly is an understatement. Beuster Bar boasts a perfect bistro kitchen that exudes French noblesse combined with an air of nonchalance. Would you care for a glass of Riesling, or for some perfectly fried octopus? Perhaps a steak tartare, lightly seared, with crispy skinny fries and a glass of Sancerre as a bona fide appetizer? The dining room is cozy, the menu small and refined, and the service swift and friendly. With squeals of pure glee over the fantastic cheesecake, I followed an espresso martini straight to the bar. At the very least, an evening here is a special taste of happiness.

Text: Ferdinand Hamsch / Photos: Daniel Farò

Beuster Bar
Weserstraße 32, 12045 Berlin-Neukölln
Daily from 18:00
beusterbar.com

EXTRA TIP

Erstklassig französisch isst man auch in Charlottenburg:
In der Brasserie Lamazère am Stuttgarter Platz 18. You
can also find first-class French cuisine in Charlottenburg:
in the brasserie Lamazère at Stuttgarter Platz 18.

SHORTLIST

ÜBERALL DORT, WO ZEITGEIST ZUHAUSE IST, ERFINDEN SICH DIE STADT UND IHRE BEWOHNER NEU – SECHS TRENDS, DIE UNS BEGLEITEN: DRINNEN, DRAUSSEN UND UNTERWEGS. WHEN ZEITGEIST MOVES IN, THE CITY AND ITS INHABITANTS CHANGE THEIR WAYS – HERE ARE SIX TRENDS THAT ACCOMPANY US, NO MATTER WHERE WE ARE: INDOORS, OUTDOORS, OR ON THE GO.

LUNETTES SELECTION
Torstraße 172
10115 Berlin-Mitte
lunettes-selection.de

FRAMEPUNK
Manteuffelstraße 48
10999 Berlin-Kreuzberg
framepunk.com

VAVA EYEWEAR
vavaeyewear.com

R.T.CO
Sanderstraße 6
12047 Berlin-Neukölln
r-t-co.com

Eine Brille rundet jedes Outfit ab: Sie
ist das perfekte Accessoire – auch
für diejenigen, die keine Sehschwäche,
sondern lediglich eine Schwäche für
getönte Gläser haben. Jedes Gestell ist
ein Stück Berliner Mentalität:
funktional, aber sexy. Momentan meint
man fast doppelt zu sehen, so viele
Brillengeschäfte und -labels gibt es
inzwischen. Diese Übersicht sorgt für
Durchblick! Glasses are the finishing
touch on any outfit, the perfect
accessory, a distillation of Berlin's
spirit: both functional and sexy.
Berlin has recently seen an explosion
of eyewear brands. All the variety
can be overwhelming. Let us help you
sift out the best picks of the bunch.

ic! berlin
Max-Beer-Straße 17
10119 Berlin-Mitte
ic-berlin.de

SPECTACULAR SPECS

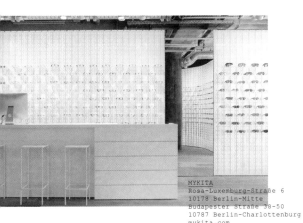

MYKITA
Rosa-Luxemburg-Straße 6
10178 Berlin-Mitte
Budapester Straße 38-50
10787 Berlin-Charlottenburg
mykita.com

PROJEKT SAMSEN
projekt-samsen.de

NUTSANDWOODS
nutsandwoods.de

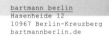

bartmann berlin
Hasenheide 12
10967 Berlin-Kreuzberg
bartmannberlin.de

Anna Badur
Donaustraße 83
12043 Berlin-Neukölln
annabadur.de

OBJECTS OF DESIRE

S H O R T L I S T

OBJEKTE UNSERER TAGE
objekteunserertage.com

Von innovativen Lampen über elegante Stühle
bis zu dekorativen Porzellantellern - vor
den Berliner Produktdesignern ist nichts
sicher, denn sie beherrschen die Kunst,
Form, Farbe und Funktion zu vereinen und
Objekte der Begierde zu kreieren. So werden
hiesige Lokale und Geschäfte schöner,
und unser Zuhause natürlich ebenso. From
innovative lamps to sophisticated chairs
and decorative porcelain plates - our
Berlin-based designers will re-think them
all. Merging shape, color, and function,
they can turn any piece into an object of
desire. Local hang-outs and shops are
beautifully decorated with their designs,
not to mention our homes.

Alex Valder
Urbanstraße 64, 2nd courtyard
10967 Berlin-Kreuzberg
alexvalder.de
maisonmariaodelga.com

GECKELER MICHELS Industrial Design
Treptower Straße 22
12059 Berlin
geckelermichels.com

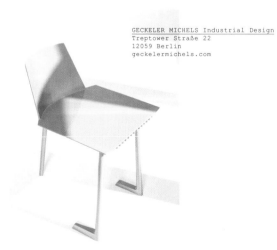

Mariusz Malecki / studio ziben
Kopenhagener Straße 66
10437 Berlin-Prenzlauer Berg
studio-ziben.de

Rainer Spehl
rainerspehl.com

MY KILOS
Leipziger Straße 65
10117 Berlin-Mitte
mykilos.com

NEW TENDENCY
Adalbertstraße 6a, 1st courtyard, left
10999 Berlin-Kreuzberg
newtendency.de

Christian Metzner
christian-metzner.com

Atelier Haußmann
atelierhaussmann.de

THE BARN Coffee Roasters
Schönhauser Allee 8
10119 Berlin-Prenzlauer Berg
thebarn.de

Five Elephant Coffee Roastery and Cake Shop
Reichenberger Straße 101
10999 Berlin-Kreuzberg
fiveelephant.com

Fjord Coffee Roasters
fjord-coffee.com

Fjord coffee is availble at
Silo Coffee
Gabriel-Max-Straße 4
10245 Berlin-Friedrichshain

Father Carpenter
Münzstraße 21, 1st backyard
10178 Berlin-Mitte
fathercarpenter.com

COFFEE CITY

Die Hysterie um Third Wave-Kaffee flaut nicht ab. Baristas und Experten verfolgen ihre Bohne bis zur Wurzel und scheuen nicht davor zurück, selbst Hand anzulegen – sei es beim Rösten, der Einrichtung ihres Cafés oder dem Design der Kaffee-Verpackungen. The third wave coffee hysteria is unstoppable. Berliners are tracking their coffee right down to the source, getting their hands dirty on every level of the process, from sourcing the beans to creating gorgeously designed coffee shops and packaging.

Friedl Rösterei & Kekse
Pappelallee 35
10437 Berlin-Prenzlauer Berg
friedlkaffee.de

KAFFEEKIRSCHE Roastery
Adalbertstraße 23
10997 Berlin-Kreuzberg
kaffeekirsche.berlin

Bonanza Roastery Café
Adalbertstraße 70
10997 Berlin-Kreuzberg

Café at Oderberger Straße
Oderberger Straße 35
Berlin-Prenzlauer Berg
bonanzacoffee.de

Concierge Coffee
Paul-Lincke-Ufer 39/40
10999 Berlin-Kreuzberg
Facebook: ConciergeCoffee

Michelberger Hotel - The Hideout
Warschauer Straße 39-40
10243 Berlin-Friedrichshain
michelbergerhotel.com

Das Stue
Drakestraße 1
10787 Berlin-Tiergarten
das-stue.com

Auch wenn die Stadt niemals schläft, muss
man selbst ab und an ein Auge zumachen.
Wieso also nicht zur Abwechslung in fremde
Betten hüpfen? Für einen Urlaub, der sich
anfühlt wie nach Hause kommen, nehmen sich
selbst Berliner eine Nacht frei. Even if
the city never sleeps, you might need to –
and why not do it in one of the city's many
fantastic accommodations? Even if you're
a native Berliner yourself, take a night
off for a little staycation.

25hours Hotel Bikini Berlin
Budapester Straße 40
10787 Berlin-Tiergarten
25hours-hotels.com

SWEET HOME BERLIN

NOMADS APT.
Rheinsberger Straße 32
10435 Berlin-Mitte
nomadsapt.com

Wallyard Concept Hostel
Lübecker Straße 46
10559 Berlin-Moabit
wallyard.de

NON Berlin - Asia contemporary art platform
Chausseestraße 11 / entrance via Tieckstraße
10115 Berlin-Mitte
nonberlin.com

Kleine Humboldt Galerie
Lichthof at Humboldt-University
Unter den Linden 6
10099 Berlin-Mitte
kleinehumboldtgalerie.de

ALTERNATIVE ART SPACES

Die Dichte an Projekträumen ist in Berlin einzigartig: Mehr
als 150 zählt die Stadt, viele werden von Künstlern oder
freien Kuratoren betrieben - meistens in leeren Ladenlokalen,
manchmal auch ohne festen Sitz. Die Betreiber verfolgen
nämlich meist ein Non-Profit-Prinzip - Kunst wird nicht verkauft,
dafür aber immer öfter auf institutionellem Niveau präsentiert. Berlin is covered in art spaces: more than 150 call this
city home, many run by artists or curators - most in empty
commercial premises, many with no permanent location. These
establishments operate on a non-profit principle - art is not
sold, but presented at an institutional level.

insitu
Kurfürstenstraße 21-22
10785 Berlin-Tiergarten
insitu-berlin.com

uqbar
Schwedenstraße 16
13357 Berlin-Wedding
projectspace.uqbar-ev.de

Frankfurt am Main
Wildenbruchstraße 15
12045 Berlin-Neukölln
frankfurt-am.com

Wild Things
Weserstraße 172
12045 Berlin-Neukölln
wildthingsberlin.de

Schwein
Elisabethkirchstraße 2
10115 Berlin-Mitte
schwein.online

jaja
Weichselstraße 7
12043 Berlin-Neukölln
jajaberlin.com

Craft Beer hat seinen Gegenspieler gefunden:
Seit Kurzem lässt man sich immer öfter
trüben Naturwein einschenken. Besonders gut
schmeckt er in den neuen Weinbars, die
sich meistens genauso sehr für die Herkunft
ihrer Flaschen wie für gute Snacks
interessieren – statt Nüssen reicht man hier
auch mal Rindertatar mit Radieschen zum
spontan vergärten Tropfen. Craft beer has
met its match: recently, it's more common
to hear a natural cloudy wine pouring.
These new juices of the vine are especially
delicious – and the snacks offered
along with them are just as interesting.
Instead of nuts, these new bars offer
dishes like beef tartare with radishes
to complement your drinks.

WINE VIBES

Allan's Breakfast Club and Wine Bar
Rykestraße 13
10405 Berlin-Prenzlauer Berg
Facebook: allansbreakfastclub

neontoaster
Seestraße 106
13353 Berlin-Wedding
neontoaster.de

Viniculture
Grolmanstraße 44
10623 Berlin-Charlottenburg
viniculture.de

Briefmarken Weine
Karl-Marx-Allee 99
10243 Berlin-Friedrichshain
briefmarkenweine.de

DER HERBST IST ERTRÄGLICH, ABER KURZ. DER WINTER DAS GEGENTEIL. ZWISCHEN OKTOBER UND MÄRZ ALSO BESSER ZU HAUSE BLEIBEN. NOTFALLPLAN GEGEN DAS FACETTENREICHE BERLINER GRAU? KUNST UND KULINARIK.

THE FALL SEASON IS BEARABLE BUT SHORT, WINTER THE OPPOSITE. SO BETTER JUST STAY INSIDE BETWEEN OCTOBER AND MARCH. WHAT'S THE MOST RELIABLE DEFENSE AGAINST THE ENDLESS SHADES OF BERLIN GREY? ART AND CULINARY DELIGHT.

BROTZEIT & HOCHPROZENTIGES
IN DER ALTEN APOTHEKE BREAD &
BOOZE IN A FORMER PHARMACY

Drei Buchstaben der alten Fassadenaufschrift leuchten noch im
Dunkeln. Sie bilden den Namen dieses Kleinods: Ora. 150 Jahre
lang beheimateten die Räume die Apotheke am Oranienplatz, ab 1860
Hoflieferant für die deutschen Kolonialgebiete und Schutztruppen.
Heute ist der eindrucksvolle Raum mit Stuckdecke, reich verzierten
Schränken aus dunklem Holz und Regalen voller Apothekerfläschchen
zu einem der schönsten Cafés Berlins geworden. Den ganzen Tag über
gibt es das hausgemachte knusprige Sauerteigbrot mit Aufstrichen
wie Rauchpaprika-Hummus oder warmem Sellerie-Apfel-Salat. Wie in
einem klassischen Wiener Kaffeehaus sitze ich dort am liebsten
den ganzen Tag. Oft bis es Zeit ist für Kaffee und Aprikosen-Apfel-
Tarte. Manchmal sogar so lange, dass ich den Abend mit einem
Drink wie dem Beelitz-Highball aus Korn, Estragon und Spargel
ausklingen lasse. Three letters from the old sign light up at
night, forming the name of the little gem Ora, the 150-year-old
pharmacy-turned-residential-space-turned-café on Oranienplatz.
Founded in 1860, it officially supplied the German colonies and
the German Colonial Army. In April 2015, the impressive stucco-
ceilinged room, with its ornate pharmacist's cabinets made of dark
wood and shelves lined with hundreds of old pharmacist's bottles,
became one of the best cafés in Berlin. You can go for breakfast,
lunch, or dinner and enjoy the homemade crispy sourdough bread
with spreads such as smoked paprika hummus or the warm celery-
apple salad. Just like in a classic Viennese coffee house, I
prefer to settle myself there all day and linger until it's time
for coffee and an apricot-apple tart, or – because time flies by –
a seasonal drink such as the Beelitz Highball, made with corn,
tarragon, and asparagus.

Text: Helen von der Höden / Photos: Daniel Farò

Ora
Oranienplatz 14, 10999 Berlin-Kreuzberg
Daily 9:30-1:00
ora-berlin.de

EXTRA TIP

Wer nach dem Besuch im Ora noch einen Film sehen will, geht ins fsk am Segitzdamm 2. Das kleine Programmkino zeigt Filme im Original. After Ora, head to fsk on Segitzdamm 2, a small cinema screening films in their original versions.

MANDELCAPPUCCINO X TOFUBAGEL
ALMOND CAPPUCCINO X TOFU BAGEL

Als ich um acht Uhr morgens verschlafen ins Black Sheep stolpere,
wundere ich mich zuerst, warum ich in dem breiten Angebot vergeb-
lich nach Milch suche. Erst als Audie Hillock, die freundliche und
talentierte Barista, die pflanzlichen Alternativen (Soja-, Hafer-,
Mandel-, Kokos- und Reismilch) aufzählt, erinnere ich mich, dass dieses
Café 100% vegan ist. Ich entscheide mich für den Mandelcappuccino und
bekomme einen der besten Kaffees, den ich in Berlin je hatte. Danach
kommt das Essen, serviert von Köchin Lucinda Darke. Köstlich - von
Tempeh-„Speck" und Avocado-Bagel (von der wöchentlich wechselnden Bagel-
Karte) bis hin zu Leckereien wie Snickers Slices und Rote Bete-
und Mandel-Brownies. Die beiden Besitzerinnen Audie und Lucinda
haben seit der Eröffnung 2016 quasi rund um die Uhr gearbeitet -
ein unermüdliches Engagement, das sich wirklich bezahlt gemacht hat!

Arriving at Black Sheep, yawning and sleepy at 8am, I struggle to
understand why finding the milk is so difficult. It's only when Audie
Hillock, the friendly and talented barista who is one half of the
team behind this place, points out the five different plant-based milks
on offer (soy, oat, almond, coconut, and rice milk) that I remember
this café is 100% vegan. I choose the almond cappuccino, and am
served one of the best coffees I've had in Berlin. The changing menu,
created by the innovative and gifted chef Lucinda Darke, is just
as delicious, from the incredible tempeh "bacon" and avocado bagel
to treats like the moreish snickers slices and the beetroot and
almond brownies. The founders have worked twenty-four-seven since
opening in early 2016, and this tireless dedication has resulted
in a truly fantastic new café that you just can't miss.

Text: Antonia Harris / Photos: Daniel Faró

Black Sheep Café
Bouchéstraße 15, 12435 Berlin-Alt-Treptow
Mon-Fri 8:00-18:00, Sat 9:00-18:00, Sun 9:00-15:00

GREY SKY

EXTRA TIP

Vegan isst man auch bei Let it be in der Treptower
Straße 90: Dieses Restaurant ist nach einem
Beatles-Song benannt und Moby, dem Musiker
und bekennenden Veganer, hat man die Crêpe mit
Apfelmus gewidmet. You can also find vegan food
at Let it be, at Treptower Straße 90: not only is the
restaurant named after a Beatles' song, the crêpe
with apple sauce is dedicated to Moby, a musician
and known vegan.

FRÄULEIN JÜNEMANNS GESPÜR FÜR STIL MISS JÜNEMANN'S SENSE OF STYLE

Dieser Laden ist meine persönliche Entdeckung in Sachen Vintage-Mode und Accessoires – denn hier werden Frauen und Männer gleichermaßen fündig. Inhaberin Gerda Jünemann hat selbst einen exzellenten Stil und trifft mit ihrer Auswahl genau meinen Geschmack. Je nach Stimmung und Anlass kann man hier ein hellblaues Herrenhemd von Jil Sander und eine Smokinghose finden, ein kleines Schwarzes von Comme des Garçons, eine Bluse mit Ananasdruck oder ein Flower-Power-Teil. Das Outfit wird schnell mit den passenden Schuhen, einer Tasche, und – wer mag – einem Hut komplettiert. Präsentiert wird die Auswahl in einem schlichten aber grandiosen Interieur, samt üppigen Blumenarrangements. The Good Store macht seinem Namen alle Ehre. This shop is my latest discovery for vintage fashion and accessories. Owner Gerda Jünemann has an exceptional personal style and a great eye for amazing finds for both sexes. Depending on the mood, you could select a light blue men's shirt by Jil Sander, a pair of tuxedo pants, a black dress by Comme des Garçons, a shirt covered in a pineapple print, or items from the flower power era. As for an ensemble, you can find shoes, bags, and matching hats too. They are all presented in a lovely minimalist interior, crowned with beautiful flower arrangements. The Good Store truly lives up to its name.

Text: Milena Kalojanov / Photos: Julia Luka Lila Nitzschke, Magnus Pettersson

The Good Store
Pannierstraße 31, 12047 Berlin-Neukölln
Mon-Sat 12:00-19:00
thegoodstore.berlin

GREY SKY

EXTRA TIP

Abends kann man sein neues Outfit um die Ecke in der Loftus Hall am Maybachufer 48 ausführen: Hier tanzt man zum Beispiel bei der Partyreihe African Acid is the Future. You can show off your new outfit in the evenings on the corner at Loftus Hall, at Maybachufer 48: dance to their party series like African Acid is the Future.

ASIATISCHE KUNST GEBUNKERT
ASIAN ART BUNKERED

Kreative Umnutzung ist noch immer Teil der Kreuzberger DNA. Da überrascht es nicht, dass in einem ehemaligen Telekommunikationsbunker am Halleschen Ufer seit 2016 nun Kunst zu sehen ist. Nach zwei Jahren Renovierung beherbergt die monumentale Betonstruktur nun die Privatsammlung von Désiré Feuerle mit Schwerpunkt auf südostasiatische und zeitgenössische Kunst. Bekannt für das Nebeneinander künstlerischer Epochen und Stile, umfasst seine Sammlung beispielsweise Khmer-Steinskulpturen aus dem 7. Jahrhundert sowie Werke von Anish Kapoor und Cristina Iglesias. Davon abgesehen sind es zweifelsohne die imposanten Räumlichkeiten, die meine Aufmerksamkeit auf sich gezogen haben: Zwei Meter dicke Mauern umschließen einen weitläufigen Raum, der nur unterbrochen wird von kolossalen Säulen, die eine noch kolossalere Decke stützen. Eine akzentuierte Beleuchtung und die traditionelle Teestube heben die schwere Atmosphäre des Raumes auf, ebenso wie die Präsenz der Sammlung selbst. Ever the neighborhood for creative repurposing, Kreuzberg saw the opening of a new exhibition space in 2016 – in a former WWII telecommunications bunker, of all places. After two years of renovation, the heavyset concrete structure houses the Southeast Asian and contemporary art collection of Désiré Feuerle. The German collector has established a reputation for curating works spanning wildly different artistic eras and styles, and the new gallery space will see the curious combination of 7th century Khmer stone sculptures alongside works by artists such as Anish Kapoor and Cristina Iglesias. That said, it's undoubtedly the renovated space that grabbed my attention the most. Within its two-meter-thick walls, the bunker comprises one room interrupted with huge columns supporting an even thicker ceiling, all made of concrete. Complete with accented lighting and a traditional tearoom, experiencing the heavy atmosphere of the space will be as rewarding as viewing the collection itself.

Text: George Kafka / Photos: Gilbert McCarragher, Nic Tenwiggenhorn

The Feuerle Collection
Hallesches Ufer 70, 10963 Berlin-Kreuzberg
By appointment only
thefeuerlecollection.org

EXTRA TIP

Eine Sammlung frühislamischer Kunst findet man in der Dependance der Bumiller Collection in der Naunynstraße 68. To see an early Islamic art collection, head to the offshoot of the Bumiller Collection at Naunynstraße 68.

GREY SKY

EXTRA TIP

Großartige Bagels gibt es auch bei Two
Planets in der Hermannstraße 230.
There are also magnificent bagels at Two
Planets on Hermannstraße 230.

RUNDE SACHE: BAGELS & BÜCHER ALL ROUND GOODNESS: BAGELS & BOOKS

Das Café Fine Bagels sollte den schönen Buchladen Shakespeare and Sons eigentlich nur ein wenig bereichern. Doch nun gibt es neben der Literatur einen gleichwertigen Grund, den Shop zu besuchen. Laurel Kratochvila, Besitzerin von Fine Bagels, war lange auf der Suche nach hausgemachten Bagels im New York-Style – bis sie beschloss, sie selbst zu servieren: Dafür lässt sie den Teig über Nacht aufgehen und bäckt die Kringel jeden Morgen frisch auf. Ob salzig oder süß, vegetarisch oder vegan – hier gibt es die Klassiker mit Cream Cheese und Lachs, aber auch Eigenkreationen mit Hummus, Erdnussbutter oder Ziegenkäse. Laurels Partner Roman ist übrigens für die literarische Seite verantwortlich. Vor 13 Jahren eröffnete er seinen eigenen Buchladen in Prag, spezialisiert auf englische und französische Literatur, mit dem er 2014 nach Berlin umzog. Hier hat man heute die Qual der Wahl – egal, ob zuerst die Bagel- oder die Bücherauswahl in Augenschein genommen wird. The Fine Bagels café was meant to be a small addition to the bookstore Shakespeare and Sons, but it's become a reason of its own to visit the place. Laurel Kratochvila, the owner of Fine Bagels, uses family recipes to create what she was missing in Berlin: authentic homemade bagels. She makes them NY-style, cold and slow-rising overnight, water-boiled, and then baked fresh every day. There are plenty of options, whether you like sweet or savory, with meat, veggie, or vegan toppings. Classics like cream cheese and smoked salmon feature alongside homemade hummus, peanut butter, avocado, or goat cheese. Laurel's partner, Roman, takes care of the literary side to this joint venture, with experience built up over 13 years of working in Prague. Specializing in English and French books, Shakespeare and Sons creates a perfect harmony of good food and culture together with Fine Bagels café. Now the only hard choice you have to make is whether to browse the book shelf or the bagel shelf first.

Text: Isabelle Kagelius / Photos: Daniel Faró

Fine Bagels
Warschauer Straße 74, 10243 Berlin-Friedrichshain
Mon-Sat 8:00-20:00, Sun 9:00-20:00
finebagels.com

ALPINER HOCHGENUSS
ALPINE HIGHLIGHTS

Ein Stück Bergwelt hat es bis nach Neukölln geschafft, denn: Ein Pfälzer und ein Südtiroler lehren hier, unweit der Barmeile Weserstraße, süddeutsche und österreichische Esskultur und Gemütlichkeit. Was als wöchentliche Abendveranstaltung in den Privatgemächern von Werner Gasser und Christian Vulpus begann, ist mittlerweile zu einem echten Restaurantbetrieb gewachsen: Mit Kreativität entwickeln die beiden Freunde verschiedene Variationen des Knödels und servieren pro Abend sieben bis acht Versionen, die nach Belieben zusammengestellt werden können. Dazu gibt es Salat, Wein oder Bier zu absolut moderaten Preisen. Für vegetarische Optionen ist stets gesorgt und Platz für eine süße Variante als Dessert. Die Topfenknödel mit Waldbeerenkompott schmecken himmlisch. Sollte man in jedem Fall lassen. A piece of Alpine life has made it to Neukölln: two men, one from Palatinate and the other from South Tyrol, have started to teach southern German and Austrian food culture. What began as a weekly evening event in the private chambers of Werner Gasser and Christian Vulpus has now grown into a real restaurant business: up to eight different types of Knödel, the German/Austrian dumpling, are served – all of which are created with passion and ingenuity. You can mix and match the different flavors as you go, and salad is served on the side with wine or beer. Vegetarians: don't worry, there are plenty of meat-free variations. And make sure to leave room for dessert: the Topfenknödel with wild berry compote taste like heaven!

Text: Astrid Bruckmann / Photos: Daniel Farò

Knödelwirtschaft
Fuldastraße 33, 12045 Berlin-Neukölln
Tue-Sun from 18:00
knoedelwirtschaft.de

EXTRA TIP

Wem es die süßen Knödelvariationen angetan haben, der wird auch bei häppies in der Dunckerstraße 85 glücklich: Hier gibt es hervorragende Germknödel. Anyone who liked the sweet variations of the classic Knödel will also enjoy häppies at Dunckerstraße 85: the Germknödel are delicious.

EXTRA TIP

Bunt geht es auch nebenan bei Tin Tan, einer
mexikanischen Taqueria in der Chausseestraße 124
zu: die Einrichtung ist minimalistisch, das Essen
authentisch. You'll also find a colorful atmosphere at
Tin Tan, a Mexican Taqueria at Chausseestraße 124:
the décor is minimalist, the food authentic.

JAMES TURRELL ERLEUCHTET DIE FRIEDHOFSKAPELLE JAMES TURRELL ILLUMINATES THE CEMENTARY CHAPEL

Alles ist erleuchtet! So scheint es, wenn man die Kapelle auf dem 250 Jahre alten Dorotheenstädtischen Friedhof betritt, wo unter anderem Christa Wolf und Bertolt Brecht ihre letzte Ruhe fanden. Seit 1993 steht das Friedhofsensemble unter Denkmalschutz, 2015 lud der evangelische Friedhofsverband den amerikanischen Künstler James Turrell ein, den Kapellenraum in neues Licht zu tauchen. Eine Stunde nach Sonnenuntergang wird er nun von farbigem Licht durchflutet. Turrell dringt in die Grenzbereiche der Wahrnehmung vor, nimmt der Architektur die Schwere und bewegt sich nah an der biblischen Vorstellung von Licht. Wenn man den Raum verlassen hat, bildet das Auge die Komplementärfarben – ein besinnlicher Moment, perfekt für graue Wintertage. For a brief time, everything will be illuminated inside a newly renovated chapel, located in the 250-year-old Dorotheenstädtischer cemetery. Here, among others, Christa Wolf and Bertolt Brecht found eternal peace, and from 1993 the historic cemetery grounds have been under a protective conservation order. Now, the Protestant Cemetery Union has invited American artist James Turrell to drench the chambers of this historic chapel in a new light. One hour after sunset, the chapel is flooded with colored light. The architecture loses its distant, untouchable feeling and becomes present under the effect of the changing lights, and the human eye, observing this, continues to generate complementary colors after leaving the chapel. A beautiful experience, perfect for Berlin's grey winter days.

Text: Milena Kalojanov / Photos: Florian Holzherr

Kapelle auf dem Dorotheenstädtischen Friedhof I
Chausseestraße 126, 10115 Berlin-Mitte
Check online for guided tours and opening hours
evfbs.de

LONGDRINKS IM ZWEITEN WOHNZIMMER LONGDRINKS IN YOUR SECOND LIVING ROOM

Das Mandy's – benannt nach der ehemaligen Wirtin – besitzt den außergewöhnlichen Charme einer ehemaligen Kiez-Kneipe, die behutsam und liebevoll von den Betreibern Thomas Longo und Yen To umgestaltet wurde. Zusammen führen die beide auch das Dr. To's in Neukölln und haben hier die perfekte Location für Drinks und Cocktails nach dem Abendessen geschaffen. Am meisten schätzen wir die besondere Atmosphäre und Gelassenheit, mit der hier der Leidenschaft für hochwertige Getränke gefrönt wird. Unbedingt probieren sollte man die Eigenkreation des Hauses, den South South East, ein Gin-basierter Cocktail mit Koriander. Named after the former owner, Mandy's has the charm of a local pub complemented by a well-styled interior renovated by Thomas Longo and Yen To. The pair, who also own Dr. To's in Neukölln, have branched out from tasty food to providing a perfect location for after-dinner drinks and cocktails. What is particularly appealing is the warm, relaxed atmosphere, which perfectly suits their expertly selected and smoothly mixed drinks. You should definitely try the South South East, their own creation of a gin based cocktail with cilantro.

Text: Sonja Gutschera & Leif Henrik Osthoff / Photos: Daniel Farò

Mandy's Cocktailbar
Reichenberger Straße 61, 10999 Berlin-Kreuzberg
Wed & Thu 20:00-3:00, Fri & Sat 20:00-6:00

ROMANTIK AUF DER LEINWAND
ROMANCE ON THE BIG SCREEN

Wer sich nach Romantik sehnt, sollte nach Paris oder Venedig fahren. Berlin ist eher etwas für zynische Singles – eine Stadt voller Darkrooms und Tinder-Dates ohne Happy End. In Berlin nach Romantik zu suchen, ist wie in einem veganen Restaurant ein Steak zu bestellen. In Wahrheit gibt es sie auch hier, man muss nur wissen wo: Seit vielen Jahren zeigt das Lichtblick Kino auf der Kastanienallee jeden Samstag um Mitternacht den gleichen Film – „Casablanca". Wer kennt ihn nicht, den Streifen über die Liebesbeziehung zwischen dem desillusionierten Rick (Humphrey Bogart) und der strahlend schönen Ilsa (Ingrid Bergman) zur Zeit des Zweiten Weltkriegs. Bekannterweise gibt es auch im Film kein Happy End. Das macht die Geschichte aber natürlich viel glaubhafter. Berlin is not exactly a city of romantics. There's Paris for that, or Venice. Berlin is a city of cynical singles and loners, right? A city of darkrooms and Tinder dates, not monogamy and forever-afters. Hoping for romance in Berlin is like going to a vegetarian restaurant in search of a steak – at least that's what the popular mythology says. In truth, romance is alive and well here: you can find it in a tiny theater on Kastanienallee. For years and years – I first went eight years ago – Lichtblick Kino has been screening the same movie every Saturday at the stroke of midnight: "Casablanca", the 1942 story of doomed love between a dashing but jaded Humphrey Bogart and a radiant Ingrid Bergman, set against a backdrop of WWII intrigue. Bogart and Bergman don't live happily ever after, but that's what makes their story feel all the more real.

Text: Hilda Hoy / Photos: Caterina Gili

Lichtblick Kino
Kastanienallee 77, 10435 Berlin-Prenzlauer Berg
Mon-Thu from 17:00, Sat & Sun from 14:00
lichtblick-kino.org

EXTRA TIP

Hinter einer unscheinbaren Fassade auf der Hermannstraße 20 versteckt sich der vielleicht schönste Kinosaal der Stadt: Im Neues Off. Behind a nondescript façade at Hermannstraße 20 is perhaps one of the most beautiful cinemas in the city: the Neues Off.

Auch das Programm des Theaterdiscounters im ehemaligen Fernmeldeamt in der Klosterstraße 44 lohnt sich – zuerst genießt man zeitgenössisches Sprechtheater, dann ein Bier in der Bar. The program of Theaterdiscounter, located in a former tele-communications office at Klosterstraße 44, is also recommended – enjoy the contemporary spoken theater, then a beer at the bar afterwards.

DAS THEATER MIT VIELEN GESICHTERN
A THEATER WITH MANY TALENTS

Aller guten Dinge sind drei – das gilt auch für das Hebbel am Ufer, kurz
HAU. Seit 2003 bereichert das Kombinat die freie Theaterszene mit gleich
drei Spielstätten – dem HAU 1, HAU 2 und HAU 3. Das kann schon mal für
Verwirrung sorgen. Ebenso wie das gewollt gesellschaftskritische
Programm oder HAU-typische Kampagnen mit Porträts von Lisztäffchen, Hyänen
und dem Rest der Tierwelt. Ohne eigenes Ensemble ist es als Plattform
für internationale Produktionen Schnittstelle für neue künstlerische Posi-
tionen aus den Bereichen Theater, Tanz, Performance, Musik und bildende
Kunst. Kulinarischen Zuwachs gab es 2005 mit dem Theatercafé WAU am Halleschen
Ufer. Die Fensterfront gewährt je nach Standpunkt des Betrachters einen
Blick auf den großzügigen Gastraum aus den Sechzigerjahren oder die Hochbahn
und den Landwehrkanal. Am Mittag gleicht es mit wechselnden Tagesgerich-
ten einer Kantine, am Abend wird es zum Club-Restaurant und bietet Platz
für Premierenfeiern. Good things come in threes, and this is definitely
true for Hebbel am Ufer, or HAU for short. Since 2003, the three venues
of HAU 1, HAU 2, and HAU 3 have enriched the independent theater scene,
although there is occasional confusion over where events are hosted. The
deliberately socio-critical program and the typical HAU campaigns with
their mysterious posters are also never quite simple, but always reveal
great content. HAU is a platform for international innovation and global
discussion in the fields of theater, dance, performance, music, and visual
arts. In 2005, HAU also expanded into the culinary arts with the theater
café WAU at Hallesches Ufer. Depending on your seat, the windows offer
either a view of the generous sixties dining room or the elevated railway
and Landwehr Canal. During the daytime, WAU balances a changing menu with
a prepared lunch, and in the evenings it becomes a club restaurant with
plenty of space for the party after the premiere.

Text: Stephanie Johne / Photos: Tim Richards

Hebbel am Ufer
HAU 1, Stresemannstraße 29, 10963 Berlin-Kreuzberg
HAU 2, Hallesches Ufer 32, 10963 Berlin-Kreuzberg
HAU 3, Tempelhofer Ufer 10, 10963 Berlin-Kreuzberg
hebbel-am-ufer.de

Wirtshaus am Ufer
WAU, Hallesches Ufer 32, 10963 Berlin-Kreuzberg
Mon–Fri from 11:00, Sat & Sun from 16:00
wau-berlin.de

GREY SKY

MIT SONNE IST ALLES BESSER IN BERLIN. ALLES. DAS IST NICHT DAS BLAUE VOM HIMMEL VERSPROCHEN, SONDERN EIN LEITMOTIV. FÜR GLANZVOLLE TAGE UND LAUE ABENDE. WHEN THE SUN SHINES, EVERYTHING IN BERLIN FEELS BETTER. WE CAN'T PROMISE BLUE SKIES EVERY DAY, BUT WE CAN TELL YOU OUR LEITMOTIF FOR TWINKLING DAYS AND LONG NIGHTS.

AMERIKA AM STIEL
ICED AMERICAN SPIRIT

Für Popsicles, also amerikanisches Eis am Stiel, muss man
nicht mehr bis zum nächsten Urlaub warten – ein Abstecher
zum Schlesischen Tor reicht aus. Die Idee, das California Pops
zu eröffnen, hatten Tom Schult und Jörg Ellmer auf einer
Südamerika-Reise. Ihr Ziel: Die Farbvielfalt der kühlen
Erfrischung mit der Qualität von italienischem Eis zu
verbinden. Das ist auf jeden Fall gelungen. In der hübschen
Theke finden sich, ordentlich aufgereiht, Sorten wie Cheesecake, Mango oder Pflaume: Nicht zu süß, sehr fruchtig und
ziemlich erfrischend. Und das Beste zum Schluss: Jedes
Eis ist hausgemacht, die Inhaltsstoffe bio! Don't wait until
your next vacation to have some popsicles, just take a
trip to Schlesisches Tor. Tom Schult und Jörg Ellmer came
up with the idea for their store on a trip to South America.
Their goal was to combine the colors of the cool refreshment with the quality of Italian ice cream – and they've
definitely succeeded. The lovely counter is filled with
beautifully arranged rows of flavors like cheesecake, mango,
and plum: not too sweet, very fruity, and pretty darn
refreshing. And last but not least: every pop is homemade
using only organic ingredients!

Text: Helen von der Höden / Photos: Daniel Farò

California Pops
Falckensteinstraße 4, 10997 Berlin-Kreuzberg
Sun-Thu 12:00-23:00, Fri & Sat 12:00-24:00

Herbert Hofmann war nach Berlin gekommen, um durchzuatmen. Zu überlegen, wo die Lebensreise hingehen sollte. Der Tiroler hatte 2008 sein Geografiestudium abgeschlossen, die Gletscherforschung reizte ihn sehr. Jedoch hatte er es seinem zweiten Interessengebiet zu verdanken, dass er, anstatt in der Antarktis Eisproben zu untersuchen, als Einkäufer und Kreativdirektor des coolen Kreuzberger Concept Stores Voo im Bereich „Human-Geografie" landete. „Warum Menschen an verschiedenen Orten der Welt leben, wie sie leben – das finde ich spannend. Die gleiche Frage begegnet mir in der Mode, mit ihren kulturellen Ausprägungen und wechselnden Trends." Auch sein Alltag im Kreuzberger Graefekiez gleicht einer urbanen Milieustudie. Denn hier sind viele Menschen aus unterschiedlichen Kulturkreisen auf einem kleinen Haufen. Beobachten kann man diese Durchmischung auch bei Sonnenschein auf der Wiese vor dem Urbankrankenhaus am Landwehrkanal. Dort treffen sich nämlich Locals aus aller Herren Länder genauso wie Touristen auf der Durchreise. Herbert Hofmann came to Berlin to breath deeply. And to consider where life's journey might take him. The Tyrolese native completed his geography studies in 2008, when glaciology piqued his curiousity. But rather than investigating ice samples in the Antarctic, he's made a career for himself in "human geography" (his second area of interest) as the curator and creative director of the cool Kreuzberg concept store Voo. "Why people live in different countries and cities, and how they live – that's what I find exciting. I encounter the same question in fashion, with its cultural characteristics and changing trends." His daily life in Kreuzberger Graefekiez resembles a study of the urban milieu, where many people with varying cultural combinations are all crammed into the same small area. You can observe this mixing on the sunlit lawn in front of the Urbankrankenhaus on the banks of the Landwehr Canal. There, locals from around the world meet tourists just passing through. →

vooberlin.com
@halloherbert
@voostore

HERBERT HOFMANN EMPFIEHLT: DEN URBANHAFEN HERBERT HOFMANN RECOMMENDS: THE URBANHAFEN

Wenn ich auf Reisen Heimweh bekomme, denke ich an meinen Kiez – und im Speziellen an das Wasser vor meinem Haus, den Landwehrkanal. Auf den grünen Uferflächen am Urbankrankenhaus trifft man sich. Dafür gibt es viele Gründe: die Kastanienbäume, die Sonnenuntergänge, die Admiralbrücke und die beste Pizza im Umkreis. Zwar ist die Brücke kein Geheimtipp mehr, für mich konserviert sie aber das Berliner Lebensgefühl. Hier stoßen Jung und Alt, Hippies und Hipster, Berliner und Urlauber mit einem mitgebrachten Bier an. Das Ungezwungene und Legere wird gefeiert. Wenn es warm ist, kann man mit dem Schlauchboot auf dem Kanal rudern, im Winter friert der Hafen manchmal zu. Dann spaziert man auf dem Eis und bekommt eine neue Perspektive auf den Kiez: die Kreuzberger Brücken von unten. Eines würde ich mir jedoch wünschen – ich träume den Tag herbei, an dem der Kanal so sauber ist, dass man darin schwimmen kann. If I get homesick while I'm travelling, I think of my district, especially the water slowly wending its way through the city just outside my door – the Landwehr Canal. The green banks on Urbankrankenhaus are a popular meeting place for many reasons: the chestnut trees, the gorgeous sunsets, the Admiralbrücke, and the best pizza in the vicinity. The Admiralbrücke has long been a well-known tourist attraction, but that doesn't detract from the charm of this spot: here young and old, hippies and hipsters, Berliners and vacationers collide, all sitting together on the street and sipping from the beers they brought along. It's a celebration of informality and leisure. In summer you can also paddle a boat up and down the canal. In winter the harbor and canal freeze. If you walk around on the ice, you're in for a whole new view of Kreuzberg: you can see the bridges from underneath. There's only one more thing I wish for: I dream of the day when the canal water will be clean enough to swim in.

Text: Herbert Hofmann / Photos: Daniel Farò

Urbanhafen
Carl-Herz-Ufer to Planufer, 10961 Berlin-Kreuzberg

EXTRA TIP

Nach vier Jahren in Kreuzberg ist auch die Räucherei
Glut & Späne nach Gerswalde gezogen: man findet
sie in unmittelbarer Nähe der alten Schlossgärtnerei,
Dorfmitte 11. After four years in Kreuzberg the
smokehouse Glut & Späne moved to Gerswalde:
search for them near the adjacent nursery gardens
on Dorfmitte 11.

DAS CAFÉ FÜR LANDSCHWÄRMER
AN ESCAPIST DESTINATION

Berlin wird voll - also muss man raus. Zumindest am Wochenende. Das
dachten sich auch die Ex-Berliner Lola Randl und Philipp Pfeiffer
und eröffneten kurzerhand in einem alten Hotel in der Dorfmitte, gegenüber der großen Feldsteinkirche, das Café zum Löwen. Hier trifft sich
ein Mix aus Ausflüglern, Uckermärkern und Exil-Berlinern. Auch am
nahegelegen Sabinensee mischt es sich. Alle anfallenden Arbeiten
im Löwen-Café wurden bisher von Lola, Philipp oder Freunden über-
nommen: Zur Zeit versorgen die Japanerinnen Ayumi Saito und Sayuri
Sakairi die Gäste mit japanischer Hausmannskost aus regionalen Zutaten
und selbstgebackenen Kuchen. Lola ist übrigens Filmemacherin und hat
ihrem neuen Zuhause eine Dokuserie gewidmet: Die „Landschwärmer" schaut
man im WDR, wenn man Sehnsucht nach ihrem Café bekommt. Berlin can
be busy, so sometimes Berliners need to escape. This was the moti-
vation for ex-Berliners Lola Randl and Philipp Pfeiffer, who opened
Café zum Löwen in an old hotel opposite a large stone church in the
center of the village. It's a place where an eclectic mix of holi-
daymakers, Uckermark locals, and former Berliners come to meet and
travel on to the beautiful lake Sabinensee. All the work in the
Löwen café is done by Lola, Philipp, and their friends: currently,
Ayumi Saito and Sayuri Sakairi have taken over the café, supplying
Japanese home cooking for guests, along with local produce and homemade
cakes. Finally, the multi-talented Lola is also a filmmaker who
turned their café into the documentary series "Landschwärmer," which
you can watch if you miss the friendly space after returning to the
big city.

Text: Elisabeth Schotte / Photo: Hirofume Abe

Café zum Löwen
Dorfmitte 7, 17268 Gerswalde
Sat 10:00-20:00, Sun 10:00-18:00
ayumisaito.com/zumlowen

AUSFLUG AN DEN BINNENSEE
A TRIP TO THE INLAND LAKE

Wer eine kleine Zugfahrt nicht scheut, sollte unbedingt
an die Müritz fahren – Deutschlands größten Binnensee.
Vom Berliner Hauptbahnhof aus geht es in eineinhalb Stunden
ohne Umsteigen nach Waren. Hier kann man bei Harry Hurtig
ein Fahrrad mieten und in den Nationalpark aufbrechen, wo
man von einem der Aussichtstürme Vögel beobachtet oder
einfach sein mitgebrachtes Picknick genießt. Am schönsten
ist die Rast auf dem Müritzhof, der zwischen Wald und
Wiesen liegt. Dort gibt es neben selbstgebackenem Brot
und Kuchen auch auf Buchenholz gereiftes Bier – der
perfekte Ausklang für einen entspannten Tagesausflug. If
you don't mind riding the train for a bit, Germany's
biggest inland lake, the Müritz, is absolutely worth a
visit. It's a 90 minute direct trip from the Berlin
Hauptbahnhof; upon arrival, rent a bike at Harry Hurtig
and cruise along the beautiful bike paths through
the national park. You can sit and birdwatch from one
of the look-outs, or sit, relax, and open your picnic
basket. The nicest area for a drink is at Müritzhof, sitting between forest and picturesque meadows. Alongside
the home-baked breads and cakes served there, the beechwood-
matured beer is a real highlight – the perfect ending
to a relaxing day trip.

Text: Lorena Simmel

Harry Hurtig
Am Seeufer 24, 17192 Waren (Müritz)
harryhurtig.de

Müritzhof
Müritz-Nationalpark, 17192 Waren (Müritz)
May-September: daily 10:00-18:00
April & October: daily 10:00-16:00
müritzhof.de

EXTRA TIP

Wer stilvoll Fahrrad fahren will, braucht robuste
Taschen: Unzer Esser stellt ebensolche in
kleinen Editionen in Kreuzberg her. To go with
our stylish bikes, we Berliners need robust and
bike-appropriate bags: Unzer Esser manufactures
small collections in Kreuzberg.

BLUE SKY

EIN NEUES KAPITEL FÜR KUCHEN-KENNER A NEW CHAPTER FOR CAKE CONNOISSEURS

Seit nunmehr 30 Jahren fördert das Literaturhaus deutschsprachige und internationale Autoren und lädt in seinem spätklassizistischen Backsteinbau zu Lesungen, Symposien und Diskussionen ein. Auch kulinarisch hat dieser Ort etwas zu bieten: Das Café im Wintergarten dieser Berliner Institution ist ein Muss für wahre Kuchenkenner - leicht erkennbar an der großen Zahl älterer Herrschaften, die keinerlei Abstriche in puncto Qualität und Geschmack von Gebäckspezialitäten machen. Besonders der Blechkuchen zu einem Kännchen Kaffee oder Tee sorgt für erhabene Gaumenfreuden in den hohen Räumen. Ebenfalls großer Beliebtheit erfreut sich die Käseplatte mit ihren erlesenen Sorten - und danach ein kurzer Besuch im Garten oder in der Buchhandlung im Untergeschoss für den perfekten Samstagnachmittag.

Over 30 years ago the Literaturhaus started to host readings, symposiums, and discussions, thus encouraging both German and international authors. The venue, a late neoclassicist brick building, is also a culinary gem - the café in the conservatory is a must for all food snobs, easily recognizable by the high numbers of older and more refined regulars who make no compromises in terms of quality and taste when it comes to the pastry specialities. The traybakes paired with a pot of coffee or tea make for a sublime culinary experience in the high-ceilinged rooms. Another favorite is the cheese platter, which boasts an exquisite variety - and after a short visit to the garden or the bookstore in the basement, the café is the perfect place to relax on a Saturday afternoon.

Text: Nella Beljan / Photos: Daniel Farò

Café-Restaurant Wintergarten im Literaturhaus
Fasanenstraße 23, 10719 Berlin-Charlottenburg
Daily 9:00-24:00

EXTRA TIP

Das Käthe-Kollwitz-Museum nebenan, Fasanenstraße 24, beherbergt rund 200 Zeichnungen, Druckgrafiken und Plastiken der Künstlerin. The Käthe-Kollwitz-Museum next door at Fasanenstraße 24, is home to around 200 drawings, prints, and sculptures by the artist.

EXTRA TIP

Paddeln kann man auch in Berlin: Im Badeschiff in
der Eichenstraße 4 bucht man beim StandUpClub
ein Board. You can also do a bit of paddling in Berlin:
rent your board at StandUpClub at Badeschiff in
Eichenstraße 4.

PADDELN IM SPREEWALD
PADDLING IN THE SPREEWALD

Paddeln im Spreewald? Hört sich nach einer Frührentner-Veranstaltung an, ist aber ein erfrischender Spaß und hat rein gar nichts mit einer Kaffeefahrt zu tun. Ganz im Gegenteil: Körpereinsatz ist gefragt! Etwas Geschicklichkeit auch. Obendrauf ist der Ausflug eine interessante Bestandsprobe für jede Art von Beziehung. Anfangen kann die Tour überall, allerdings sollten Boote in der Hauptsaison immer vorab reserviert werden. Im Kajak sitzt man zu zweit oder zu dritt und maximal zu viert im Kanadier. An hoch frequentierten Wochenenden helfen einem die sogenannten Schleusenkinder mit YouTube-hitverdächtigen Gesangseinlagen dabei, die Wassertore zu meistern. An manchen Stellen geht es lustig-tumultig zu, aber es gibt im weit verzweigten Wasserrouten-Netz auch idyllische Anlegepunkte und das ein oder andere versteckte Ferienparadies zu entdecken. Kayaking in the Spreewald? While it may sound like an excursion for the elderly, it's actually truly refreshing daytime fun, far from being a boring booze cruise. On the contrary – it's a rather strenuous physical activity that requires a fair amount of skill and definitely tests relationships out on the water. You can begin the tour anywhere, although in high season you should reserve the boats in advance. The kayaks can fit between two or three people, while the larger Canadian canoes can hold four. On busy weekends, so-called watergate kids help you through the locks while singing potential YouTube hits, so be sure to have some change handy. In certain areas it can get entertainingly tumultuous, but there is a wide network of waterways and space for an idyllic, relaxed afternoon. You'll also discover piers and hidden slices of paradise for your trips ashore.

Text & Photos: Stephanie Franzius

Spreehafen Burg
Am Hafen 1, 03096 Burg (Spreewald)
spreehafen-burg.de
More boat rentals: Bootshaus Conrad or Burg im Spreewald
burgimspreewald.de
Take a break at Fiedermannhof
fiedermannhof.de

MITTAGS IN MITTE: WILLKOMMEN IM KLUB! LUNCH IN MITTE: WELCOME TO THE KLUB!

Das Mekka der Lunch-Liebhaber liegt in Mitte: The Klub Kitchen. Die Gründerin Ha Duong setzt auf kreative Crossover-Küche und verarbeitet vorwiegend saisonale Produkte von regionalen Lieferanten. Auf der Karte stehen neben Quinoa-Salat auch pochierte Eier mit Joghurt und geräucherter Paprika-Butter. Die wöchentlich wechselnde Karte mit täglichen Specials und die ruhige Lage haben The Klub Kitchen in die Top Drei meiner Lunch-Charts katapultiert – langweilig wird das Menü nämlich nie. Wer am Nachmittag eine Auszeit vom Trubel in Mitte sucht, ist hier auch gut aufgehoben. Ha kann nicht nur kochen, sondern auch backen und Chia-Apfel-Minz-Säfte mixen. Und entspannt in der Sonne sitzen, geht hier – mitten in Mitte – hervorragend, wenn man einen Platz vor der Tür ergattert. Mulackstraße holds Mitte's new mecca for healthy lunch enthusiasts – The Klub Kitchen. Founder Ha Duong runs a creative fusion-style kitchen, using mostly seasonal produce from regional farmers. On the changing weekly menu you might find quinoa salad and poached eggs, with yogurt and smoked pepper butter alongside a wide range of daily specials. Ha is also hugely skilled at crafting refreshing drinks, with homemade lemonade and chia-mint-apple juice being just a couple of her specialties. As Mulackstraße is a quiet street, The Klub Kitchen is the perfect spot to spend a relaxing lunch break. If you're lucky, you might be able to grab a seat outside and rejuvenate with delicious food while basking in the sunlight.

Text: Fee Gross / Photos: Chiara Bonetti

The Klub Kitchen
Mulackstraße 15, 10119 Berlin-Mitte
Mon-Sat 10:00-19:00
theklubkitchen.com

EXTRA TIP

Açaibeeren, Chiasamen und Avocado? Genau! Gesund zu Mittag essen kann man in Mitte auch bei Superfoods & Organic Liquids, Weinbergsweg 23. Açai berries, chia seeds, and avocado? Exactly! Head to another healthy lunch spot in Mitte: Superfoods & Organic Liquids at Weinbergsweg 23.

MAX LIEBERMANNS GARTEN
MAX LIEBERMANN'S GARDEN

1909 ließ sich der Maler Max Liebermann einen Sommersitz am
Wannsee bauen, im damals vornehmsten Villenviertel der Stadt.
Der 7000 Quadratmeter große Garten wurde schnell zu seiner
Inspirationsquelle: Er machte die Blumenterrassen und den
Birkenhain nicht nur zu Motiven seiner Gemälde, sondern pflegte
sie auch selbst. Heute sind Haus und Garten dauerhaft als
Museum geöffnet. Während die ständige Ausstellung im Obergeschoss
Pastelle und Grafiken zeigt, die Liebermann am Wannsee umsetzte,
ist sein Garten so wiederhergestellt, wie er ihn einst angelegt
hat. Auf der Terrasse sitzend, kann man den Blick über das
Wasser und die vorbeiziehenden Boote schweifen lassen. Und die
Ruhe genießen, die schon der Hausherr zu schätzen wusste.

In 1909, the painter Max Liebermann built a summer residence
in Wannsee, the most prestigious residential area of the city.
The 7000-square-meter garden quickly became his source of inspira-
tion: he made his flowered terraces and birch groves not only the
frequent subjects of his paintings, but carried out the gardening
work himself. Today, the house and garden are open to the public
as a museum and a permanent exhibition upstairs displays the pastels
and graphics once created at Wannsee. Liebermann's garden is
restored just as he once planned it, and sitting on the terrace
you can let your eye wander over the waters and passing boats while
enjoying the peace the homeowner once loved so much.

Text: Milena Kalojanov

Liebermann-Villa am Wannsee
Colomierstraße 3, 14109 Berlin-Wannsee
April-September: Mon, Wed, Sat 10:00-18:00, Thu & Sun 10:00-19:00
October-March: Wed-Mon 11:00-17:00
liebermann-villa.de

EXTRA TIP

Max Liebermanns Stadthaus direkt neben dem
Brandenburger Tor, am Pariser Platz 7, kann man
ebenfalls noch besichtigen – zweimal im Jahr
werden hier Ausstellungen gezeigt. You can also
still visit Max Liebermann's townhouse, just next
to the Brandenburg Gate, at Pariser Platz 7, where
exhibitions are shown twice a year.

MIT DEM RAD ZUM HABERMANNSEE
RIDE YOUR BIKE TO HABERMANNSEE

Jeden Sommer dasselbe: Welcher See ist der beste, um sich abzukühlen? Normalerweise suche ich einfach auf Google Maps nach den „blauen Flecken" auf der Landkarte, die im Umland von Berlin zu erkennen sind. Oft fällt unsere Wahl auf den Habermannsee, den man ganz einfach mit der Straßenbahn oder dem Rad erreichen kann. Für mich ein idyllischer kleiner See, der nicht überfüllt ist und viele schöne Plätze am Ufer bietet – Liegewiesen für die Großen und sandige Buchten mit flachen Ufern für die Kleinen. Every year, there's a hype about Berlin's best secret lake to cool down in on hot summer days. I usually just browse through online maps and search for the "blue spots" that surround the city in their hundreds. However, if I want to go to a lake that's not too far and reachable by tram or bike, then I end up at Habermannsee, the perfect place for me. It's dotted with plenty of great sunbathing areas all around the shore, grassy areas for the grown-ups, and sandy beaches with a good stretch of shallow water for the little ones.

Text: Sven Hausherr / Photos: Daniel Farò

Habermannsee
Kressenweg, 12623 Berlin-Mahlsdorf

EXTRA TIP

Wer noch länger an der frischen Luft bleiben will: auf in die Gärten der Welt im Erholungspark Marzahn (Eisenacher Straße 99). If you want to stay in the open air a little longer, Gärten der Welt in Erholungspark Marzahn (Eisenacher Straße 99) is the perfect place for you.

BOR
N&
BR
ED

DEM LOKALPATRIOTISMUS
GESCHMACKVOLL
AUSDRUCK ZU VERLEIHEN
IST MÖGLICH. MIT
BERLINER KREATIONEN
VON BETONMÖBELN BIS
ZU NATURKOSMETIK.
THERE'S A STYLISH
WAY TO PARADE YOUR
LOCAL PATRIOTISM:
WITH QUINTESSENTIALLY
BERLIN CREATIONS, FROM
CONCRETE DESIGNS TO
NATURAL COSMETICS.

DRAPIERTE ELEGANZ
DRAPED SOPHISTICATION

Den Shop von Michael Sontag zu betreten, fühlt sich an, wie ein Musikalbum von vorne bis hinten zu hören: Ich verstehe die Idee seiner Kollektion, bin angezogen von der Klarheit, der Reduziertheit, den Farben. Bekannt für sein Draping insbesondere bei Kleidern, kann man hier aber auch endlich die Vielseitigkeit und Tragbarkeit seiner Kollektionen entdecken. Ich habe mich verliebt und für ein rotes stone-washed Seidenoberteil, ein dunkelgraues Rippoberteil mit schwarzen Satinstreifen und natürlich eines seiner berühmten Kleider entschieden. Die Gestaltung des Shops folgt eben-falls der Idee des Modemachers: Die Ladenfront ist konse-quente Transparenz, die Aufteilung klar und reduziert, ohne kühl zu sein. Nichts ist angestrengt, die Lässigkeit überwiegt. Hier ist sie, eine Welt, die immer noch zählt.

Entering Michael Sontag's store feels like listening to a whole record. I began to understand the idea of his collec-tion: its simplicity, the color palette. His store offers a comprehensive look at the diversity and wearability of his collections, known best for timelessly stylish dresses and draping. I can't help falling in love with a red stonewash silk top and a dark grey ribbed alternative with black sateen stripes. And, of course, one of his famous draped dresses. The store itself matches his fashion designs perfectly and is strictly transparent, and the inner partitions are precise and minimal. A spirited coolness outweighs any possibility of becoming tired or overwhelmed. Here another world awaits you beyond the threshold.

Text: Kirsten Hermann / Photos: Daniel Farò

Michael Sontag Shop
Muskauer Straße 41, 10997 Berlin-Kreuzberg
Sat 11:00-16:00, Thu 15:00-20:00, Tue, Wed, Fri: 13:00-18:00 and by appointment
michaelsontag.com

EXTRA TIP

Rund zehn Minuten dauert es zu Fuß in die
Manteuffelstraße 48 zu Platz doch!, einem Restaurant für osteuropäisches Slow Food. It only takes 10
minutes to walk to Manteuffelstraße 48, where you'll
find Platz doch!, a restaurant for East-European
Slow Food.

KUNST FÜR ALLE: GRAFIK, MUSIK & MULTIPLES ART FOR ALL: GRAPHICS, MUSIC & MULTIPLES

Rund um die Spichernstraße trafen sich schon einmal die Intellektu-
ellen und Künstler der Stadt. Erich Kästner schrieb hier Kinderbücher
und Vladimir Nabokov frühstückte in der Prager Diele. 1964 öffnete
René Block, mit gerade mal 22 Jahren, in der Gegend seine erste
Galerie. Er zeigte damals noch unbekannte Künstler wie Joseph Beuys,
Nam June Paik und Gerhard Richter. Zwei Jahre später gründete er die
Edition Block: einen Raum für Druckgrafik, Multiples und Schallplat-
ten. An der Idee der Edition hielt er auch nach Zwischenstopps in New
York und Kassel fest – jeder sollte in der Lage sein, Kunst nicht nur
betrachten, sondern kaufen zu können. Neben neuen Arbeiten junger
Künstler sieht man heute auch Werke alter Bekannter wie KP Brehmer,
den Block schon in seiner ersten Galerieausstellung präsentierte. At
the beginning of the twentieth century, the area around Spichernstraße was a meeting ground for the city's intellectuals and artists.
Erich Kästner wrote children's books here, and Vladimir Nabokov
breakfasted in the Prager Diele. In 1964 René Block, 22 years old,
opened his first gallery in the area. At first he showed then-unknown
artists like Joseph Beuys, Nam June Paik, and Gerhard Richter. Two
years later, he founded Edition Block, a space for prints, multiples,
and records. After taking a few years' break from Berlin in New York
and Kassel, Block continued to hold fast to his founding beliefs
that everyone should be able to buy art instead of only seeing it in
galleries and museums. Now, next to new pieces from up-and-coming
names you can also see the works of established artists such as
KP Brehmer, whom Block featured in his very first gallery exhibition.

Text: Laura Storfner / Photos: Uwe Walter

Edition Block
Prager Straße 5, 10779 Berlin-Wilmersdorf
Thu & Fri 11:00-18:00, Sat 12:00-16:00
editionblock.de

EXTRA TIP

10 Fußminuten entfernt, in der Ludwigkirchstraße 11, befindet sich das Manzini,
ein kleines Bistro mit Kronleuchtern,
Stuckdecken und leckerem Club-
Sandwich. It takes 10 minutes by foot to
get to Manzini at Ludwigkirchstraße 11,
a small bistro with chandeliers, stucco
ceilings, and a great club sandwich.

BORN & BRED

SAISONALE KÜCHE IM KLEINEN GARTEN
SEASONAL COOKING IN A LITTLE GARDEN

Früher wurde in dem ehemaligen Ballhaus getanzt, seit 2015 kann man im Laden Buchholz-berlin saisonale Küche genießen. Der Laden, soviel verrät bereits der Name, ist ein Gemeinschaftsprojekt der Architektin und Designerin Katja Buchholz und den Machern des Restaurants namens Lokal, Maren Thimm und Gary Hoopengardner. Auf der Karte stehen unter anderem Flatbread, Salate und Suppen. Im Frühjahr und Sommer kommen die Zutaten aus dem eigenen Garten. Die Einrichtung stammt aus Katjas Hand – von den massiven Holztischen bis zu den Holzschalen und -brettern, in und auf denen das Essen serviert wird. Natur rundum, denn das Holz wird ausschließlich aus den Wäldern Brandenburgs bezogen! Und das Beste: Alle Produkte können vor Ort gekauft oder online bestellt werden. Previously filled with dancers as a former Ballhaus, in summer 2015 it was transformed into a venue for seasonal cuisine: Laden Buchholzberlin – a joint project by the designer and architect Katja Buchholz and the makers of Lokal, Maren Thimm and Gary Hoopengardner. The menu offers delicious flatbreads alongside refreshing salads and hearty soups. In spring and summer, the ingredients come directly from their own homegrown garden, which is located in the cozy backyard of the shop. The interior has Katja's touch everywhere, from the massive wooden tables to the wooden bowls and boards on which the food is served. The connection between nature thrives inside as well, the wood comes exclusively from regional surrounding forests. And the best part? All the products can be purchased directly or ordered from their shop.

Text: Katharina Pencz / Photos: Daniel Farò

Laden Buchholzberlin
Joachimstraße 20, 10119 Berlin-Mitte
Tue-Sat 12:00-22:00
buchholzberlin.com

EXTRA TIP

Nomen est omen: Die Mozzarella Bar um die Ecke, in der Auguststraße 34, serviert fantastische Burrata. The name says it all: The Mozzarella Bar on the corner at Auguststraße 34 serves fantastic burrata.

ATELIERS & KUNSTWORKSHOPS IM KLINKERBAU ART STUDIOS & WORKSHOPS IN AN OLD BREWERY

Die vier Schornsteine der ehemaligen Schultheiss-Brauerei erblickt man schon von Weitem. Dass der Klinkerbau im Gewerbegebiet Schöneberg bis in die Neunzigerjahre die größte Malzproduktionsanlage Europas war, sieht man ihm heute aber nicht mehr an. Heute werden die größtenteils noch original erhaltenen Verwaltungsgebäude, Maschinenräume und Lagerhallen als Ateliers und Ausstellungsorte genutzt. Berliner Künstler wie Julian Charrière und Julius von Bismarck arbeiten hier, Kreativität und Forschung gehen Hand in Hand: Neben der von Frank Sippel gegründeten District Kunst- und Kulturförderung, die halbjährlich ein öffentliches Atelier- stipendium explizit an Frauen vergibt und regelmäßig Work- shops anbietet, ist das Gelände auch als Veranstaltungsort beliebt – der Berlin Art Prize wurde hier gefeiert und auch das Project Space Festival kehrt immer wieder hierher zurück. Im Sommer lockt nicht nur das Programm, sondern auch das renaturierte Brachland mit seinen zwei Teichen, in denen man baden kann. The four chimneys of the former Schultheiss Brewery are visible even from afar. Now, however, it's hard to tell that up until the nineties this old brick building in the commercial district of Schoeneberg was the biggest malt-production factory in Europe. Today, most of the original administrative buildings, machine rooms, and ware- houses have been preserved and are used as studio and exhi- bition spaces, with Berlin artists such as Julian Charrière and Julius von Bismarck working here. Creativity and education go hand in hand: in addition to the District Art and Culture Foundation, founded by Frank Sippel, a semi- annual public studio scholarship is explicitly reserved for women, and regular workshops are offered. The site is also a popular event venue: the Berlin Art Prize has been celebrated here and the Project Space Festival frequently returns. In summer it's not just the program that entices you to explore between the brick walls – the reclaimed wasteland has two ponds in which you can take a swim and cool off.

Text: Laura Storfner / Photos: Emma Haugh

District Berlin
Bessemerstraße 2-14, 12103 Berlin-Schöneberg
Tue-Sat 14:00-18:00 during exhibitions or by appointment
district-berlin.com

EXTRA TIP

Noch mehr Natur erlebt man im angrenzenden Schöneberger Südgelände, Prellerweg 47-49, einem Park, der früher als Rangierbahnhof genutzt wurde. If you want to explore more nature, go to the adjacent Schöneberger Südgelände, Prellerweg 47-49, a park once used as a switchyard.

EXZELLENTES AUS DER REGION
SUPER LOCAL SUPPER

Dieses Restaurant sollte man besuchen – am besten zu zweit. Man
wird einen unvergesslichen Abend erleben, was zum einen am
fantastischen Essen, zum anderen am charismatischen Gastgeber
liegt. Billy Wagner ist nämlich nicht nur ein exzellenter
Sommelier, sondern auch ein begnadeter Entertainer. Jeder Wein
wird mit einer Anekdote serviert – die professionelle Getränke-
begleitung zum wechselnden Menü ist daher ein Muss. Während der
Herr des Hauses von Rhabarber-Moussierendem bis zu Bier
Überraschendes eingießt, werden die Gerichte aus regionalen
Zutaten von den jeweiligen Köchen direkt an den Platz gebracht:
Fleisch grillt man hier schon mal über Rebenholz und Forelle
wird in kalt gepresstem Spinatsaft angerichtet. Man sitzt also
da, auf sehr bequemen Stühlen, bewundert eben noch das schöne
Buttermesser und das aparte Geschirr, dann heißt es auch schon
wieder: probieren, was man so noch nie gegessen hat. Bis man nach
Hause geht, vielleicht mit dem Duft von grünem Hafer in der Nase.

A visit to this dining establishment is highly recommended, ideally
as a pair. It's sure to be an unforgettable evening – thanks
partly, of course, to the fantastic food. However, Nobelhart &
Schmutzig is more than just a local restaurant, as the light box
in the window suggests. It's a restaurant with a concept and a
charismatic owner – the excellent sommelier and gifted entertainer Billy Wagner. Every wine comes with a story, and tasting
the recommended beverage that accompanies the changing menu is
a must. While the head of house pours surprising potions, from fizzy
rhubarb to special beer, the cooks bring the dishes to the table
themselves: meat grilled over vine shoots, trout in cold-pressed
spinach juice. So visit, recline on your comfortable chair in a
space with fantastic acoustics, and you will barely have time to
admire the beautiful butter knife and striking china before it's
time to taste something prepared in a completely unique way before
you go home, maybe with the scent of green oat in your nose.

Text: Nina Trippel / Photos: Sven Hausherr, Caroline Prange, Marko Seifert

Nobelhart & Schmutzig
Friedrichstraße 218, 10969 Berlin-Kreuzberg
Tue-Sat 18:30-22:30
nobelhartundschmutzig.com

EXTRA TIP

Produkte von Und Gretel Naturkosmetik kauft man zum Beispiel in Jacks Beauty Department, Kastanienallee 19. You can buy Und Gretel Naturkosmetik products from Jacks Beauty Department, located at Kastanienallee 19.

HIGH-END KOSMETIK IN DEN FARBEN DER NATUR LUXURY COSMETICS MADE ALL-NATURAL

Christina Roth weiß, was das Gesicht einer Frau braucht: Aufmerksamkeit. Nährstoffe. Und Farbe. Kurz: Make-up, das pflegt und aufhübscht. Klingt wie ein Traum, aber Christina – ihres Zeichens Make-up Artist - und ihre Business-Partnerin Stephanie Dettmann haben ihn wahr gemacht. Das Ergebnis: Und Gretel. Eine Kosmetiklinie, deren Produkte altdeutsche Namen wie Sunne oder Lieth tragen. Meine Favoriten sind die hochpigmentierten Mono-Lidschatten in satten Farben und Ilge, der hauchzarte, transparente Puder im kleinen Spiegeldöschen, der den Teint mattiert und sich mit jedem Make-up kombinieren lässt. Spaß machen die extragroßen Lipglosse, bei denen man kaum glauben mag, dass diese leuchtenden Farben ohne schädliche Chemie hergestellt werden. Stimmt aber! Und Gretel ist ehrliche Naturkosmetik im High-End-Segment. Christina Roth knows what a woman's face needs. Attention. Nutrients. Color. In other words, cosmetics that are given in perfect nuances and doses, soothing and celebrating your skin at the same time. Sounds like a dream? Not anymore. Roth, a trained makeup artist, and her business partner Stephanie Dettmann have brought this vision to life. The result: Und Gretel – a cosmetic line whose products are given traditional German names like Sunne and Lieth. My favorites are the highly pigmented mono eye shadows in deep colors and the transparent powder Ilge that works on every skin tone. The extra big lip glosses are also fun. It's hard to believe that these bright colors are made without using anything noxious. But take my word for it. Und Gretel products are high-end, yet all natural.

Text: Nina Trippel / Photos: Sarah Radowitz

Und Gretel Naturkosmetik
undgretel.com

DIE WUNDERKAMMER DES FRANK LEDER FRANK LEDER'S CHAMBER OF WONDER

Ein Besuch beim Modedesigner Frank Leder fühlt sich an, als würde man bei einem guten Freund vorbeischauen, der zufällig im Museum wohnt. In seinem Charlottenburger Atelier kann man Stunden verbringen und Neues entdecken: das Projekt „Gebackenes Hemd in Salzkruste" vor dem Kamin oder Pferdehaar, das auch als Füllung seiner Bomberjacken Verwendung findet, die große Sammlung von Weckgläsern oder Öle und Shampoos seiner Kosmetiklinie Tradition, die in Österreich hergestellt werden und Namen wie Deutsche Eiche und Weizenbier tragen. Der Showroom wird durch einen Shop ergänzt: Im zweiten Stock erwirbt man seine Mode – Hemden und Hosen aus groben Woll- und Baumwollstoffen sowie Pullover und Strickjacken, in denen man sich „zuhause" fühlt und trotzdem anständig angezogen ist. Entering Frank Leder's showroom makes you feel like you're visiting an old friend who is living in a museum. At the designer's Charlottenburg showroom, you can spend hours studying every little detail of his products, like a cabinet of curiosities. You'll see his project called "Baked Shirt in Salt Crust" near the fireplace and the horsehair he uses to pad his bomber jackets, as well as a collection of canned jars and his own cosmetic line called Tradition – shower gels and oils named Weizenbier (wheat beer) or Deutsche Eiche (German oak). The showroom has a sister shop on the second floor, where you can buy the designer's fashion collection: pants made from thick wool, cotton shirts that embrace your body, and knitted sweaters and cardigans that evoke a feeling of homeliness.

Text: Milena Kalojanov / Photos: Daniel Farò

Frank Leder
Kantstraße 139, 2nd floor, 10623 Berlin-Charlottenburg
Mon-Fri 11:00-18:00
frank-leder.com

EXTRA TIP

Stilvolle Herrenmode gibt es auch im Kreuzberger Maßatelier von Purwin & Radczun am Tempelhofer Ufer 32. You can also find bespoke men's style in a Kreuzberg Atelier, at Purwin & Radczun at Tempelhofer Ufer 32.

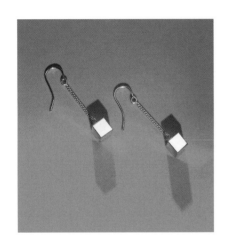

DIE KLEINE BOUTIQUE FÜR FILIGRANE PREZIOSEN THE LITTLE BOUTIQUE FOR FILIGREE JEWELRY

Die zeitlosen Designs von Felicitas Seidlers Schmuckkollektionen lassen mich jedes Mal, wenn ich die Schröderstraße entlanggehe, vor ihrem Schaufenster Halt machen. Man merkt, dass Felicitas eigentlich ausgebildete Architektin und Goldschmiedin ist, denn der Schmuck verbindet ihre Vorliebe für klare, einfache Linien mit ihrem Interesse an zart und fein gestalteten Stücken. Die Ringe, Halsketten, Broschen und Armbänder, die allesamt in ihrem Berliner Studio aus ausgewählten Materialien entstehen, zeugen von ihrer Fähigkeit, elegante und verspielte Kollektionen zu entwerfen. Sie runden lässige Outfits ab und machen jeden Look noch einen Tick schöner. The timeless designs of Felicitas Seidler's jewelry collections draw my eye every time I walk down Schröderstraße. Trained as an architect and a goldsmith, Seidler combines an architect's love of clean, simple lines with a goldsmith's penchant for delicate, beautiful pieces. The rings, necklaces, brooches, and bracelets, all made in Seidler's Berlin studio with painstakingly chosen materials, are testaments to her ability to create collections with both elegance and a sense of fun. The pieces are perfect as the finishing touches for any look.

Text: Milena Kalojanov / Photos: Johann Clausen, Filine Fink

Felicious
Schröderstraße 14, 10115 Berlin-Mitte
Wed-Fri 14:00-19:00, Sat 14:00-18:00
felicious.com

EXTRA TIP

In der Alpenstück-Manufaktur nebenan, Schröderstraße 15, trifft man sich zum Mittagessen (Speck-, Semmel- und Brezn-Knödel, Quiches und Suppen) oder kauft hausgemachte Schmankerl für daheim. In the neighboring Alpenstück-Manufaktur at Schröderstraße 15, you'll find lunch (bacon, bread, and pretzel Knödels, quiches and soups), or get a homemade Schmankerl to take home.

AUF EIN STÜCK OPERNTORTE NACH RIXDORF TO RIXDORF FOR A PIECE OF OPERA CAKE

Die beiden talentierten Köchinnen Sarah Hallmann und Friederieke Klee haben das Abenteuer vom gemeinsamen Restaurant gewagt. Seither servieren sie in ihren hellen Räumen mit urigem Holzboden, weiten Fenstern und freiem Blick in die „Wunderkammer" Küche originelle und äußerst liebevoll angerichtete Speisen, wie etwa die Variation aus gebackener Kartoffel und Püree mit gebratenen und roh-marinierten Radieschen. Ebenso köstlich sind die Backwaren: Es gibt französisch inspirierte Desserts wie Rhabarber-Baiser und Operntorte mit Kaffee, Schokolade und Sesam, die im Mund geradezu zerschmelzen. Die Kreationen der beiden sind ausbalanciert und fein abgestimmt. Abgerundet wird alles mit dem Blick auf den Böhmischen Platz, wo es besonders im Frühjahr schön ist, wenn die Kirschbäume in Blüte stehen. Sarah Hallmann and Frizzi Klee, two talented German chefs, decided to branch out and begin their own joint venture. Their daytime restaurant Hallmann & Klee is airy with beautiful windows, rustic wooden floors, and a view into the magic of the kitchen, where original and lovingly prepared dishes are created, with options such as smoky roasted and pureed potato with marinated radish. The baking is equally delicious, with some French-inspired desserts such as a coffee, chocolate, cocoa, and sesame opera cake, and a rhubarb meringue pie that will melt in your mouth. Both creations are balanced and finely tuned. The view of the lovely Böhmischer Platz rounds out the experience, especially in spring when the cherry trees are in full bloom.

Text: Antonia Harris / Photos: Daniel Farò

Hallmann & Klee
Böhmische Straße 13, 12055 Berlin-Neukölln
Wed-Sat 9:30-22:00, Sun 9:30-20:00
hallmann-klee.de

BETON-KREATIONEN NACH MASS
BESPOKE CONCRETE CREATIONS

Im Café Barini in Neukölln baumelt ein Kronleuchter aus Beton von der
Decke und im Kontor Eismanufaktur in Prenzlauer Berg lässt sich ein
robuster Tresen aus dem schroffen Material bewundern, genau wie im
Le Bon. Alle drei Elemente wurden von Accidental Concrete entworfen
und produziert, einer kleinen Firma für handgefertigte Objekte und
maßgefertigte Möbel aus Beton. Dahinter steht Jonas Klock, ein
Architekt aus Berlin, der sich mit seinem Herzensprojekt selbständig
gemacht hat. Zu dem aktuellen Sortiment gehören kubistische Hänge-
lampen, Kerzen, diverse Vasen, Tische und Wandregale. Bisweilen teilt
er sein Wissen auch mit Nicht-Profis: Im Rahmen der Cee Cee Lessons
hat Jonas 15 Workshop-Teilnehmern gezeigt, wie man aus Glasflaschen
Betonvasen herstellt. Wer ein Objekt für Zuhause sucht, schaut auf
seine Webseite oder schreibt ihm, denn am liebsten entwickelt Jonas
seine Produkte mit den Kunden. At Café Barini a concrete chandelier
hangs from the ceiling; at Eismanufaktur a giant counter also made
from the stark material draws attention and admiration; at Le Bon
another such counter serves as the centerpiece. All these bespoke
pieces are designed and produced by Accidental Concrete, a small
company that fashions concrete objects and furniture. Jonas Klock,
a young architect from Berlin, stands behind this ambitious project,
spending his time experimenting with materials and following his
heart's designs. Finely crafted cubist droplights, candles, and
vases complement stark tables and shelves. Sometimes he even shares
his expertise with non-professionals: he showed 15 participants in
one of our Cee Cee Lessons how to make a concrete vase from a glass
bottle. If you're looking for a creation of your very own, check
out the website or write to him: besides his ready-made articles,
Jonas often develops products on-site.

Text: Mira Starke / Photos: Daniel Farò, Jonas Klock

Accidental Concrete
accidentalconcrete.com

EXTRA TIP

Wem Accidental Concrete zu kubisch daherkommt,
dem gefallen vielleicht die Keramikkreationen
von Livia Polidoro, die man in ihrem Atelier in der
Berliner Straße 80–82 erstehen oder in Auftrag
geben lassen kann. If Accidental Concrete is a little
too cubic for you, you may like the ceramic bowls
of Livia Polidoro. See them in her studio at Berliner
Straße 80–82 or commission them individually.

GLÜCKSGEFÜHLE IN KUCHEN-FORM JOY IS A PIECE OF CAKE

Kuchen – eine große Liebe! Ich habe mich oft genug verführen lassen, um sagen zu können: bravo Bravko ist das Paradies. Egal, ob Orientalische Orange, Birne-Mohn oder Pistazien-Mousse – ich hatte sie alle, Baby! Und jeder war auf seine Art grandios. Zumal hier auch das Setting stimmt, innere Werte sind schließlich nicht alles. Auf Wanddekoration wird verzichtet, stattdessen gefallen wuchtige Industrielampen, abgeblätterte Metallstühle und die Theke mit den blauen Fliesen, die vorher den Boden bildeten. Realen Flirts helfen die zwei langen Tafeln auf die Sprünge, an denen die Gäste Platz nehmen. Der Eigentümer, Dubravko Dordevic, beliefert Cafés in der ganzen Stadt, aber nur in seiner Werkstatt mit Café kann man einen Blick in die Backstube erhaschen. Obwohl man gerade glücklich mit seinem Stück ist, schielt man bereits Richtung Vitrine für die nächste süße Liaison. Monogamie wird überbewertet. Cake! It's my greatest love. I've been seduced many a time, so trust me – bravo Bravko is a true paradise. Choose between oriental orange, pear-poppy seeds and pistachio mousse cakes: baby, I've had them all, and every single one was wonderfully unique and delicious. I love the interior design of this place too, how the bare walls accentuate the heavy industrial lights, old metal chairs, and the reclaimed blue tiles of the counter while the long tables unite customers as they enjoy their sweets. The owner, Dubravko Dordevic, also delivers to cafés all over town. Only at his Kreuzberg location, however, can you gain a glimpse into the bakery while you eat. Sitting there with a piece in front of you, you may feel completely confident in your choice. However, as soon as you lift your head to see the others being put out on display you might have a change of heart. Monogamy is overrated.

Text: Eva Biringer / Photos: Lotte Ostermann

bravo Bravko Kuchenwerkstatt
Lausitzer Straße 47, 10999 Berlin-Kreuzberg
Daily 9:00-19:00
bravo-bravko.de

FRISCHGEZAPFTES FÜR ZUHAUSE
TAKE YOUR GROWLER HOME

In Neuengland, wo ich aufgewachsen bin, gehört es zum guten Ton, Growler – dickbäuchige Bierkrüge oder Flaschen – in die eigenen Lieblingsbrauereien mitzunehmen, um sie dort mit Fass-bier füllen zu lassen. Die Besitzer des Craft Beer-Shops Lager Lager, Robyn Anderson und André Gifkins, bringen dieses Konzept nun nach Neukölln – und zwar mit einer kleinen, aber feinen Auswahl, die frisch gezapft wird. Das Sortiment besteht aus einer farbenfrohen Auswahl an Flaschen- und Dosenbieren: Neben den Stars der Berliner Szene, wie dem Heidenpeters der Markthalle Neun und Spent Brewer's Collective, gibt es auch internationale Sorten, die man sonst nur selten findet. Ob für zu Hause oder einen Nachmittag am Kanal – dieser Laden macht dem bestsortiertesten Späti Konkurrenz. Growing up in New England, I loved the ritual of taking a growler – these potbellied beer jugs – to my favorite local breweries for refills of fresh draft beer. Lager Lager owners Robyn Anderson and André Gifkins bring this neighborhood-esque option to Neukölln, with a small, diverse array of rotating taps waiting to re-plenish your very own growler or smaller bottle. The shelves are filled with a colorful variety of bottled and canned beer. Next to stars of the Berlin scene like Markthalle Neun's Heidenpeters and Spent Brewer's Collective are harder-to-get international varieties. Lager Lager is in serious danger of ruining your relationship with any well-equipped Späti.

Text: Mason Dean / Photos: Daniel Farò, Janar Siniloo

Lager Lager
Pflügerstraße 68, 12047 Berlin-Neukölln
Mon-Wed 12:00-22:00, Thu 12:00-23:00, Fri 12:00-24:00, Sat 11:00-24:00
lagerlagerberlin.de

EXTRA TIP

Wer zum Trinken einen Grund braucht, der isst vorher bei Jimmy Woo in der Friedelstraße 24: Das Curry und der Papayasalat sind extrem lecker und scharf. Danach schmeckt das Bier doppelt so gut. If you need a reason to drink, eat at Jimmy Woo at Friedelstraße 24: the curry and the papaya salad are really delicious and extremely spicy. After that, the beer tastes twice as good.

LIVE & LEARN

ENDLOS SCHAUEN UND
BETRACHTEN IST EINFACH
IN BERLIN. ERKUNDEN UND
MITMACHEN EBENFALLS.
DANN WIRD DIE STADT
ZUM BEKANNTEN UND DIE
BEWOHNER ZU FREUNDEN.
IT'S EASY TO PLAY BERLIN
AS A SPECTATOR SPORT,
BUT SO IS PARTICIPATING
AND EXPLORING. THEN
THE CITY WILL BECOME
YOUR COMPANION
AND ITS INHABITANTS
YOUR FRIENDS.

LESEN, LERNEN & VERWEILEN
LINGER IN THE READING ROOM

Kaffee trinken und lesen – das geht im westberlin, dem
Café und Mediashop des Architekten Kai Bröer, Hand in
Hand. In seinem hellen Ladenlokal verkauft er eine ex-
zellente Auswahl an Publikationen rund um Mode, Kunst
und Design – von Achtung bis Wired und kleineren Indie-
Heften. Berlin-Lektüre ergänzt das Sortiment und macht
das Café zum idealen Zwischenstopp auf einer Tour mit
Freunden von außerhalb – und das nicht zuletzt weil das
westberlin unweit des Checkpoint Charlie liegt. Auf der
Karte steht u.a. Espresso mit Bohnen der Rösterei Drop
Coffee Roasters, daneben frische Säfte, Kuchen und salzige
Snacks. Eine erstklassige Anlaufstelle mit kleiner
Sonnenterrasse am wenig beachteten, südlichen Ende der
Friedrichstraße. Having a cup of coffee and reading a
magazine is a perfect leisurely pastime. westberlin, run
by architect Kai Bröer, provides such an experience: a
café where you can purchase your magazine and enjoy it
right there. You'll find an excellent selection of reads,
from fashion to design titles, like Achtung or Wired magazine. Furthermore, there are also select Berlin books,
meaning the café is a great stopping point on a tour of
the city with friends – not to mention its great location,
only a few minutes from Checkpoint Charlie! Fantastic
espresso from Stockholm's Drop Coffee Roasters is served
alongside fresh juices, cakes, and snacks. A first class
location with a lovely sun terrace. It's a great addition
to the southern end of Friedrichstraße.

Text: Massimo Hartmann / Photos: Daniel Farò

westberlin coffeebar & mediashop
Friedrichstraße 215, 10969 Berlin-Kreuzberg
Mon-Fri 8:30-19:00, Sat & Sun 10:00-19:00
westberlin-bar-shop.de

EXTRA TIP

Ruhig, aber nicht weniger aufregend als am
Checkpoint Charlie geht es im Galerienhaus an
der Charlottenstraße zu: hier haben die Galerie
Barbara Thumm und Carlier I Gebauer ihren Sitz.
More peaceful but no less exciting than Checkpoint
Charlie is the Galerienhaus on Charlottenstraße,
with Galerie Barbara Thumm and Carlier I Gebauer.

GETÖPFERTE REDUKTION
MOLDED MINIMALISM

Töpfern? Ja, tatsächlich: töpfern! Und zwar japanisch reduziert – ohne Esoterik und Klimbim. Das zeigt schon der erste Blick in den geflochtenen Korb, der vor dem Laden Bender Keramik steht: Vasen, Schalen und Teller aus der Manufaktur mit winzigen, wunderschönen Unregelmäßigkeiten – und deshalb zu reduzierten Preisen. Verkauft werden sie von Anemone Richter, geb. Bender, die in ihrem Geschäft auch Kurse an der Drehscheibe gibt. Wer den Einsteigerkurs von vier Veranstaltungen à zwei Stunden absolviert hat, kann sich stundenweise die Drehscheibe mieten. Für Kinder stehen Tonfiguren zum Bemalen bereit. Auf Wunsch entwickelt Anemone auch Sonderanfertigungen in filigraner Handarbeit, wie hängende Blumentöpfe oder Aufbewahrungsgefäße für den Kühlschrank. Ein Besuch lohnt sich – nicht nur wegen der Schätze im Korb. Pottery? Yes: pottery! Simple, Japanese-style pottery, free of showy extras or twee pieces. Inside the store, you'll discover the beautiful irregularities that make each of the handmade vases, bowls, and plates unique. Anemone Richter, née Bender, sells not only her own handcrafted pieces but also offers back-to-basics pottery classes. Once you've mastered the four two-hour beginner classes, you can even book the studio and work on your own. For the younger visitors there are also clay figurines just waiting to be painted. Special orders and individual designs for delicate hand-worked decoration can be requested, among other items such as flowerpots, clay pots, and small pans. It's not only a place for things to be sold, but also to be personalized in a lovely creative setting.

Text: Christina Hoffmann / Photos: Janar Siniloo

Bender Keramik
Reuterstraße 90, 12053 Berlin-Neukölln
Check online for opening hours
benderkeramik.de

EXTRA TIP

Schön und praktisch sind auch die Vasen und Zuckerdosen von feuer zeug keramik in der Mariannenstraße 48: Töpfern und Glasieren lernt man in der Werkstatt in der Lenaustraße 23. The vases and sugar bowls made by feuer zeug keramik are both beautiful and practical. Check them out at Mariannenstraße 48, or head to Lenaustraße 23 to learn about creating pottery and glaze your creations yourself in the workshop.

ACHTUNG, HIER KOMMEN DIE DINOSAURIER! BEWARE: HERE THERE BE DINOSAURS!

Wer das Museum für Naturkunde in Berlin besucht, nimmt vor allem die Dinosaurier-Sammlung wahr: Das liegt an Tristan, dem 66 Millionen Jahre alten T. rex, der seit Dezember 2015 die große Haupthalle beherrscht. Das sehr gut erhaltene Skelett wurde 2010 in den USA ausgegraben und gilt aufgrund der Menge an gefundenen Knochen als weltweit einmaliger Fund. Aber die Urzeit-Echsen sind bei Weitem nicht der einzige Schatz. Hinter den Kulissen des Museums lagert gut behütet eine der größten Sammlungen der Welt, mit über 30 Millionen zoologischer Artefakte. Wer es vermeiden kann, kommt nicht am Wochenende, wenn Kinder staunend und raunend durch die Räume wuseln, sondern unter der Woche ab 15 Uhr – die beste Zeit, um ungestört zum Forscher zu werden. Visitors to the Museum of Natural History in Berlin are always especially impressed by the dinosaur collection. Naturally Tristan, the 66 million-year-old T. rex who has dominated the great hall since December 2015, occupies most of their attention. The skeleton, which was found in 2010 in the USA, is one of the best-preserved specimens in the world. However, it's well worth taking a look around the rest of the museum, because the prehistoric lizards are not the only treasure to be found within its walls. Behind the scenes is one of the largest natural collections in the world, with over 30 million zoological artifacts. Try to avoid visiting at peak times, especially during the weekend when children run wild through the rooms. It is usually quiet from midweek, around three in the afternoon, and then you can wander about undisturbed by anyone but researchers.

Text: Helen von der Höden / Photos: Daniel Farò

Museum für Naturkunde
Invalidenstraße 43, 10115 Berlin-Mitte
Tue-Fri 9:30-18:00, Sat & Sun 10:00-18:00
naturkundemuseum.berlin

Noch mehr Edelsteine kann man in den Mineralo-
gischen Sammlungen der Technischen Universität
am Ernst-Reuter-Platz 1 bewundern. You can admire
even more gems in the mineral collections of the
Technische Universität at Ernst-Reuter-Platz 1.

DIE WELT IM OBEREN JURA

DIE WELT DER RISOGRAFIE
BRINGING BACK THE RISOGRAPH

Wenn es um Risografie geht, bin ich ein Enthusiast. Das Druckver-
fahren, das ähnlich wie Siebdrucktechnik mit Schablonen
arbeitet, die Farbe jedoch ohne Chemikalien und Hitze aufs
Papier bringt, ist genial, und nach meinem ersten Besuch
bei We make it ist meine Begeisterung sogar noch gewachsen.
Franziska Brandt und Moritz Grünke haben ihr Studio 2012
im Wedding eröffnet und sich auf die individuellen Wünsche
von Künstlern und Designern spezialisiert. Auch Bücher und
Zines werden hier direkt geschnitten und gebunden. Ein Besuch
lohnt sich schon alleine wegen der wechselnden Ausstellungen
und der hauseigenen Sammlung an Risografien – eine wunderbare Inspirationsquelle. I've always been a big fan of the
risograph. Real ink, fewer chemicals – they're an enduring
miracle of the print world. The Wedding-based print studio
We make it has made me even more enthusiastic. Set up by
Franziska Brandt and Moritz Grünke in 2012, We make it places
an emphasis on DIY ethics. The founders provide years of
experience and knowledge to artists, designers, and writers
who are looking to get their zines, posters, books, and
editorial work to print. Along with printing, the studio also
has finishing facilities for binding, cutting, foiling,
and scoring. It's also worth a visit to see their temporary
exhibitions and in-house collection of risograph prints –
definitely an inspirational trip.

Text: Janar Siniloo / Photos: Moritz Grünke, Son Ni, Janar Siniloo

We make it
Malplaquetstraße 17, 13347 Berlin-Wedding
Appointments only
we-make.it

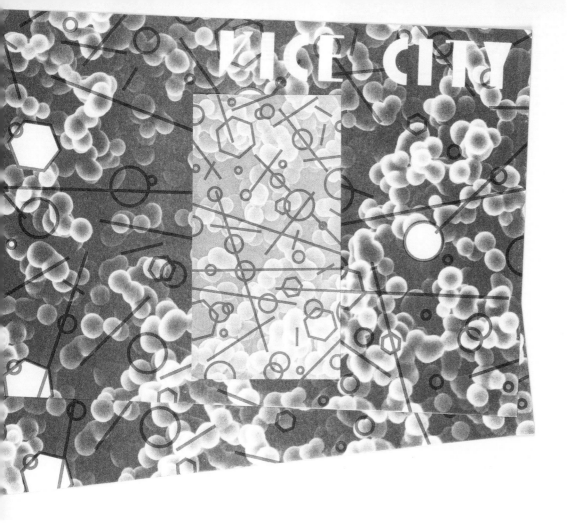

EXTRA TIP

Selbst tätig werden kann man auch im Sonder 54 in der Rheinsberger Straße 54: In der Werkstatt lernt man beispielsweise, wie Suminigashi-Papier hergestellt wird. Keep yourself busy with a trip to Sonder 54 at Rheinsberger Straße 54: in the workshop you can learn, for example, how Suminigashi paper is made.

KOCHKURS IM SCHLARAFFENLAND
CLASSES IN CULINARY WONDERLAND

Neben dem Hauptstandort am Helmholtzplatz betreibt Goldhahn und Sampson auch eine Dependance im Westen: Dort gibt es viel Platz für Feinkost, Kochbücher aus aller Welt, ein Café und vor allem für eine große Küche, in der Kurse zu Themen wie Japanische Klosterküche oder Persische Sommerküche angeboten werden. Auf dem Menü der French Bistro Class standen französische Klassiker wie Salade Niçoise, Lammrücken und Tarte au Citron. Mit einem Glas L'Oustalet Blanc gelang die Zubereitung spielend. Nur eines habe ich bereut: Als ich spätabends aus dem Laden ging, hätte ich zu gerne noch ein paar Köstlichkeiten gekauft, wie zum Beispiel das Brot von Sironi oder die Schokolade von Retos Candy Farm – Grund genug, wiederzukommen. Following the success of their Prenzlauer Berg store, food enthusiasts Goldhahn und Sampson have opened another shop in West Berlin. The spacious interior holds a café, a large deli stocked with delicacies, cookbooks from around the world, and on top of this a fully equipped kitchen which hosts cooking classes such as Japanese Kitchen or Persian Summer Cooking. I tested their French Bistro class, and spent an evening making a traditional menu of salade niçoise, roast lamb, and tarte au citron. Accompanied by a large glass of L'Oustalet Blanc, the cutting and the preparation was swiftly underway. I regret only one thing: when I left the store late that night, filled with joy and drink, I should have thought to purchase some of their incredible food, such as the Sironi bread or chocolate from Retos Candy Farm – but on the bright side, that's the perfect excuse to come back for another visit.

Text: Helen von der Höden / Photos: Mani Bakhshpour

Goldhahn und Sampson
Wilmersdorfer Straße 102/103, 10629 Berlin-Charlottenburg
Mon-Sat 8:00-21:00
Dunckerstraße 9, 10437 Berlin-Prenzlauer Berg
Mon-Fri 8:00-20:00, Sat 9:00-20:00
goldhahnundsampson.de

EXTRA TIP

Bei der Initiative Über den Tellerrand kochen in der Roßbachstraße 6 lernt man Rezepte von Geflüchteten, z.B.: aus Syrien kennen und bereitet sie gemeinsam zu. Learn recipes from refugees, e.g.: from Syria, and prepare meals to share at Über den Tellerrand at Roßbachstraße 6.

PERFECT DAY

PER
FE
CT
DAY

IMMER AUF DER SUCHE NACH DEM SCHÖNEN LEBEN. DABEI LIEGT ES SO NAHE. WIR SAGEN: BIS BALD.

ENDLESSLY HUNTING FOR THE GOOD LIFE EVEN THOUGH IT'S RIGHT HERE AT YOUR DOORSTEP. SEE YOU SOON.

DEM ZEITGEIST SEIN HAUS
A HOUSE FOR THE ZEITGEIST

Beim Halleschen Tor raus und rein ins Hallesche Haus – genauer gesagt ins Paradies von Jillian May, Michelle Casciolo und Oliver Cayless, wo es Produkte gibt, die jedes Zuhause schöner machen. Ich schlendere durch das historische Gebäude, in dem früher ein Postamt untergebracht war, und begutachte die Haushaltsartikel, Terrarien, Schreibwaren und allen voran die Sukkulenten und bestelle an der Bar einen Kaffee. Unter der Woche gibt es auch Mittagessen und am Wochenende Brunch: Man hat die Wahl zwischen Lunch Bowls, frisch zubereiteten Salaten oder Kuchen – natürlich auch glutenfrei und vegan. Samstags wird die Karte um French Toast und Breakfast Burritos erweitert. Im Garten sitzend, genießt man sein Frühstück und die Sonne. Ein Grund mehr, in diesem wunderbaren Haus vorbeizuschauen. Step out of Hallesches Tor and in through the arches of Hallesches Haus, otherwise known as a paradise for home accessories curated by Jillian May, Michelle Casciolo, and Oliver Cayless. Strolling through the historic building formerly known as Postamt 61, you'll find joyful terrariums, household tools to ensure those chores get done, stationary, and Pendleton blankets to ward off the harshest Berlin winter. In between browsing the artfully stocked store, pick up a coffee and try their snacks, lunch or weekend brunch, with offerings like lunch bowls, freshly prepared salads, and gluten free or vegan cakes. Furthermore, on Saturdays come for French toast or breakfast burritos, both of which can be enjoyed in the sunny garden. Just one more reason to pop by this multifaceted store!

Text: Elizabeth Rushe / Photos: Daniel Farò

Hallesches Haus
Tempelhofer Ufer 1, 10961 Berlin-Kreuzberg
Mon-Fri 9:00-19:00, Sat 11:00-16:00
hallescheshaus.com

Wer den Tagesausflug ausweiten möchte, besucht
die Amerika-Gedenkbibliothek am Blücherplatz 1
gegenüber. Extend your day trip and explore the
Amerika-Gedenkbibliothek on Blücherplatz 1.

BARCELONA AM KOTTI
BARCELONA BY THE KOTTI

Die vielen von der Decke hängenden Blumen sind das Erste, was man beim Eintreten wahrnimmt. Sie verleihen der Bar namens Das Hotel ihren ganz eigenen Charme. Kerzenschein, das Klavier in der Ecke und die große Fensterscheibe zur Straße tragen ihr übriges dazu bei. Man fühlt sich ein bisschen wie in Barcelona oder einer mediterranen Miniatur-Villa, die nur zufällig in Kreuzberg steht. Alte, vergessene oder unentdeckte Songs tönen aus den Lautsprechern, das Stimmengewirr ist laut. Man kommt ins Gespräch mit seinen Sitznachbarn oder anderen Gästen, die am Tresen stehen, denn klein ist sie, diese Bar. Zu später Stunde wird auch schon mal zwischen den Tischen getanzt. Am Wochenende kann man dafür auch in den Keller gehen, wo DJs auflegen - mehr Platz gibt es dort allerdings auch nicht. Aber genau dafür kommt man ins Hotel: jeder Besuch ist ein Kurzurlaub, neue Bekanntschaften inklusive. It's the many flowers hanging from the ceiling that are the first sign of the atmosphere at Das Hotel. Flickering candlelight, the piano sitting quietly in the corner, and the windows opening onto the street add to the overall decor - you feel as though you're in Barcelona or a miniature Mediterranean villa that just happens to be in Kreuzberg. Old, forgotten or undiscovered tunes play constantly through the hanging speakers with a loud buzz. You stand there, chatting to your neighbors or other guests crowded around the tiny bar. As it grows later, people begin to dance between the tables. On weekends, head down to the basement, where DJs play - not that there's any more room down here. But that's exactly why you come here: everyone's looking for a short vacation, new acquaintances included.

Text: Massimo Hartmann / Photos: Daniel Farò

Das Hotel
Mariannenstraße 26a, 10999 Berlin-Kreuzberg
Bar: daily from 16:00
Club: Fri & Sat from 23:00

UNSER LIEBSTES TÄGLICH BROT
OUR BELOVED DAILY BREAD

Bis vor kurzem wäre Kreuzkölln ein weißer Fleck auf der Landkarte gewesen - zumindest in Sachen gutes Brot. Seit der dänische Brot-Connoisseur Magnus Grubbe seine Bread Station im Jahr 2015 eröffnet hat, ist das glücklicherweise anders. In der Küche stehen nun eine Getreidemühle mit integriertem Mahlstein, ein riesiger Teigmixer und verschiedene Backöfen. Die Zutaten sind bio und alles ist, natürlich, mit Liebe gebacken. Typisch deutsche Brötchen gibt es allerdings nicht, stattdessen kauft man hier große Laibe Brot - innen luftig, außen mit Kruste. Um sechs Uhr morgens kommt der erste Schwung in den Ofen und lockt mit seinem unwiderstehlichen Duft die Kunden an. Ein Besuch lohnt auch wegen der köstlichen Croissants, Zimtschnecken und, wie ich finde, der besten Himbeer-Schnitten der Stadt. It could be argued that Kreuzkölln was once something of a dead spot for good, simple, freshly baked bread, but this all changed with the opening of The Bread Station. The bakery-cum-café was opened by Danish bread-connoisseur Magnus Grubbe in 2015. Creating the bakery itself was a true labor of love, with Magnus spending months installing a fully functional corn mill, complete with a grinding stone, a giant dough mixer, and multiple baking ovens. The bread is freshly prepared and baked on the premises using organic ingredients, but you'll find no typical German Brötchen here - only hefty, crusty-on-the-outside, fluffy-on-the-inside loaves. The bakers put the first batch in the oven at six in the morning, meaning a steady stream of locals are drawn in by the irresistible smell of fresh loaves as the doors open one hour later. There's also a mouthwatering selection of fresh croissants, cinnamon rolls, and the best raspberry slices in the city.

Text: Caroline Stephenson / Photos: Daniel Faró

The Bread Station
Maybachufer 16, 12047 Berlin-Neukölln
Mon-Fri 7:00-19:30, Sat & Sun 8:00-16:00

EXTRA TIP

Ausgezeichnetes Brot gibt es auch beim Kiez-Bäcker Hacker - einem Traditionsbetrieb in der Stargarder Straße 69. Besonders wegen der Splitterbrötchen kommt man hierher. Excellent bread is also baked at the Kiez bakery Hacker - a traditional company at Stargarder Straße 69. Many come just for their yummy Splitterbrötchen.

KLEINE AUSZEIT AM NEUEN SEE
TIME OUT AT THE NEUEN SEE

Während sich das Wasser leise am Ufer bricht, sitzt man von
Bäumen umgeben, mit einem Bier in der Hand im Café am
Neuen See und vergisst beinahe, dass man immer noch mitten
in Berlin ist. Versteckt im weitläufigen Tiergarten, bekommt
man an diesem Ort weder vom städtischen Lärm noch von der
Hektik etwas mit. Von den Bäumen hängen Lichterketten,
deren Reflexionen abends auf dem See tanzen, während die Rümpfe
der bunten Ruderboote sanft an der kleinen Anlegestelle
auf- und abschaukeln, wo sie im Sommer vermietet werden.
Serviert wird köstliche deutsche Küche: goldbraune Schnitzel, Flammkuchen und, zur Saison, Pfifferlinge in allen
Variationen. Wer weniger auf deutsche Tradition setzt, muss
sich keine Sorgen machen – Pizza und Pasta gibt es ebenfalls.
Aber egal, was man letztendlich bestellt: Ein deutsches Bier
gehört dazu! Sitting at the Café am Neuen See, beer in hand,
surrounded by trees, with the lake lapping gently at the
edges of the shore, it's easy to forget that you're in the
middle of Germany's capital. Tucked away in the sprawling
Tiergarten, the café is completely insulated from urban noise
and bustle. In the evenings, strings of lights hang overhead, their reflections dancing in the lake, disturbed by
the hulls of the brightly colored row-boats bobbing gently
by the small docks which you can rent in summer for a quick
ride on the Neuen See. Delicious and authentic German
food like golden-brown schnitzel, tarte flambée as well as
a seasonal chanterelle-menu, a German favorite, is being
served. If classic German food isn't your speed, not to
worry – delve into the more international offerings like
wood-fired pizza and pasta. And don't forget to wash it down
with a traditional German beer!

Text: Esmé Rocks / Photos: Daniel Farò

Café am Neuen See
Lichtensteinallee 2,10787 Berlin-Tiergarten
Restaurant: daily from 9:00
Biergarten: daily from 11:00, Sat & Sun from 10:00
cafeamneuensee.de

EXTRA TIP

Ein anderer schöner Biergarten befindet sich in der
Hobrechtsfelder Dorfstraße 30a in Panketal/
Zepernick: Nach einem Ausflug zum Gorinsee kehrt
man bei James Biergarten ein. Another great beer
garden is at Hobrechtsfelder Dorfstraße 30a in Panketal/
Zepernick: after a trip to lake Gorin take a break at
James Biergarten.

ITALIENISCHES DINNER MIT FREUNDEN
AN ITALIAN DINNER WITH FRIENDS

Das Restaurant Caligari ist herrlich unkompliziert und jeder fühlt sich willkommen. Das liegt zum einen an den drei herzlichen Besitzern, Andreas de Blasi, Michelangelo Contini und Nandhan Molinaro; sie stammen aus Apulien und der Lombardei, haben sich in Berlin kennengelernt und vor zwei Jahren ihr eigenes Restaurant im Schillerkiez eröffnet. Unprätentiös, aber geschmackvoll eingerichtet, trägt auch das Interieur zum lässigen Flair bei. Nicht zu vergessen das Essen: Auf der wechselnden Karte, die in Form eines losen Blattes gereicht wird, findet jeder etwas. In der Küche stehen die drei meistens selbst, und wenn nicht sie, dann ihr Koch Jacopo Ghiggini. Vorspeisenfans können neben Klassikern wie Burrata und Carpaccio immer auch etwas Überraschendes wählen. Vegetarier schätzen den großen Salat mit Ziegenkäse und Feigen. Alle, die Appetit auf italienische Pasta-Klassiker haben, werden ebenso satt und glücklich. Beim Dessert bin ich wenig experimentell: das Tartufo muss auf den Tisch – mit mindestens zwei weiteren Löffeln für die Freunde. Wer darum bittet, bekommt es mit einem Espresso übergossen. Wenn es Zeit ist zu gehen, weiß man, dass man zurück-kommen wird, einfach weil man sich fühlt wie ein gern gesehener Gast – in Berlin bisweilen leider noch immer keine Selbstverständlichkeit. Anyone would feel comfortable and welcome at Caligari. The relaxed attitude comes from the three owners, Andreas de Blasi, Michelangelo Contini, and Nandhan Molinaro from Apulia and Lombardy. They got to know each other in Berlin, and two years ago they opened the restaurant in Schillerkiez. Unpretentious but furnished with good taste, the interior boasts a casual flair. And let's not forget about the food: the changing menu, printed on a loose sheet of paper, has something for everyone. The three founders usually work in the kitchen themselves or with their cook, Jacopo Ghiggini. Fans of starters can always order something unique and exciting next to old classics like burrata and carpaccio. The fig and goat cheese salad is certainly not just for vegetarians, and those with an appetite for classic Italian pasta dishes shall be satisfied too. When it comes to dessert, I'm hardly experimental; I always order the tartufo ice cream with at least two spoons for sharing. If you ask, they'll pour an espresso over it. When evening comes to an end and it's time to head home, you know you'll be coming back, simply because you always feel welcomed here – still an all too rare feeling in Berlin.

Text: Nina Trippel / Photos: Daniel Farò

Caligari Bistro
Kienitzer Straße 110, 12049 Berlin-Neukölln
Daily 18:00-23:00
caligariberlin.de

CEE CEE'S GUEST: LISA FELDMANN

Wenn jemand weiß, was Frauen wirklich wollen, dann Lisa Feldmann. Nach Stationen bei Magazinen wie Elle und Cosmopolitan war sie zehn Jahre lang Chefredakteurin der schweizerischen Zeitschrift Annabelle und hat dort bewiesen, dass Konsum, Kultur und ein kritischer Blick auf das aktuelle Zeitgeschehen die perfekte Symbiose eingehen können. Nach einer Dekade am schönen Zürichsee zog sie an die raue Spree. Einem Intermezzo bei Interview folgte das Engagement als Chefredakteurin der ersten deutschen Version des französischen Hochglanzmagazins L'Officiel. Seither macht sie von ihrem Büro am Gendarmenmarkt aus wieder das, was sie am besten kann: ein Modemagazin für kluge Frauen. Abends verlässt sie Mitte dann gerne gen Westen. Wer ihr auf Instagram folgt, sieht sie mit Freunden wie Moritz von Uslar in der Paris Bar. Abends folgt ihr meist Dackel Kelly über den Savignyplatz. Und öfters auch bis ins Petit Royal – mit Sicherheit einem der stilvollsten Orte der Stadt.

If there's one person who knows what women really want, it's Lisa Feldmann. After positions at magazines like Elle and Cosmopolitan, she was the editor-in-chief of the Swiss magazine Annabelle, where she proved that consumerism, culture, and a critical outlook can enter into a perfect symbiotic relationship. After a decade on the picturesque Zürichsee, she moved to the rough Spree. A short stint at Interview was followed by her engagement as editor-in-chief of the first German edition of the French glossy magazine L'Officiel. Since then, she's done what she does best from her office on Gendarmenmarkt: creating a fashion magazine for clever women. After a day of work, she happily leaves Mitte for the West. If you follow her on Instagram, you'll see her with friends like Moritz von Uslar in the Paris Bar. In the evenings she brings her dachshund Kelly to Savignyplatz and often into Petit Royal – certainly one of Berlin's most beloved spots. →

lofficiel.de
@lofficielgermany
@lisafeldmann_

EXTRA TIP

Auch ein anderes Mitte-Urgestein hat es in den Westen verschlagen: Die Galerie Contemporary Fine Arts lädt in die Grolmanstraße 32/33 zur Vernissage. Another Mitte veteran is in the West: the gallery Contemporary Fine Arts at Grolmanstraße 32/33 is definitely worth a visit.

LISA FELDMANN EMPFIEHLT: LE PETIT ROYAL LISA FELDMANN RECOMMENDS: LE PETIT ROYAL

Wer im Westen Berlins zu Hause ist, hatte es bisher nicht leicht. Zumindest wenn es um Essen in interessanter Gesellschaft ging. Nun wurde unser Repertoire um ein Restaurant erweitert, das schon im Namen die Hoffnung auf ein wenig Mitte-Flair birgt. Denn mit dem Petit Royal hat ein Ableger des Grill Royal im Herzen Charlottenburgs eröffnet. Das Restaurant bietet eine reduzierte, verfeinerte Version der Speisekarte des großen Bruders, mehr Fisch als Fleisch ist im Angebot, dazu erlesene Weine, aber auch Hummersuppe und Austern. Ich bin über Nacht zum Stammgast geworden. Was nicht heißt, dass ich jeden Abend hier sitze, sondern vielmehr, dass ich schon in jeder mir lieben Konstellation hier war: geschäftlich, mit meinen Freundinnen nach dem Theater, mit meinem Mann, allein an der Bar. Statt uns in ein Taxi Richtung Mitte zu setzen, leinen wir jetzt den Dackel an und „ziehen um die Häuser". Und so war es doch mal gedacht, das Ausgehen in Berlin. For those who, like me, feel at home in West Berlin, things haven't been easy, particularly when it comes to food paired with good company. Now our collection of restaurants has expanded with a restaurant whose name itself expresses the spirit of Mitte. Petit Royal is an offshoot of the famous Grill Royal in the heart of Charlottenburg. The restaurant offers a refined, reduced version of its big brother's menu, more fish than meat, with select wines as well as clam chowder and oysters. I became a regular overnight. I've passed countless hours here with many different constellations of acquaintances: business dinners, on the way to the theater with friends, with my husband, or alone at the bar. Instead of sitting in a taxi, we put the dog on a leash and roam the streets. This is going out in Berlin as it was once meant to be.

Text: Lisa Feldmann / Photos: Daniel Farò

Le Petit Royal
Grolmanstraße 59, 10623 Berlin-Charlottenburg
Mon-Sat from 18:00-23:00
lepetitroyal.de

DER CHARMANTE KLEINE LUNCH-SPOT THE CHARMING LITTLE LUNCH SPOT

Dieses Lokal auf der Weserstraße verleiht dem Konzept Take-away eine ganz neue Bedeutung. Hier füllt man seine Lunchbox zum Beispiel mit den berühmten Sesamnudeln New York-Style, doch Vegetarier und Veganer kommen gleichermaßen auf ihre Kosten: Sandwiches, Suppen, selbst gebackene Pop-Tarts und Greenies – grüne Versuchungen mit Matcha, Macadamia und weißer Schokolade – liegen am Tresen bereit. Sobald man seine Favoriten ausgewählt hat, wird alles in eine Lunchbox gepackt, mitgenommen oder direkt vor Ort gegessen – einen Besuch ist das Stella aber schon wegen der Cafeteria mit der tropischen Tapete von Dorothy Draper wert, die sich als Selfie-Kulisse bewährt hat. Die Wanddekoration ist allerdings nur eines der schönen Details, das den Laden von Köchin Suzy Fracassa ausmacht, die die Berliner Gastro-Szene übrigens schon seit mehr als einer Dekade bereichert. This eatery on Weserstraße is giving new meaning to the phrase "dine and dash." Pop in and fill your Stella lunchbox with the already famous NY style sesame noodles. Vegetarians and vegans will find plenty of choices as well: there are sandwiches, soups, and homemade baked sweets like pop-tarts and matcha macadamia nut white chocolate "greenies." Pick your favorites and eat them on-site or have them packed to go. And don't miss the tropical cafeteria in the back adorned with Dorothy Draper wallpaper – a popular selfie spot. The interior of Stella was designed with loving attention to detail by proprietor and chef Suzy Fracassa, who has been part of Berlin's food scene for more than a decade!

Text: Elizabeth Rushe / Photos: Elizabeth Rushe, Jochen Arndt

Stella - Ready Dishes/Take-away/Catering
Weserstraße 166, 12045 Berlin-Neukölln
Tue-Sat 12:00-18:30

EXTRA TIP

Suzy Fracassa lädt auch ab und zu in ihren Supper Club Fortuna's Feast Private Dining in der Weserstraße 58 ein oder kümmert sich mit Fortuna's Table um Caterings. Suzy Fracassa also sometimes invites guests to her Supper Club Fortuna's Feast Private Dining at Weserstraße 58 or caters with Fortuna's Table.

PERFECT DAY

EXTRA TIP

Im Keller treffen sich hier auch Yoga-Klassen –
Meditation und Kinderkurse gibt es zur Auswahl.
Anmeldung über: yoga@distriktcoffee.de
Yoga classes are held in the basement: there are
options including meditation and courses for kids.
Register at: yoga@distriktcoffee.de

EIN CAFÉ ZUM VERWEILEN
A CAFÉ FOR QUALITY TIME

Bei Sophie Hardy und ihrem Freund Hannes Haake steht
nicht nur der Kaffee, sondern der Genuss desselben im
Vordergrund, weswegen ein schönes Interieur und leckere
Speisen in ihrem vor zwei Jahren eröffneten Distrikt
Coffee selbstverständlich sind. Im Sommer kann man
draußen die Sonne genießen, im Herbst und Winter
laden die Ledersofas, Backsteinwände und natürlich
auch die warmen Suppen und Heißgetränke dazu ein,
es sich innen gemütlich zu machen. Ob Açai-Bowl oder
American Pancakes – die Entscheidung fällt schwer.
Bei einem Besuch bleibt es nicht! For Sophie Hardy and
her boyfriend Hannes Haake, the experience of drinking coffee is just as important as the coffee itself –
beautiful interior design and delicious food should
accompany the drink, and to this end they opened
Distrikt Coffee two years ago. In summer you can enjoy
the sun outside, while in fall and winter the leather
sofas, brick walls, and of course hot soups and drinks
invite you inside to make yourself cozy. Debating
between an Açai Bowl or American Pancakes is a difficult
decision. One visit isn't enough!

Text: Isabelle Kagelius / Photos: Sven Hausherr, Ana Santl

Distrikt Coffee
Bergstraße 68, 10115 Berlin-Mitte
Mon-Fri 8:30-17:00, Sat & Sun 9:30-17:00
distriktcoffee.de

KÄSE MIT PEP CHEESE WITH PEP

„Sweet dreams are made of cheese", heißt es ja bekanntlich, und bei Peppikäse gibt's den Beweis. In dem kleinen Käse-Feinkostladen im Neuköllner Weichselkiez erlebt der Rohmilchkäse sein Revival und hat seinen Platz zwischen Blauschimmel- und Frischkäse, Schweizer und österreichischen Spezialitäten auf den kleinen Holztischen gefunden. Bei Inhaber Georg Weishäupl bringt das Zusammenspiel der Aromen erst den Geschmack, und deshalb findet man in seinem Sortiment neben dem Käse ausschließlich hochwertige Begleiter - wie zum Beispiel Brandenburger Säfte, regionalen Birnenschnaps und cremige Alpenbutter. Sich von Weishäupl beraten zu lassen, macht Appetit, vor allem, weil er die Produzenten seiner Ware noch persönlich kennt. Peppis Claim ist „Rohmilchkäse rockt". Wir sagen: Peppi rockt!

"Sweet dreams are made of cheese" is a well-known fact, and Peppikäse is the proof. In the little Neukölln cheese shop, raw milk cheese is currently experiencing a revival. Visitors meander among blue cheese and cream cheese, Austrian and Swiss specialties and more, all set out on small wooden tables. For owner Georg Weishäupl, only the interplay of flavors can fully bring out the taste of the cheeses, so high quality companions are also offered, such as juices from Brandenburg, regional pear brandy, and creamy alpine butter. His advice will only make you hungrier - no one is better equipped to create the most delicious combinations than Weishäupl, who knows all his producers personally. To Peppi's claim that raw milk cheese rocks, we say: Peppi rocks!

Text: Leonie Haenchen / Photos: Daniel Farò

Peppikäse
Weichselstraße 65, 12043 Berlin-Neukölln
Wed 14:00-20:00, Thu & Fri 10:00-20:00, Sat 10:00-18:00
peppikaese.de

PERFECT DAY

EXTRA TIP

Wunderbar schmeckt der Käse auch bei Blomeyer's Käse in der Pestalozzistraße 54a: In der Theke liegen u.a. Bärlauchcamembert und Gepfeffertes Ärschle. The cheese at Blomeyer's Käse at Pestalozzistraße 54a is also fantastic: try the wild garlic camembert and peppered Ärschle.

NACH KÖNIGSWALDE ZUM BADEN
A LAKE FAVORITE IN KÖNIGSWALDE

Die idyllische Kulisse aus dichtem Wald, zahllosen Seerosen und türkisfarbenem, klarem Wasser machen diesen Ausflug und Sprung ins kühle Nass unvergesslich. Der Sacrower See liegt an der Stadtgrenze zwischen Berlin und Potsdam und ist umgeben vom Königswald, einem wunderschönen Naturschutzgebiet. Erreichbar ist das Seeufer nur zu Fuß und über zwei Badestellen; um den See führt ein Wanderweg. Das bekanntere Ufer liegt nördlich, und wer hier ankommt, wird nicht nur von einer schönen Liegewiese begrüßt, sondern auch von Sonnenschirmen, Eis, Pommes und Alsterwasser. Die zweite Badestelle befindet sich am Ostufer – hier ist weniger los, nur ein kleiner Waldpfad führt zum Wasser. Wer diese Bucht findet, wird nie wieder an einen anderen See fahren wollen! The beautiful scenery of dense forests, countless water lilies, and turquoise waves is the perfect backdrop for a memorable leap into the cold, clear waters. The Sacrow lake is located at the Berlin-Potsdam border and is surrounded by the forest of Königswald, a beautiful nature reserve. The lakefront is only accessible by foot and has two swimming spots. One is located on the northern shore, with a fantastic view of the lake and other perks including sunshades, fries, ice cream, and shandy – the classics for a day by the lake. The second swimming site is an insider's tip, located on the eastern shore and reached via a small forest path. If you find it, you'll never want to visit another lake again.

Text: Milena Kalojanov / Photos: Daniel Farò

Sacrower See
14469 Potsdam
By bus 638 from Berlin-Spandau or Potsdam Hauptbahnhof to F.-Günther-Park; from there to the northern swimming: 15mins walk

EXTRA TIP

Wer anschließend Kunst sehen will, besucht eines der
schönsten Museen Potsdams – die Villa Schöningen in
der Berliner Straße 86, wenige Meter von der Glienicker
Brücke entfernt. If you want to see more art, visit
Potsdam's most beautiful museum: Villa Schöningen in
Berliner Straße 86, a few meters from Glienicker Brücke.

MÄNNERMODE & BÜRGERSTEIGGELAGE
MEN'S FASHION & BLOCK PARTIES

Hier müssen Männer nicht traurig auf der Couch warten und die Einkaufstüten der
Freundin hüten: der Soto Store hat sich ganz auf die modischen Bedürfnisse der
männlichen Großstadtbewohner eingestellt. Zwischen internationalen Marken wie
Acne Studios und Raf Simons hängen und liegen auch Teile deutscher Labels wie
A Kind of Guise oder Accessoires von PB1001 (designt von Christian Metzner S. 54, 123).
Weil das Konzept der Gründer Philip Gaedicke (S. 270), Omer Ben-Michael und David
Fischer gut aufging, gesellte sich einige Zeit später noch der kleine Bruder
dazu: Soto 2. Und die doppelte Power gibt auch mindestens zweimal so viel Anlässe,
eine kleine In-Store Party zu schmeißen. Spätestens dann, wenn Menschentrauben,
DJ-Pulte und Foodtrucks die Torstraße vor den Geschäften bevölkern, weiß man: hier
feiert Mann die Mode. Here, there's no need for men to wait sadly on the couch for
their girlfriends to finish browsing: Soto Store is fully dedicated to the needs
of the modern urban man. The racks stock international brands such as Acne Studios
and Raf Simons as well as German fashion and accessory brands like A Kind of Guise
or PB1001 (designed by Christian Metzner, pp. 54, 123). Because the concept, developed
by Philip Gaedicke (p. 270), Omer Ben-Michael, and David Fischer, worked out so
well, they opened a little brother just next door: Soto 2. Ever since this double
joint venture has offered twice as many reasons to throw in-store parties. So now
if you spot crowds surrounding food trucks parked at Torstraße with a DJ set-up
outside, you'll know: here's a place where men can celebrate fashion.

Text: Massimo Hartmann / Photos: Robert Wunsch

Soto Store Berlin
Torstraße 71 & 72, 10119 Berlin-Mitte
Mon-Fri 12:00-20:00, Sat 11:00-20:00
sotostore.com

EIN HEIM FÜR DELIKATESSEN
HOME OF IRRESISTIBLE DELICACIES

Halb Deli, halb süchtig machender Feinkostladen: Candy on Bone vereint die kulinarische Kompetenz des Partner-Restaurants Katz Orange und die Nachhaltigkeit des Mutterschiffs Contemporary Food Lab. An der Theke gibt es neben frischem Fleisch und Käse auch Salate mit Haselnuss, Petersilie und Birne sowie Sandwiches, belegt mit der Spezialität des Hauses – langsam geröstetem Schweinefleisch. Im angeschlossenen Laden findet man eine Auswahl an Lebensmitteln und Küchenutensilien. Alles wird von kleinen Manufakturen bezogen: Meersalz-Flocken mit Lakritz der Marke Nordur aus Island, elegant verpackte Gewürze von Pfeffersack & Soehne sowie Eigenkreationen von Candy on Bone, darunter unser Liebling: ein Bacon Jam Chutney. Beim nächsten Spaziergang am Landwehrkanal sollte man hier auf jeden Fall vorbeischauen. Part deli, part addictive cookery shop, Candy on Bone channels both the culinary expertise of sister restaurant Katz Orange and the principles of sustainability inherent to its founders at Contemporary Food Lab. The combination is enchanting; from sandwiches filled with Katz Orange's famous slow-roasted pork to parsley and pear salad, the brightly lit counter offers simple yet immaculately prepared dishes alongside a selection of fresh meats and cheeses. Next door, ingredients, liquor, cookbooks, and kitchen essentials are arranged in a kaleidoscope of flavors and colors; there's Nordur liquorice salt from Iceland and elegantly packaged spices from Pfeffersack & Soehne. Dotted around the store are also Candy on Bone's own range of granolas, nuts, and sauces, including our favorite: Bacon Jam Chutney. It's a cathedral of devotion to gastronomy, and it's definitely worth a visit during your next canal-side stroll.

Text: Antonia Harris / Photos: David Gauffin

Candy on Bone
Planufer 92b, 10967 Berlin-Kreuzberg
Mon-Fri 12:00-21:30, Sat 10:00-21:30, Sun 10:00-19:00
candyonbone.com

EXTRA TIP

Für Feinkost aus Italien besucht man den Amore Store in der Sanderstraße 12: Hier gibt es auch die legendäre rote Parmesanreibe von Rigamonti, die Lust auf Urlaub macht. For delicacies from Italy visit the Amore Store at Sanderstraße 12: you'll find the legendary red parmesan graters from Rigamonti. You're sure to leave with a craving for a holiday.

SAVOIR VIVRE IM SCHILLERKIEZ
SAVOIR VIVRE IN SCHILLERKIEZ

Unweit des Tempelhofer Felds liegt das kleine Restaurant L'eustache. Besitzerin und Köchin Justine Daufresne kreiert wöchentlich wechselnde Gerichte und verbindet ihre französischen Wurzeln mit internationalen Einflüssen. Die Gerichte sind fantastisch – auf der Karte stehen dann Pâté de campagne neben Oktopus-Ragout auf Kichererbsen und Sablé Breton neben einem warmen Schokoladenküchlein. Die Inneneinrichtung ist simpel, aber charmant: Der alte Holztresen bildet das Herzstück, gegessen wird an einfachen Tischen vor dunkelgrün getünchter Wand. Liebevoll arrangierte Pflanzen schmücken die Fensterbank, die Lampen erinnern an eine Schiffskajüte und der Service ist sehr persönlich. Kurz: Das L'eustache hat Charakter! Close to Tempelhofer Feld, Justine Daufresne's small French restaurant L'eustache offers a changing weekly menu of French dishes tweaked with Mediterranean influences. The dishes are sensational – an example menu being pâté de campagne side by side with octopus ragout on a chickpea stew, and desserts such as sablé breton and warm chocolate cake that will keep you enchanted throughout the evening. The atmosphere is simple yet charming, with wooden stools and tables crowded between the dark green walls and plants lining the window ledges. In short, L'eustache is full of character!

Text: Michaela Wölfel / Photos: Daniel Farò

L'eustache
Weisestraße 49, 12047 Berlin-Neukölln
Wed-Sat from 18:00

EXTRA TIP

Wer in der Gegend nach einem Platz zum Frühstücken sucht, wird bei No.58 Speiserei in der Weisestraße 58 glücklich: Avocado-Brot, steirische Eierspeise und weitere Leckereien stehen auf der Karte. Anyone looking for a breakfast spot in the area should test out No.58 Speiserei at Weisestraße 58: the menu offers avocado bread and Styrian eggs, among other dishes.

LEIPZIGER STRASSE, MITTE

GÖRLITZER PARK, KREUZBERG

STAHLHEIMER STRASSE, PRENZLAUER BERG.

NIGHT FALL

BERLIN SCHLÄFT NIE. SOGAR IN DEN GRELLEN MORGENSTUNDEN WEISS DIE STADT ZU UNTERHALTEN. OB STILVOLL ODER VERWEGEN — DIE NACHT HAT VIELE GESICHTER. BERLIN NEVER SLEEPS. EVEN IN THE BRIGHT LIGHT OF MORNING, THE CITY KNOWS HOW TO ENTERTAIN. WHETHER THE STYLISH OR FOOLHARDY — THE NIGHT HAS MANY FACES.

MEIN CAFÉ, MEIN CLUB, MEIN BLOCK
MY CAFÉ, MY CLUB, MY BLOCK

Zwischen Betonblocks und Dönerbuden, direkt am Pulsschlag des Kottbusser Tors, verteidigt die Südblock-Bar ihren Kiez. Angesichts der wachsenden Schwulenszene Kreuzbergs eröffneten Richard Stein und Tülin Duman vor einigen Jahren mit der Bar ihren eigenen kleinen Melting-Pot der Kulturen und des Austauschs. Das Ziel: Einen Raum der Begegnung schaffen – für langjährige Anwohner und tolerante Hedonisten auf der Durchreise. Jeder Gast kann hier seine Geschichte erzählen und wird dafür, wenn nötig, mit ausreichend Bier versorgt. Respekt wird im Südblock groß geschrieben, doch auch wenn deshalb der Außenbereich abends zum Wohl der Nachbarn geschlossen wird, heißt das noch lange nicht, dass drinnen nicht bis in die Morgenstunden getanzt werden kann. Between concrete buildings and kebab shops, directly at the pulsing heart of Kottbusser Tor, Südblock Bar defends its district. Amid the growing gay scene in Kreuzberg, Richard Stein and Tülin Duman opened the bar as a small melting-pot of cultures and exchanges. Their goal: to create a meeting space for longtime locals and hedonists just passing through. Each guest can tell his story, and, if necessary, remain well-stocked with beer. Respect is taken very seriously at Südblock, and even though the outdoor section of the bar is closed in the evenings out of sympathy for the neighbors, the indoor is open for dancing well into the wee hours.

Text: Leonie Haenchen / Photos: Daniel Farò

Südblock
Admiralstraße 1-2, 10999 Berlin-Kreuzberg
Daily from 10:00
suedblock.org

EXTRA TIP

Gefeiert wird auch im Kultclub SchwuZ in der ehemaligen Neuköllner Bierbrauerei an der Rollbergstraße 26. You can also party in the cult club SchwuZ in the former Neukölln brewery at Rollbergstraße 26.

GEHOBENE BARKULTUR UNTER DEN S-BAHN-BÖGEN HIGH-END BAR CULTURE UNDER THE TRAIN TRACKS

Stammgäste kommen durch den Hintereingang. Unterbewusst nahmen wir wohl deshalb auch diesen Weg in die Bar Zentral, die von Torsten Bender und Sebastian Mathow betrieben wird. Ihr Herzstück ist ein langer Holztresen, die Rückwand wird nicht von Flaschen gekrönt, sondern von einem eleganten Regalsystem – damit die Besucher nicht den ganzen Abend auf Logos starren, sondern sich stattdessen auf ihre Unterhaltung konzentrieren können. Für das Design wurde das Berliner Büro Hidden Fortress engagiert, das von den Lampen bis zu den Metallleisten am Tresen alle Details sorgsam durchdacht hat. Die exzellenten Drinks werden unter anderem vom Ex-Würgeengel-Barkeeper Max Engler gemixt. So saßen wir also dort mit einem Prince of Wales und einem Wodka Collins, stießen an, vergaßen die Zeit – und wissen, dass auch wir bald als Stammgäste, und nicht als Neulinge, durch die Hintertür hineinkommen.

We'd heard that the regulars like to come through the back door. Maybe that's why we subconsciously chose this door as well. But no matter which entrance you choose at Bar Zentral, run by Torsten Bender and Sebastian Mathow, you will be standing in front of a huge wooden bar and a backdrop made of sophisticated black shelves, which means rather than staring at bottle logos all night long, you're encouraged to concentrate on the lovely person next to you. That's just one of many ideas that studio Hidden Fortress came up with – the design studio created the refined interior concept, with details ranging from metal slats at the bar to custom lamps. The drinks are perfectly mixed and one of the bartenders might seem familiar to you: Max Engler worked at Würgeengel bar before coming to Bar Zentral. We enjoyed a perfect Prince of Wales, a superb Vodka Collins, and other delicacies from the drinks menu and forgot all about the passing time, knowing that we'd definitely be back through the back door as regulars.

Text: Nina Trippel / Photos: Daniel Farò

Bar Zentral
Lotte-Lenya-Bogen 551, 10623 Berlin-Charlottenburg
Daily from 17:00
barzentral.de

EXTRA TIP

Auch der hintere Raum, der besten Bar in Mitte, das Buck and Breck in der Brunnenstraße 177, wurde vom Designstudio Hidden Fortress im Jahr 2016 neu gestaltet. The back room of Buck and Breck, the best bar in Mitte, was also redesigned by the studio Hidden Fortress in 2016. Go for a drink at Brunnenstraße 177.

EXTRA TIP

Vor der Party im Acud stärken? Los geht's zu
Tommi's Burger Joint in der Invalidenstraße 160.
Need a little fortification before partying at
Acud? Go to Tommi's Burger Joint a few houses
down at Invalidenstraße 160.

DAS KULTURZENTRUM NEU ERFUNDEN CULTURE HUB RELOADED

Früher als Acud e.V. bekannt, hat das Kulturzentrum, das sich in einem Hinterhof in Mitte befindet, die Wende bis heute überdauert und ist das letzte seiner Art. Dank der Initiative „Acud macht Neu" konnte es vor der Schließung bewahrt werden; in Eigenregie bauten die Kulturschaffenden die Räumlichkeiten aus und öffneten ihre Türen für alle Kulturinteressierten. Theater und Kino, Galerie und Club, Studio und Radio teilen sich die gemeinsame Fläche und bieten den Besuchern eine geballte Ladung aus Lesungen, Workshops, Tanz und Konzert – so vielfältig wie die Räume selbst. Formerly known as Acud e.V., this cultural center, hidden away in a back courtyard in Mitte, is now the only of its kind left standing. It was saved from closing its doors permanently thanks to the initiative "Acud macht Neu." Cultural workers organized the scheme themselves, updating the premises and opening their doors to cultural interests of all kinds. Theater and movies, gallery and club, studio and radio all share the building, offering visitors an interdisciplinary cornucopia of readings, workshops, dance performances, and concert – a selection as varied as the rooms themselves.

Text: Leonie Haenchen

Acud Macht Neu
Veteranenstraße 21, 10119 Berlin-Mitte
acudmachtneu.de

TAPAS AUF JAPANISCH
TAPAS TOKYO-STYLE

Darf sich eine Stadt ohne Izakaya-Bars Metropole nennen? Ich finde nicht. Aber mit dem Zenkichi hat Berlin in diesem Punkt aufgeholt und eine fantastische japanische Tapas-Lokalität dazugewonnen: Motoko Watanabe und Shaul Margulies haben den Keller ihres Restaurants House of Small Wonder komplett umgebaut und in ein schummriges Labyrinth verwandelt, das sich im typischen Izakaya-Style aus kleinen, privaten Separees zusammensetzt. Zwischen dunklem Holz und Bambuspflanzen isst man und trinkt Sake (bis zu 30 Sorten sind im Angebot) – und vergisst schon mal die Zeit. Unbedingt bestellen sollte man das Hamachi Sashimi, den hausgemachten Tofu und das Tempura Shiso-Maki. Oder einfach das Omakase, ein wechselndes Prix-fixe-Menü, zusammengestellt vom Chef, um die ganze Bandbreite der leckeren Kleinigkeiten zu genießen. Bahnt man sich schließlich seinen Weg zurück in die Berliner Realität, fühlt es sich fast an, als käme man aus einem Tokioter Parallel-Universum. Is a city without authentic Japanese Izakayas a true metropolis? Well, not for me. Luckily Berlin has finally caught up to this with the opening of Zenkichi, serving Japanese-style tapas alongside a selection of over 30 types of sake. Owners Motoko Watanabe and Shaul Margulies had the basement of House of Small Wonder completely transformed; once you open the unassuming door, you'll find yourself lost in a dimly lit labyrinth of glowing lanterns, dark burnished wood, and bamboo pillars. In typical Izakaya style, the secluded tables nestle in tiny booths for privacy. Must-have dishes include the hamachi sashimi, homemade tofu, and tempura shiso-maki. Alternatively, place your trust in the expert chef and opt for the changing Omakase fixed menu to enjoy a truly immersive experience with a varied array of delicious dishes. Leaving Zenkichi feels like crawling slowly back into the real life of Berlin after a true taste of Tokyo.

Text: Rei Matsuoka / Photos: Daniel Farò

Zenkichi
Johannisstraße 20, 10117 Berlin-Mitte
Daily from 18:00–24:00
zenkichi.de

EXTRA TIP

Die Kuratorin Anna-Catharina Gebbers lädt in unregelmäßigen Abständen um die Ecke, in der Ziegelstraße 2, in ihre „Bibliothekswohnung" zu Ausstellungen und Vorträgen ein. Curator Anna-Catharina Gebbers periodically invites guests around the corner to her "Bibliothekswohnung" at Ziegelstraße 2 for exhibitions and lectures.

Cristian Niculescu kennt Zeiten der Unfreiheit und der Unterdrückung: Im einst dikatorisch-kommunistischen Rumänien wurden ihm Konzertreisen ins Ausland erst ab dem 18. Lebensjahr gewährt. Heute pendelt der freie Musiker zwischen Auftritten in Konzertsälen weltweit und Engagements in Berlin. Aufzuzählen wo der gebürtige Bukarester und Wahl-Berliner schon konzertiert hat, würde Seiten füllen. Auftritte mit den Berliner Symphonikern, der Cleveland Chamber Symphony und natürlich dem Philharmonischen Orchester „George Enescu" sind nur einige Beispiele. Kurz: Cristian ist ein gefragter Musiker. Neben seiner Karriere als Solo-Künstler ist er auch Gründungsmitglied des Dinu Lipatti Trio Berlin und fester Pianist des ensemble contempo paris. Wer so fleißig ist, lebt und übt im stillen Kämmerlein? Mitnichten! Man trifft ihn auch auf Parties und als perfekten Gastgeber seiner eigenen Bühne (s. S. 59). Einer seiner liebsten großen Veranstaltungsorte ist der wunderschöne Konzertsaal des Konzerthauses am Gendarmenmarkt. Natürlich spielt er dort auch selbst regelmäßig (s. S. 240).

Cristian Niculescu knew times of oppression and constraints: he grew up in the former Communist dictatorship of Romania, which denied him permission to travel abroad for concerts until he was 18. Today the Bucharest-born adoptive Berliner swings between performances in large concert houses worldwide and smaller engagements in Berlin. If you tried to count all the venues he's filled with music, you'd cover multiple pages. The Berliner Symphoniker, Cleveland Chamber Symphony and of course the Philharmonic Orchestra "George Enescu" are just a few examples in his long list of credits. In short: Cristian Niculescu is a world-renowned musician. On the side, he's co-founder of Dinu Lipatti Trio Berlin and the fixed pianist of the ensemble contempo paris. Cristian lives and breathes music, right but you might as well meet him at a party, and he himself is an excellent host, with his own stage for events and music. (s. p. 59) One of his favorite big stages is the gorgeous Konzertsaal in the Konzerthaus on Gendarmenmarkt. Of course, he performs here as well regularly. (s. p. 59). →

studioniculescu.com
@cristi_niculescu

CRISTIAN NICULESCU EMPFIEHLT:
DAS KONZERTHAUS CRISTIAN NICULESCU
RECOMMENDS: THE KONZERTHAUS

Das Konzerthaus Berlin gibt es unter diesem Namen erst seit 1994. Entworfen hat das Gebäude vor fast hundert Jahren der Meisterarchitekt des Klassizismus, Karl Friedrich Schinkel. Das einstige Königliche Schauspielhaus und spätere Preußische Staatstheater wurde im Zweiten Weltkrieg beschädigt und 1984 von der DDR-Regierung nach stilgerechten Umbauten als Konkurrenz zur Westberliner Philharmonie eröffnet. Pro Jahr finden heute um die 550 Veranstaltungen in vier Konzertsälen statt – darunter thematische Konzertzyklen, Alte und Neue Musik sowie Kinderkonzerte. Während im Großen Saal zu Sinfoniekonzerten mit dem hauseigenen Konzerthausorchester, der Staatskapelle Berlin, geladen wird, führt man Kammerkonzerte im Kleinen Saal auf. Ich selbst habe Konzerte im Konzerthaus gegeben und mag besonders den multifunktionalen Werner-Otto-Saal, der vom Architekturbüro Peter Kulka als modernes Pendant zur Schinkelschen Sachlichkeit gestaltet wurde. It was only in 1994 that the Konzerthaus Berlin got its current name. The building was designed by the master neoclassical architect Karl Friedrich Schinkel. Nearly a hundred years ago, formerly the Royal Theater and later the Prussian State Theater, it was damaged in World War II and re-opened in 1984 by the East German government as an answer to the opening of the Westberliner Philharmonie. Today, the four halls of the Konzerthaus host 550 events a year, including thematic concert cycles, classical and contemporary music, and children's concerts. Symphonies are performed by the Konzerthaus's own orchestra, the Staatskapelle, in the Großer Saal, while chamber concerts are held in the Kleiner Saal. I've held concerts myself in the Konzerthaus – my favorite is the multi-functional Werner-Otto-Saal, designed by architect Peter Kulka as a modern counterpart to Schinkel's realism.

Text: Cristian Niculescu / Photos: Marco Borggreve, Sonja Gutschera & Leif-Henrik-Osthoff

Konzerthaus Berlin
Gendarmenmarkt, 10117 Berlin-Mitte
konzerthaus.de

DIM SUM BIS ZUM MORGENGRAUEN
DIM SUM FROM NOON 'TIL DAWN

Wenn es in Berlin dunkel wird, wird es im Aroma in Charlottenburg
hell. Spotleuchten, Aquarien und falsche Mingvasen sorgen für
das kitschig-authentische Ambiente, das man von Asia Restaurants
kennt. Auf der Suche nach Gemütlichkeit ist man hier falsch,
für beste kantonesische Küche hingegen richtig. Die Gerichte erklären
sich dank ausführlicher Bebilderung auf der Karte fast von
selbst, was die ohnehin schwere Wahl erleichtert. Auch die Kellner
beantworten Neugierigen gerne ihre Fragen – oder der Tischnachbar,
der aller Wahrscheinlichkeit nach hier Stammkunde ist. Ein Muss:
die gedämpften Lotusblätter, gefüllt mit Klebreis und Fleisch,
die frittierten Sojateigrollen mit Schweinefleisch und das hausgemachte
Dim Sum. Kulinarische Abenteurer sollten sich den Quallensalat
nicht entgehen lassen. Falls das etwas Überwindung bedarf, Zeit
ist kein Problem – das Aroma hat bis drei nachts geöffnet. It's
dark in Berlin, but Aroma in Charlottenburg is as light as
ever. Spotlights, aquariums, and fake Chinese vases create an
authentically kitschy Asian-restaurant ambience. If you're looking
for a cozy atmosphere, you're in the wrong place, but if you're
hunting for authentic Cantonese cuisine then look no further.
The dishes are pictured in the menu, which helps you make the
difficult choice between all the excellent options. The waiters
are also happy to answer your questions – or if they're busy, your
neighbor, who's probably a regular, is surely delighted to help.
The steamed lotus leaves filled with sticky rice and meat,
the fried soy dough rolls with pork, and the homemade dim sum
dumplings are all unmissable. Culinary adventurers shouldn't
miss out on the jellyfish salad. If you have to convince yourself to
eat it, take your time – Aroma is open until three in the morning.

Text: Stephanie Johne / Photos: Daniel Farò

Aroma
Kantstraße 35, 10625 Berlin-Charlottenburg
Daily 12:00-3:00

EXTRA TIP

Wer das Aroma schon kennt, schaut bei
Good Friends, einem anderen Chinesen auf
der Kantstraße 30 vorbei. If you already know
Aroma, try out Good Friends, another
Chinese restaurant at Kantstraße 30.

WOHNZIMMER MIT TANZFLÄCHE
LIVING ROOM WITH A DANCE FLOOR

Für Neulinge ist es ja nicht leicht am Kotti - besonders wegen all dieser Treppenaufgänge, die dicht beieinander liegen. Zur Paloma Bar führt nicht eines der engen Treppenhäuser, sondern quasi die Königin der Kotti-Treppen: freiliegend und offen - obschon leider meist zugemüllt mit Junkie-Utensilien, fettigen Döner-Papieren oder getrashten Fernsehern, lockt sie Ausgehwütige in die erste Etage des Wohnblocks. Den Müll hinter sich gelassen, wirkt die wohnzimmergroße Paloma Bar umso mehr wie eine gute Stube, die Musik ist noch dazu angenehm und verdrängt den Lärm von draußen. Die Getränke tun ihr Übriges und die Gäste sind zur Abwechslung mal nicht zu jung. 2006 eröffnet, wird sie von den Machern des Monarch und der Fahimi Bar (zu erreichen über besagte Treppenhäuser) betrieben. Beliebt ist die kleine Bar als Startpunkt für alle, die danach noch in einen „richtigen" Club gehen wollen. Oder als letzte Station vor dem Heimweg. Schade! Man sollte den ganzen Abend hier verbringen und das Weiterziehen einfach knicken, denn diese Location kann alle Bedürfnisse erfüllen: mit Freunden feiern, tanzen, trinken, ausgelassen sein, und spätestens wenn die gelbe U-Bahn vor der schrägen Fensterfassade vorbeirauscht das ultimative Großstadtgefühl erleben.

Kotti can be confusing to newcomers - all those intersecting stairwells are like a maze. But to get to Paloma Bar, you don't need to negotiate your way around the narrow staircases. It's located on the quasi-queen of the Kotti-steps: exposed and open, though sadly littered with junkie relics, greasy Döner papers, or broken TVs. Despite this, it seems to draw party-goers like moths to a flame. Leaving the trash behind, the living-room sized Paloma Bar seems like a friendly parlor, and the good music drowns out the noise outside. The drinks do the rest, and for once, the guests aren't too young. Opened in 2006, the creators also own the Monarch and Fahimi Bar (opened on the mentioned stairwells). The little bar is a favorite start to the evening for all, especially for those who want to go to the "right" club afterwards. Alternatively, it makes a great last stop on the way home. And that's too bad! You should try spending the whole evening here, instead of going someplace else. This venue has everything you need for a fantastic evening: you can celebrate with friends, dance, drink, and - at the latest when the yellow U-Bahn rushes past the oblique window façades - have the ultimate big-city experience.

Text: Nina Trippel / Photos: Daniel Farò

Paloma Bar
Skalitzer Straße 135, 10999 Berlin-Kreuzberg
Summer: Thu-Sat from 23:00, Winter: Thu-Sat from 22:00

GRENZÜBERSCHREITUNG UND DIE KUNST DER UNTERHALTUNG
THE ART OF CROSSING BORDERS

Betritt man das Neu West Berlin, kann man sich sicher sein, von einer bunten, polyglotten Künstlergruppe begrüßt zu werden. Der Raum ist voll von Dingen, die so unterschiedlich sind wie die Menschen, die hier verkehren - von zahllosen Porzellan-Teekannen der Marke Rosenthal über unterschiedliche Holzstühle, die nicht zusammenpassen, bis hin zu großformatigen Gemälden, die noch im Entstehen begriffen sind. Das Neu West Berlin weiß um seine Geschichte, richtet das Augenmerk auf die Berliner Mauer und updated zugleich die glamouröse Künstlerszene West-Berlins - daher der Name. Während ich mir Pizza mit den Stammgästen teile, kommt ein junger Musiker herein, um Patrice Lux, dem Co-Betreiber und Gründer des Neu West Berlins zu sagen, dass er und seine Band gleich ein Konzert im Laden geben werden. Patrice scheint die Idee zu gefallen. Dies ist nicht nur ein Ort, an dem sich Künstler profilieren können, er ermöglicht auch Köchen aus der ganzen Welt, für das hauseigene Pop-up-Restaurant Floinc zu kochen: Dem Ruf folgten bislang Küchenteams aus u.a. Galizien, Schweden, Italien und Island. Ähnlich wie die Künstler sind auch die Köche begeistert am Werk und verleihen ihren Gerichten eine eigene, einzigartige Note. When you walk into Neu West Berlin, prepare to be greeted by a motley group of artists speaking any number and mixture of languages. The space is filled with a group of objects as eclectic as the people, from countless porcelain teapots from the Rosenthal factory to mismatched wooden chairs to large paintings-in-progress. Neu West Berlin respects its history, placing an emphasis on the Wall and recreating a modern take on the glamorous, creative culture of the old West Berlin - hence the name. As I share a slice of pizza with the regulars, a young musician strolls in to let co-founder Patrice Lux know that his band is putting on a concert. Patrice seems delighted with the idea. In addition to providing a space for artists to hone their craft, Neu West Berlin's restaurant, Floinc, features a rotating cast of international chefs, hailing from all over Europe, such as Galicia, Sweden, Italy, and Iceland. The chefs are just as much craftsmen as any of the artists here, each bringing their own unique touch to the food they serve.

Text: Esmé Rocks / Photos: Markus Braumann

Neu West Berlin
Yorckstraße 86, 10965 Berlin-Kreuzberg
Variable opening hours
neuwestberlin.com

GEPFLEGTE DRINKS IM GROSS-STADTDSCHUNGEL FINE DRINKS IN THE URBAN JUNGLE

Mit dem Basalt ist dem harten Pflaster des Weddings ein Bar-Pflänzchen entsprungen, das man gut und gerne nach Mitte umtopfen könnte. Die Bar der Inhaber Kieran Mac Devitt und Matthias Heumeier, die sich als „Weddinger Interpretation eines botanischen Gartens bei Nacht" versteht, ist – um im Jargon des Großstadt-Botanikers zu bleiben – eine im Berliner Norden immer noch selten anzutreffende Gattung. Allerlei Grünpflanzen versprühen im dunkel gehaltenen Barraum Dschungel-Stimmung. Kleine Details wie smaragdgrüne Fliesen aus der Außenfassade runden das visuelle Erlebnis ab. Auch die Drinks sollten einem Großstadt-Tarzan zu Gaumenfreuden verhelfen: Der erfrischende Basilisk, ein mit Basilikum und Holunder-sirup versetzter Grey Goose-Wodka, lässt mich sehnlichst von lauen Berliner Sommernächten träumen. Eine Bar, die man eigentlich sofort unter Naturschutz stellen möchte. A bar has sprouted from the rough streets of Wedding that you may well want to repot in Mitte. The bar owner duo Kieran Mac Devitt and Matthias Heumeier, who see themselves as a "Weddinger interpretation of a botanical garden at night" are – to continue the city-botanist theme – a species rarely seen in the north of Berlin. All sorts of green plants radiate a jungle atmosphere in the bar, which is kept dark. Small details like emerald green tiles, salvaged from the external wall, complete the visual experience. The drinks are a treat for any urban dweller: the refreshing Basilisk, which offsets Grey Goose Vodka with basil and elderberry syrup, makes me dream ardently of warm summer nights in Berlin. The bar has its own unique little ecosystem that you immediately want to protect.

Text: Daniela Ihrig / Photos: Tabea Mathern

Basalt
Utrechter Straße 38, 13347 Berlin-Wedding
Tue-Sat 19:00-2:00, Sun 19:00-1:00

EXTRA TIP

Wer sich vor dem Barbesuch stärken will, bestellt gegenüber bei Parma di Vini Benedetti in der Utrechter Straße 31 Schinken, Salami und Brot direkt aus dem Ofen. If you want a quick snack before heading to the bar, order ham and salami and bread fresh from the oven from Parma di Vini Benedetti, across the street at Utrechter Straße 31.

EIN TOAST AUF DIE NACHT!
A TOAST TO NIGHT-TIME!

Einst als Ausstellungsraum konzipiert, zählt das Kumpelnest,
in dem früher einmal ein Bordell untergebracht war, heute
wahrscheinlich zu den berühmtesten und berüchtigsten Spe-
lunken Tiergartens - zwar sind die Rotlichttage gezählt,
doch verrucht geht es heute immer noch zu. Gegründet von
Techno-Produzent Mark Ernestus, wurde die Bar mit dem
herrlich exzentrischen Interieur schnell ein zweites Wohnzimmer für Transvestiten, Trinker, Partygänger und Nacht-
eulen. Zwischen den kitschigen Lampen, Spiegeln, dem Glitzer
und Konfetti scheint der Zigarettenrauch der letzten 25
Jahre noch immer an den Wänden zu hängen – ein Ort, der
resistent jeder Konvention widersteht. Once intended as
an exhibition space, the Kumpelnest went on to become a
brothel, and is today perhaps one of Tiergarten's most
notorious drinking dens. Its red light days might be over,
but the kitsch and the kooky remain. Founded by techno
producer Mark Ernestus, the bar has become synonymous with
an eccentric style that attracts transvestites, alcoholics, party preachers, and disco dancers for random all-
nighters. Swathed in glitter and mirrors, a blanket of
cigarette smoke from the last 25 years clings to the walls
of this establishment, a place that has seemingly
resisted every convention in the book to remain what it
has always been.

Text: Victoria Pease / Photos: Kilian-Davy Baujard

Kumpelnest 3000
Lützowstraße 23, 10785 Berlin-Tiergarten
Sun-Thu 19:00-5:00, Fri & Sat from 19:00
kumpelnest3000.com

EXTRA TIP

Legendär sind auch die Vernissage-Abende in der
Galerie Gillmeier Rech um die Ecke in der
Körnerstraße 17. The opening evenings of the gallery
Gillmeier Rech, located at Körnerstraße 17, are
also legendary.

PERSPECTIVES

AUS DER VOGELPERSPEKTIVE KANN MAN EINE STADT MANCHMAL AM BESTEN VERSTEHEN. ODER DURCH FREMDE FENSTER SEHEN UND NEUE WELTEN ENTDECKEN. A BIRD'S-EYE VIEW CAN BE THE BEST WAY TO UNDERSTAND A CITY — OR TO DISCOVER NEW WORLDS FROM SOMEONE'S WINDOWSILL.

SONNTAGSBLICK SUNDAY VIEWS

Einer der besten Orte, an dem man einen Sonntagnachmittag verbringen kann, ist das Turmgeschoss der Zionskirche. Erbaut 1866 vom Architekten August Orth im Stil des Berliner Historismus, handelt es sich hier um eine der prachtvollsten Kirchen Berlins. Auch „Dom des Nordens" genannt, liegt die Kirche auf dem höchsten natürlichen Punkt der Stadt, einem alten Weinberg. Wer den Turm besteigen will, schaut sonntags vorbei und erklimmt die enge Treppe zur 67 Meter hohen Kirchturmspitze. Oben angekommen, steht man mit dem Kopf (fast) in den Wolken und hat einen wunderbaren Blick über die Stadt. Ein Tipp ist auch die Imkerei an der Zionskirche, deren Bienenstöcke in den Eckpfeilern der Kirche untergebracht sind. Wer ein Glas Honig mit nach Hause nehmen möchte, kauft es in der Kirche oder im Café Kapelle direkt am Platz. One of the best places to spend a lazy Sunday afternoon is inside the spire of the Zionskirche. Built in 1866 by the architect August Orth in the Berliner Historicism style, the Zionskirche is one of the most magnificent churches in town. Also known as the "Dome of the North," the church sits on the highest natural hill in the city, the old Weinberg. Climb up the narrow stairs in the 67-meter octagonal spire and enjoy the expansive 360 degree view of the capital. Our secret tip is the Zion's apiary. Bees produce tasty honey in the beehives located inside the arched openings on the building's façade. The honey can be purchased at the church or at Café Kapelle on Zionskirchplatz.

Text: Milena Kalojanov / Photos: Daniel Faró, Filine Fink

<u>Zionskirche</u>
Zionskirchplatz, 10119 Berlin-Mitte
Sun 12:00–17:00
zionskirche-berlin.de

EXTRA TIP

Fleißige Bienen gibt es in Mitte jede Menge – am Kraftwerk in der Köpenicker Straße 70 zum Beispiel: ihren Tresorhonig kauft man im gleichnamigen Club. Mitte is filled with hardworking bees – for example, at Kraftwerk in Köpenicker Straße 70, you can buy their pure honey at the club Tresor.

P E R S P E C T I V E S

Wer ihn bei einer seiner Performances erlebt, bekommt fast ein bisschen Angst – denn Christians Falsnaes macht „Ansagen" mit Nachdruck. Der 1980 geborene Künstler animiert Menschen in Museen, Galerien und auf Kunstmessen wie der Art Basel Dinge zu tun, die man sich als Erwachsener in der Öffentlichkeit ansonsten eher selten traut: Fremde umarmen, sich nackt ausziehen oder auf Händen durch den Raum tragen lassen. Er selbst steht dabei bisweilen wie eine Mischung aus TV-Moderator, Ferienclub-Animateur und Rockstar im Mittelpunkt „seiner" Gruppe – ein künstlerisches Konzept, für das er 2015 mit dem Preis der Nationalgalerie nominiert war. Privat ist er zurückhaltender, aber nicht minder unterhaltsam. Und vielleicht der einzige Däne in Berlin, der Deutsch mit Wiener Akzent sprechen kann, denn bevor er nach Berlin zog, hat der gebürtige Kopenhagener in der österreichischen Hauptstadt studiert. Die nächste Station ist New York. Sightseeing wird er dort nicht betreiben, sondern Menschen beobachten, denn um die geht es ihm, in seiner Kunst und der Freizeit. In Berlin geht das seiner Meinung nach auch gut am Hauptbahnhof. Oder im Tiergarten – vor oder nach dem Besuch der Akademie der Künste, einem seiner Lieblingsorte.

Anyone who's seen one of his performances is almost frightened of Christian Falsnaes – he makes his "announcements" emphatically. The artist, born in 1980, motivates his audiences in museums, galleries, and art fairs such as Art Basel to do things that, as an adult in the public sphere, you'd rarely dare to try: hug strangers, strip naked, let people carry you on their hands through the room. He himself seems like a mixture of a TV host, vacation group leader, and rock star, standing in the middle of "his" flock – an artistic concept for which he was nominated for the Preis der Nationalgalerie in 2015. Privately, he's more reserved but no less entertaining. Aside from all this, Christian is maybe the only Dane in Berlin who could speak German with a Viennese accent: before he moved to Berlin, the Copenhagen native studied in Austria's capital. The next stop on his journey is New York City. Sightseeing will not be on his list; instead, he will be people-watching, because that's his real passion, both in art and in his free time. Hauptbahnhof is one of Berlin's best people-watching locations, says Christian. Or the Tiergarten – before or after a visit to the Akademie der Künste, another of his favorite places. →

falsnaes.com / psm-gallery.com
@christianfalsnaes

CHRISTIAN FALSNAES EMPFIEHLT:
DIE AKADEMIE DER KÜNSTE
CHRISTIAN FALSNAES RECOMMENDS:
THE AKADEMIE DER KÜNSTE

Einer meiner liebsten Ausstellungsräume in Berlin ist die Akademie der Künste am Hanseatenweg. Ich liebe die funktionale Architektur, die Kombination aus Ausstellungsfläche und Theaterraum, sowie die Lage in unmittelbarer Nähe der modernen Häuser des Hansaviertels. All das macht diesen Ort so besonders! Die Akademie der Künste besticht mit einem ambitionierten Veranstaltungsprogramm aus Ausstellungen, Theateraufführungen, Konzerten und Talks - ich habe hier einige wirklich gute Schauen gesehen. Auch wenn man sich nicht so sehr für das Programm interessiert, sind die Lage und das Gebäude an sich Grund genug für einen Besuch. Den Hofgarten und den Theaterraum, dessen Sitzplätze auf beiden Seiten der Bühne angebracht sind, mag ich besonders. Auch der Tiergarten gehört zu meinen Lieblingsplätzen in Berlin, wenn man anschließend nach einem Platz sucht, um ein wenig in der Sonne zu sitzen. One of my favorite exhibition spaces in Berlin is Akademie der Künste at Hanseatenweg. I love the functional architecture. The combination of exhibition and theater space, as well as its location, surrounded by the modern homes of the Hansaviertel, makes it quite unique. The Akademie der Künste houses an ambitious program of exhibitions, stage productions, concerts, and talks - I've seen several really good shows there. Even if the program doesn't interest you, the location and building are reasons enough for a visit. I especially enjoy the courtyard garden and the theater space with seats for spectators on both sides of the stage. Plus, it's located right next to the Tiergarten, one of my favorite places in Berlin to hang out in the sun.

Text: Christian Falsnaes / Photos: Manfred Mayer

Akademie der Künste
Hanseatenweg 10, 10557 Berlin-Tiergarten
Building: daily 10:00-22:00, Exhibitions: Tue-Sun 11:00-19:00
adk.de

EXTRA TIP

Einen Eingang weiter, in der Ritterstraße 2a, ze
die Galerie Chert neben jungen Künstlern auc
Werke von Pionieren der Siebzigerjahre, wie d
von Ruth Wolf-Rehfeldt. Next door, at Ritterstra
2a, gallery Chert shows pioneers from the 70s li
Ruth Wolf-Rehfeldt alongside young artists.

PASTRAMI-EXPERTISE IM DESIGN-DELI THE DESIGN DELI WITH PASTRAMI EXPERTISE

Rote Wände, klare Linien. Dazu sonnenhell funkelnde Tische, türkisfarben wie kleine Swimming Pools. Hello Palm Springs! Oder: Welcome to Louis Pretty! Im Deli von Oskar Melzer stimmt alles: vom Design über das Essen bis hin zum Service. Der Wahl-Berliner bietet einmal mehr jüdische Delikatessen an, mit dem Fokus auf Pastrami. Jenes Sandwich mit Rindfleisch hat er mit 13 auf einer Bar-Mizwa in New York zum ersten Mal probiert. Fortan ließ ihn der Geschmack dieses geräucherten Fleisches nicht mehr los. Meine Begleitung delektierte das Reuben-Pastrami in gefühlten fünfzehn Millisekunden. Meine Veggie-Variante mit Baby Leaf, Guacamole, Chipotle und eingelegten Zwiebeln: würzig, leicht scharf, köstlich. Zum Dessert gibt es Brownies mit Karamellsauce und Salzsplittern – zum Niederknien. Zusammen mit einer Tasse Filterkaffee (American Style mit Free Refill) der perfekte Abschluss.

Red walls, clean lines, and sunlit tables topped with dappled turquoise that look like little swimming pools: hello, Palm Springs! Or, alternatively, welcome to Louis Pretty! In Oskar Melzer's new deli, everything is perfect, from the design right through to the service. A Berliner by adoption, he serves the finest Jewish delicacies, with a big focus on pastrami. Melzer tried the special beef sandwich for the first time when he was just 13 years old at a Bar Mitzvah celebration in New York. From that moment on, he was hooked on the smoked red meat, and he finally brought it back with him to Berlin! My dinner date clearly enjoyed the Reuben Pastrami, finishing it after what felt like fifteen milliseconds. My veggie variety, made with baby leaf salad, guacamole, chipotle, and pickled onions, was spicy, slightly hot, and delicious. We topped off the evening with brownies with caramel sauce and salt crystals, alongside classic American filter coffee, American-style with free refills, of course – the perfect ending.

Text: Nella Beljan / Photo: Steve Herud

Louis Pretty
Ritterstraße 2, 10969 Berlin-Kreuzberg
Mon-Sat 11:00–22:00
louispretty.com

EXTRA TIP

Schön ist die Aussicht auch vom Müggelturm im Osten der Stadt: Zunächst erklimmt man den Kleinen Müggelberg, dann den 30 Meter hohen Turm. The view from the Müggelturm, in the east of the city, is also gorgeous: first climb the small Müggelberg, then the 30 meter tower for a view of the city.

AUSFLUG MIT AUSSICHT
EXCURSION WITH A VIEW

Schon der Weg Richtung Flatowturm macht Spaß: Der Landschafts-
architekt Peter Joseph Lenné legte den Babelsberger Park 1833
an, und folgt man heute seinem Pfad, taucht das Bauwerk mal rechts,
mal links auf. Ein Besuch lohnt sich natürlich wegen des
fantastischen 360-Grad-Blicks auf Sehenswürdigkeiten wie das
Belvedere oder die Kuppel des Marmorpalais im Neuen Garten.
Das ehemalige Gästehaus von Kaiser Wilhelm I beheimatet allerlei
Kuriositäten: Wunderbar ist der Paustisch im obersten Stock –
mit einer Linse wird die umliegende Landschaft auf einen
Tisch projiziert. Stift und Papier liegen bereit und man kann
sich künstlerisch austoben. Der Audioguide ist interessant, besonders nett ist es aber, sich auf einen Schwatz mit dem Museums-
aufseher einzulassen. Just a few steps away from the Babelsberg
train station, you'll find a park that shares its name. Make no
mistake, it is its own entity, and every aspect of your visit
there promises fruitful discoveries. Take the winding path,
designed by Peter Joseph Lenné in 1833, to Flatow Tower, which
appears to be on your left at certain moments and right at
others. The experience doesn't exactly plateau either. The 360
degree view, including landmarks like Belvedere and the dome
of the Marble Palace in the New Garden, are major highlights.
The indoor exhibition is equally wonderful. The former guest
house of Friedrich Wilhelm I hosts curiosities from all over the
world. I had loads of fun with the layout table on the top floor:
the surrounding countryside is projected onto a table through a
lens. Pen and paper are provided as a portal for those feeling
inspired and creative. While the audio-guide is interesting, leave
time to chat with the museum guard.

Text & Photos: Helen von der Höden

Flatowturm
Park Babelsberg 12, 14482 Potsdam
May-October: Sat & Sun 10:00-18:00
psg.de/schloesser-gaerten/objekt/flatowturm

PERSPECTIVES

ARCHITEKTUR ALS ZEICHNUNG
ARCHITECTURAL SCRIBBLES EXHIBITED

Als guter Architekt oder Designer muss man das Zeichnen von Hand beherrschen, die Kunst, erste Ideen aus dem Kopf direkt aufs Papier zu übersetzen. Vage Scribbles, schnelle Striche und Perspektiven, die nach einem langen Prozess zu gelungener Architektur werden – das sind in meinen Augen die schönsten Zeichnungen. Diese Tatsache im Gedächtnis, gründete Architekt, Zeichner und Sammler Sergei Tchoban 2009 die Tchoban Foundation. Den Schwerpunkt seines Museums bildet eine umfangreiche Sammlung an Architekturzeichnungen. Das Spektrum reicht von Arbeiten alter Baumeister bis hin zu den ersten Skizzen der leider zu früh verstorbenen Star-Architektin Zaha Hadid. In der hauseigenen Bibliothek können die Liebhaber der feinen Linie noch tiefer in die Recherche einsteigen. I don't know any good artists or designers who can't translate their ideas onto paper with their hands. In my eyes those are the most beautiful drawings, the vague scribbles and rapidly laid down lines of the first ideas and perspectives, the beginning of a long process of a (hopefully) successful piece of architecture. Sergei Tchoban, architect, illustrator, and collector, founded the Tchoban Foundation in 2009 with this principle in mind. An impressive collection of architectural drawings forms the main focus of the museum – the spectrum ranges from designs created by the old masters to the first sketches of star architect Zaha Hadid. Meanwhile, the library presents a fantastic research opportunity for any lovers of drawing, design, and fine lines.

Text: Milena Kalojanov / Photos: Roland Halbe, Patricia Parinejad

Tchoban Foundation – Museum für Architekturzeichnung
Christinenstraße 18a, 10119 Berlin-Mitte
Mon-Fri 14:00-19:00, Sat & Sun 13:00-17:00
tchoban-foundation.de

EXTRA TIP

Anschließend stärkt man sich um die Ecke bei Momos in der Fehrbelliner Straße 5, wo es vegetarische, dampfgegarte nepalesische Teigtaschen gibt. Refresh yourself around the corner at Momos at Fehrbelliner Straße 5, and eat steamed vegetarian Nepalese dumplings.

EXTRA TIP

Wer anschließend eine Stärkung braucht, besucht
das Hofcafé bei Mutter Fourage in der Chausseestraße
15 in Wannsee, wo es saisonale Küche gibt.
If you're low on energy afterwards, go to the Hofcafé
bei Mutter Fourage: you'll find seasonal cooking
in the yard of a former animal feed factory, at
Chausseestraße 15 in Wannsee.

TAGESAUSFLUG INS PARADIES
DAY TRIP TO PARADISE

Kaum zu glauben, aber Berlin hat mehr als 34 Inseln im Stadt-
gefüge. Eine davon grenzt an Potsdam und liegt in der Havel:
die Pfaueninsel. Mit einer Größe von 67 Hektar und einem ural-
ten Baumbestand von rund 400 Eichen ist sie zweifellos eine
der Meisterleistungen des Landschaftsarchitekten Peter Joseph
Lenné. Im April und Mai ist der Ausflug mit der Fähre auf das
Eiland besonders schön. Dann bahnt sich nicht nur die Natur
ihren Weg durch die Erde und die ersten Obstbäume haben sich
„in Blüte geworfen", sondern auch die Namenspatronen stellen sich
zur Schau: über 30 bunte und weiße Pfauen leben hier. Mit ihrem
prächtigen Gefieder beeindrucken sie kleine und große Stadt-
kinder. Ebenfalls faszinierend ist der Ausblick nach Sacrow,
Glienicke und zum Neuen Garten. Fazit: Ein kleines Spazier-
Paradies ganz ohne Autos und Räder. Believe it or not, Berlin
has more than 34 islands included in its territory. One of them
adjoins Potsdam at the Havel river: the Pfaueninsel (peacock
island). The island measures 67 hectares, and with the ancient
forest of 400 oak trees, it's an absolute masterstroke by land-
scape architect Peter Joseph Lenné. We traveled to this stunning place on a little ferry. The trip to the island is particularly beautiful in April and May as nature awakens and the
blossoming trees and magical creatures that lend the isle its
name make themselves known. Over 30 white and colorful peacocks
live here and impress visitors by showing off their ostentatious
feathers. Also impressive: the view of Sacrow, Glienicke, and the
Neuer Garten. It's a walkers' paradise – without bikes and cars.

Text: Milena Kalojanov / Photos: Daniel Farò

Pfaueninsel
Nikolskoer Weg, 14109 Berlin-Wannsee
spsg.de/schloesser-gaerten/objekt/pfaueninsel

KAL EID OSC OPE

DIE STADT STRAHLT GRÜN
IM SOMMER, IM WINTER
TRÄGT SIE HIMMELGRAU.
ABER SCHÖNE DINGE
LEUCHTEN IN ALLEN
NUANCEN. UND WOLLEN
MIT NACH HAUSE KOMMEN.

BERLIN IS GREEN IN
SUMMER AND GREY IN
WINTER. BUT THESE
PLACES ARE RAINBOW-
COLORED ALL YEAR
AROUND. TAKE SOME HOME
WITH YOU.

MODE FÜR MUTIGE & SHOPPING MIT SPASSFAKTOR FASHION SHOPPING FOR THE BOLD & HAPPY

Berlin mag Schwarz: schwarze Kleidung, schwarze Accessoires, schwarzen Kaffee. Doch der Happy Shop Global Alliance auf der Torstraße schlägt andere Töne an. Das Credo von SJ Ballantyne, der den Laden 2015 neu konzipierte, lautet: Farbe satt! Komplexe Muster, ungewöhnliche Stoffe sowie hochwertige Design-objekte von Miharayasuhiro, Interzoo und Onar Studios ergänzen die bunte Palette. Was im Hinterhof aussieht wie ein Container, entpuppt sich als kleiner Co-Working Space mit dem Namen Curro und als hauseigenes Café, casita. Hier stehen neben Kuchen und Keksen eine wunderbare Tee-Selektion auf der Karte, und auch der beliebte Kaffee von Square Mile, einer Rösterei aus East London, wird angeboten. Wieder ist der Kaffee schwarz, aber der Happy Shop lässt Mitte wahrlich farbig erstrahlen. Berlin tends to have a predilection for black: black clothes, black accessories, black third wave coffee … But Torstraße's Happy Shop Global Alliance goes against the grain. Head of concept SJ Ballantyne, who carried out the rebranding of the store in 2015, does not limit the products to the monochrome. The store values gorgeously rich tones in every shade, alongside intricate patterns, uncommon fabrics, and high quality materials from designers such as Miharayasuhiro, Interzoo, and Onar Studios. Exit through a sliding door, and you'll see what appears to be a shipping con-tainer conspicuously dumped in the back yard, repurposed to serve as a home to casita, their coffee shop, which serves a selection of organic cakes and cookies coupled with delicious teas and coffee blends like East London's Square Mile. The space also holds Curro, their co-working space open seven days per week. The coffee may be black, but the Happy Shop still adds a real splash of color to Mitte.

Text: Antonia Harris / Photos: Daniel Farò

Happy Shop Global Alliance
Torstraße 67, 10119 Berlin-Mitte
Tue-Fri 11:00-19:00, Sat 12:00-19:00

casita
Café: Tue-Fri 10:00-17:00, Sat 12:00-17:00
Bar: Tue-Sat 17:30-22:00
happyshop-berlin.com

EXTRA TIP

Glücklich macht auch La Cucina, Schönhauser Allee 187: Ein kleiner, unscheinbarer italienischer Feinkostladen mit freundlichem Personal und dem niedlichsten Hund der Welt. A visit to the corner at Schönhauser Allee 187, where La Cucina lies, will also keep you happy; a small, unassuming Italian deli with friendly personnel and the cutest dog in the world.

PIZZA IN PERFEKTION PIZZA PERFECTION

Seinen stolzen Namen trägt dieses Lokal zu Recht. Die hier servierte Pizza schmeckt unvergleichlich, und wer erst einmal davon gekostet hat, kann fortan ähnlich aussehende, von anderen servierte „Fladen" nicht länger als Pizza bezeichnen wollen. Keinem anderen Gericht aus dem kulinarischen Welterbe als der Pizza wurde durch die prinzipiell lobenswerte Erfindung des Schockfrostens mehr Schaden angetan, und zwar genau als 1930 in den Vereinigten Staaten die ersten Tiefkühlprodukte auf den Markt kamen. Aus dem großen Versprechen einer Pizza für Jedermann wurde so in Wahrheit die Pizza für Niemanden, denn mit der ursprünglichen Pizza neapolitanischer Machart, wie sie nun im Standard serviert wird, hat eine im heimischen Ofen aufgebackene nicht nur nicht viel, sondern gar nichts zu tun. Das liegt nicht allein an den erstklassigen Zutaten, dem hausgestampften Pesto, dem Schinken und den Käsesorten, die verwendet werden, sondern vor allem an der infernalischen Hitze, mit der ein gemauerter Kuppelofen von allen Seiten auf Teig und Beläge einwirkt. Die Standard-Pizza kommt wenige Minuten nach der Bestellung auf den Tisch. Im Ofen selbst hat sie dabei – wer mag, soll auf die Uhr sehen – gerade 60 Sekunden verweilt. Die vom Belag unbelasteten Ränder der Pizza erscheinen nun zu einem Ring aufgetrieben, den appetitlich dunkle Sprenkel zieren. Die saftige Fracht besteht im Falle einer Taste of Brandenburg aus gegarten Scheiben einer fruchtigen Kartoffelsorte, geräuchertem Fior di latte (Mozarella) und Salsiccia vom Wildschwein. Nadeln frischen Rosmarins bleiben durch ihren Gehalt ätherischer Öle bei der kurzen Hitzeschockbehandlung vor dem Verbrennen geschützt und können so ihr Aroma entfalten. Der Räucherkäse und die hervorragend gewürzte Wurst ersparen selbst eingefleischten Nachsalzern den Griff zum Streuer. Für eine ausschließlich auf Pizza spezialisierte Küche legt man im Standard übrigens eine angenehm kurze Karte vor. Auch die Getränkeauswahl ist wohlüberlegt. Das einzig rustikale Element der Einrichtung besteht in besagtem Kuppelofen, der in dieser Umgebung jedoch skulptural erscheint, wie ein archäologisches Fundstück. This restaurant has every right to its proud name. The pizza served here is incomparable – a towering standard. After your first taste, any pizza made by the hands of another, even though it might look similar, will no longer designate "pizza." 1930 saw the first frozen-food products on US shelves. The grand promise of a pizza for everybody soon descended into a pizza for nobody; frozen pizza has nothing to do with its original Neapolitan style. Cutting against this regretful descent, Standard resurrects the pizza's true form. It is not only because of the first-class ingredients – the homemade pesto and select cheeses and ham. Rather, it has to do with the infernal heat of the oven. After placing your order the pizza will arrive at your table only a few minutes later, having stayed in the oven – you can clock it on your watch – for just 60 seconds. In this time the crust will have become a brown ring, speckled with appetizing dark spots. In the case of having chosen the Taste of Brandenburg, among its juicy cargo you will find succulent potato slices, smoked fior di latte, and salsiccia made from wild boar. Rosemary needles, saved from burning because of their essential oils and the heat-shock treatment, grace the air with their tempting aroma. Smoked cheese and the masterfully spiced sausage saves even the most devoted "salter" the effort of reaching for the saltshaker. For a kitchen that specializes in pizza, Standard's menu is very short and well considered. Their selection of drinks is also thoughtful. As for the furnishings, the oven is the only rustic feature, which, in this environment, impresses like a sculpture or an archaeological find.

Text: Joachim Bessing / Photos: Daniel Farò

Standard - Serious Pizza
Templiner Straße 7, 10119 Berlin-Mitte
Tue-Fri 18:00-24:00, Sat & Sun 13:00-24:00
standard-berlin.de

PROGRESS
ON
PERFECTION

ÜBERRASCHUNGEN ZUM DRAUF-HAUEN BINGE ON ART

Ob in Form eines quietschgrünen Dinosauriers oder als silbern funkelnde Ziffer – Piñatas sind das perfekte Mitbringsel für Klein und Groß, Geburtstage, WG-Parties oder Bürofeiern. Die aus Südamerika stammende Tradition, mit einem Piñata-buster (einem kleinen Stock) auf die Piñata einzuhauen, bis sie zerbricht und es Überraschungen regnet, findet auch hierzulande immer mehr Fans. Man kann die Piñata selbst basteln oder einfach Stefanie Wilhelm von der Piñateria fragen. Sie fertigt die bunten Wunderwerke von Hand an, und wer das Rund-umsorglos-Paket will, lässt seine Objekt auch gleich von ihr befüllen. Whether in the form of a squeaky green dinosaur or a sparkling silver number, piñatas are the perfect gift for children big and small, for birthdays, house-warming parties, or office celebrations. The tradition of beating the piñata with a piñata buster (a small stick) until it rains surprises down on its attackers originally comes from South America but has gained many fans all over the world. You can tinker with making your own – or just ask Stefanie Wilhelm from the Piñateria to do it. She makes the colorful marvels by hand. For the full package, let her fill the piñata with treats as well.

Text: Nina Trippel / Photos: Daniel Farò

Piñateria - Die Piñata Manufaktur
(at Kinderschuh am Platz) Schönleinstraße 8, 10967 Berlin-Kreuzberg
Mon-Fri 11:00-19:00, Sat 11:00-16:00
pinateria.de

SÄFTE FÜR FORTGESCHRITTENE
JUICING FOR THE ADVANCED MIND

Ins Glas oder die Flasche für den Smoothie to go kommen bei
Nils Bernau nur kaltgepresster Saft in fein abgestimmten
Kompositionen, vollgepackt mit Nährstoffen – und, passend zum
Namen, natürlich meistens in grün. Morgens zählt der Brain
Juicer mit Petersilie und Avocado zu den Favoriten. Wer nach-
mittags eine gesunde Alternative für etwas Süßes sucht, nimmt
den Dr. Snuggles mit rohem Kakao, Avocado und Basilikum. Ein
Saftladen mit dem besten aus dem Garten Eden! Nils Bernau's
personal goal is to provide nothing but top-notch quality
juice: it's nutrition packed, cold-pressed for superior taste,
and almost always based on green ingredients. Early birds fuel
up with the Brain Juicer, and customers looking for a healthy
alternative to sweets opt for Dr. Snuggles, packed with raw
cocoa, avocado, and basil. This shop-and-café lives up to its
name, offering the best of the Garden of Eden.

Text: Massimo Hartmann

Liquid Garden
Stargarder Straße 72, 10437 Berlin-Prenzlauer Berg
Summer: Mon-Fri 8:00-18:00, Sat 10:00-19:00, Sun 11:00-19:00
Winter: Mon-Fri 10:00-18:00, Sat 10:00-18:00, Sun 12:00-18:00
liquidgarden.berlin

EXTRA TIP

Wer eine eiskalte Erfrischung bevorzugt, schaut
nebenan bei Hokey Pokey, Stargarder Straße 73,
vorbei: für Sorten wie Bergamotte-Blutorange mit
weißer Schokolade lohnt sich das Schlange stehen!
If you're looking for an ice-cold refreshment, try
out Hokey Pokey, Stargarder Straße 73: the promise
of creations like bergamot-blood orange with white
chocolate will make standing in line bearable!

CEE CEE'S GUEST: PHILIP GAEDICKE

Ohne ihn wäre die Torstraße nicht das, was sie ist, denn wenn es in den letzten Jahren ein Bordsteingelage gab, war Philip Gaedicke mit Sicherheit beteiligt. Ob Blockparty oder Event einer Modemarke (s. S. 214), der gebürtige Frankfurter ist bestens connected, und wenn er ruft, dann kommen sie alle: die Influencer, die Follower, die Freunde. Sein Netzwerk basiert nicht zuletzt auf seiner Tätigkeit. 2012 gründete Philip das Kollektiv BAM, das deutschen und internationalen Brands in Kommunikations- und Imagefragen als Partner zur Seite steht. So reicht Philip allen die Hand: den Medien, den Marken und den Menschen, die die Produkte am Ende kaufen. Hinzu kommt, dass er mit seiner offenen Art den Geist der Stadt perfekt verkörpert: Support statt Konkurrenz, heißt sein Motto. Daher bereichert der Mitinhaber des Soto Stores (s. S. 214) den Cee Cee-Newsletter und dieses Buch immer mal wieder mit Tipps für besondere Geschäfte. Seine Empfehlung für Objekte, die das Zuhause schöner machen, ist der Concept Store namens Bazar Noir.

Torstraße wouldn't be as exciting without him. All those moments when people flocked to the sidewalk here – he was definitely involved. Whether a block party or fashion event (s. p. 214) – Philip's perfectly connected in this city. When he calls they all come running: influencers, followers, and friends. It's thanks to his profession that his network is so widespread. In 2012 Phil founded the collective BAM, with a client list of several German and international lifestyle brands. This way the Frankfurt native is linked to the brands, the makers, and the consumers. All of this comes with a very endearing attitude: mutual support rather than competition. So it makes sense that the Soto Store (s. p. 214) co-owner recommends other people's businesses on a regular basis in the Cee Cee newsletter and this book. A highlight among his tips is a store selling beautiful homewares called Bazar Noir. →

bam-berlin.com
sotostore.com
@phil_g
@bam_berlin
@sotostore

PHILIP GAEDICKE EMPFIEHLT: BAZAR NOIR PHILIP GAEDICKE RECOMMENDS: BAZAR NOIR

Auf den Concept Store Bazar Noir bin ich zufällig gestoßen. Bei einem Spaziergang vorbei am Viktoriapark Richtung Tempelhof linste ich durchs Schaufenster. Der in Schwarz gehaltene Shop von Catherine Pfisterer wurde vom Büro Hidden Fortress aufwendig gestaltet. Auf die Kunden wartet eine stilsichere Auswahl an Objekten und Möbeln von Designern wie Andree Weissert, Ben Storms oder Berlins Local Hero Sigurd Larsen. Der Shop ist klein, aber man kommt aus dem Staunen gar nicht mehr heraus, wenn man sich die Produkte ansieht, zum Beispiel die handgemachten Deko-Pfeile vom New Yorker Kreativ-Duo Fredericks & Mae, und das Gefühl zieht sich beim Gang durch den gesamten Laden; immer wieder bleibt man hängen, um das eine oder andere Objekt zu bewundern. Und wie es so ist mit Dingen, die man unglaublich schön findet: sie sind auch unglaublich teuer. Aber das ist vielleicht auch ganz gut so. I stumbled across Bazar Noir by chance while walking trough my neighborhood, passing Viktoriapark towards Tempelhof. Even though the little shop looks uninteresting from the outside, it caught my attention and I peeked through the window. The inside of this concept store, run by Catherine Pfisterer, is quite the contrary – all black and striking, designed by Hidden Fortress. You will find a stylish selection of furniture pieces by Andree Weissert, Ben Storms, and Berlin's local hero Sigurd Larsen. Although the shop isn't very big, you can't help but stop and look at each one of the unique objects inside – handmade arrows by New York's creative duo Fredericks & Mae are just one example. The feeling of astonishment will stick with you as you explore the shop. And as it always is with items you admire incredibly, things here are also incredibly expensive. But maybe that's not such a bad thing.

Text: Phillip Gaedicke

Bazar Noir
Kreuzbergstraße 78, 10965 Berlin-Kreuzberg
Mon by appointment, Tue-Fri 11:00-16:00, Sat 11:00-18:00
bazar-noir.com

DIE EMILIA-ROMAGNA MITTEN IM WRANGELKIEZ EMILIA-ROMAGNA IN THE HEART OF WRANGELKIEZ

Bosco bedeutet Wald auf deutsch, und schon vor meinem Besuch ahnte ich, dass ich hier in guten Händen sein würde. Durchs kulinarische Dickicht führen nämlich zwei Experten der italienischen Küche: Federico Testa und Francesco Righi. Los geht es mit dem Gruß aus der Küche: Spuma di Mortadella, also Mortadellaschaum, der luftiger nicht sein könnte, sowie Thunfisch-Steak mit Radicchio und Mango als Antipasti. Danach folgte ein Gang, für den die beiden Inhaber bekannt sind: hervorragende Trüffel aus Cesena von Francescos Mama, serviert in Kombination mit einem auf niedriger Temperatur gekochten Wachtelei und Risotto. Köstlich! Die Erinnerung an das Dessert begleitet mich noch auf meinem Heimweg – deliziös war es, aber mehr sei an dieser Stelle nicht verraten. Selbst probieren, lautet die Devise! Bosco means forest in Italian, but I knew I wouldn't get lost as I wandered into this culinary wilderness. I am being led through the woods by two experts in Italian cuisine: Federico Testa and Francesco Righi. The journey begins with spuma di mortadella, or mortadella foam, whipped and light on the tongue. Following this, a tender tuna steak with radishes and mango for antipasto continues the adventure. Next comes the treat the duo is particularly well known for: truffles straight from Cesena, from Francesco's Mamma, served with lightly-cooked quail eggs and risotto. One word sums it up: fantastic! A lingering, sweet impression of the dessert stays with me on my trudge back home. My experience cannot be expressed merely in words – go find out for yourself.

Text: Milena Kalojanov / Photos: Daniel Faró

Bosco
Wrangelstraße 42, 10997 Berlin-Kreuzberg
Wed-Sat from 19:00
boscoberlin.com

LOKALE MODE ZWISCHEN INTER-NATIONALER HIGH FASHION
LOCAL DESIGN MEETS INTER-NATIONAL HIGH FASHION

„Manche dieser Marken findet man sonst nirgendwo in Berlin", sagt Jochen Drewes, der sympathische Inhaber des Chrome Store, während er mir ein Kleidungsstück von Sissi Götze zeigt. Zwischen neuen Entwürfen von Berliner Designern wie Xenia Bous und Thone Negrón hängen Vintage-Teile für Männer und Frauen – die Auswahl reicht von High Fashion-Marken wie Jil Sander und Prada bis zu Stücken kommerzieller Labels wie COS und American Apparel. Der Shop an sich ist minimalistisch gehalten, mit schwarzen Wänden und chromfarbenen Kleiderständern. Alle Kleidungsstücke wirken brandneu, der einzige Unterschied zu einer exklusiven Boutique sind die niedrigeren Preise. Vieles ist de facto auch nur einmal getragen worden: bei einem Fashion-Shooting. "Some of these brands you won't find anywhere else in Berlin," says Jochen Drewes, showing me a garment from Sissi Goetze. Among them are new collections by Berlin designers, such as Xenia Bous and Thone Negrón, mixed with contemporary vintage fashion for both women and men. The repurposed pieces are mainly high fashion brands such as Prada or Jil Sander, but also sit alongside items from more mainstream brands like COS or American Apparel, if they fit in with the quality and vision of the store. The interior is clean and minimalist with sleek black walls and chrome racks. All the clothes look brand new, with the lower price being the only thing that differs from the usual exclusive boutique. Some of the clothes have been worn only once: for a photo shoot.

Text: Isabelle Kagelius / Photos: Jochen Drewes

Chrome Store
Lenaustraße 10, 12047 Berlin-Neukölln
Mon-Fri 13:00-20:00, Sat 11:00-19:00
chrome-store.com

EXTRA TIP

Das Outfit lässt sich ein Stück weiter bei Aura, in der Sanderstraße 13, vervollständigen: Hier warten Bikinis aus den Siebzigern und japanische Kimonos. Your outfit just needs one finishing touch from Aura on Sanderstraße 13: bikinis from the seventies and Japanese kimonos await your discovery.

GENUSS & GASTFREUNDSCHAFT PAR EXCELLENCE HOSPITALITY & DELIGHT

„Sieh doppelt, was Du liebst", steht auf der Tafel, die die Außenfassade des Kreuzberger Speiselokals Tulus Lotrek ziert. Diesen Rat beherzigen wir gerne, und so folgt dem Begrüßungsimperativ der –aperitif, ein Doppel-wacholder-Gimlet, der uns von Gastgeberin Ilona Scholl und Koch Maximilian Strohe gereicht wird. Wir lassen ihn uns am Holztresen im Barraum schmecken, der wie die beiden Gasträume offen, gemütlich, und trotzdem schick ist – nicht zuletzt aufgrund der eigens fürs Lokal gezeichneten Tapete. Wir schlemmen uns durch ein phänomenales Sechs-Gänge-Menü mit mariniertem Hühnchen sowie Kirschrisotto mit Räucheraal, wobei wir mithilfe der großartigen Weinbegleitung für die angeratene Sichterweiterung sorgen. Alternativ gibt's grandiose Einzelgerichte auch à la carte. Weit später als geplant verlassen wir diesen besonderen Ort, beseelt und erfüllt: Die wissen hier wirklich, was sie tun – und das tun sie von Herzen. "Look twice at the things you love" is the wise advice found written on the board outside the Kreuzberg-based Tulus Lotrek, run by hostess Ilona Scholl and cook Maximilian Strohe. We certainly followed this advice upon entering the restaurant. We were immediately welcomed with an aperitif, which we enjoyed seated at an old, central, wooden-topped bar. Leading off from the bar are two separate eating spaces, large and cozy but with chic and eye-catching wallpaper. We feasted on the delicious six-course menu, eating cherry risotto with smoked eel as well as marinated chicken. And the perfected list of accompanying wines completely changed our perspective on the dishes. As expected, we left tulus lotrek feeling full of satisfaction and fantastic food. They know just what to do – and they know it by heart.

Text: Veronika Aumann / Photos: Daniel Farò

Speiselokal Tulus Lotrek
Fichtestraße 24, 10967 Berlin-Kreuzberg
Tue-Sun 18:00-24:00
tuluslotrek.de

EXTRA TIP

Gegenüber liegt der Fichtebunker – der älteste und einzige erhaltene Steingasometer Berlins. Im Rahmen von Führungen kann man ihn besichtigen. Opposite is the Fichtebunker – the oldest and only surviving stone gasometer in Berlin. Take a tour and explore!

Aufgemischt hat sie Berlin. Oder wachgeküsst. Auf jeden Fall geht einiges mehr, seit sie in dieser Stadt wohnt: Kavita Meelu. Im Jahr 2008 zog die gebürtige Engländerin mit indischen Wurzeln der Liebe wegen von London nach Berlin. Die neue Heimat bot dann auch genug Platz für ihre persönliche Leidenschaft – Kochen und Essen. Die Vielfalt der Londoner Streetfood-Szene begann sie allerdings schnell zu vermissen, weswegen sie beschloss, die Sache selbst in die Hand zu nehmen. Mit der Supperclub-Reihe Mother's Mother begann ihre Erfolgsgeschichte – gemeinsam mit Freunden kochte Kavita Rezepte ihrer und anderer Großmütter nach. Inzwischen ist sie Patin vieler erfolgreicher Projekte: Sie war es, die den Streetfood Thursday in der Markthalle Neun und die Event-Reihe Burgers & Hip-Hop initiierte. Vielleicht gründet ihr Erfolg auf der Tatsache, dass sie einen Abschluss in Wirtschaft von der International University of London in der Tasche hat. Oder es liegt einfach an ihrer grenzenlosen Energie, ihrem Wissen und Qualitätsanspruch. Deswegen weiß sie natürlich auch, wo es die schwer zu findenden Zutaten für internationale Gerichte gibt – bei Azzam in Neukölln. She's mixed Berlin up. Or kissed it awake. No matter how you put it, something interesting is happening since she's lived in this city: Kavita Meelu. In 2008 the Indian-rooted Englishwoman followed love from London to Berlin. Her new home had plenty of space for her personal passion – food. She quickly began to miss the diversity of London's street food scene, though, so she decided to take matters into her own hands. Her success story began with her supper club series Mother's Mother – a group composed of friends, with whom Kavita cooked recipes from both her own and other grandmothers. Meanwhile, she's godmother to many successful projects: it was she who began Streetfood Thursday in Markthalle Neun and the event series Burgers & Hip-Hop. Maybe her success stems from her degree in Economics from the International University of London. Or, perhaps, it lies simply in her boundless energy, knowledge, and her unfailing sense for quality. Thus she also knows where to find the best ingredients for international dishes – at Azzam in Neukölln. →

@kavitagoodstar
markthalleneun.de/street-food-thursday
facebook.com/burgersandhiphop
@burgersandhiphop

KAVITA MEELU EMPFIEHLT: AZZAM
KAVITA MEELU EMPFIEHLT: AZZAM

Ich weiß noch, wie ich 2013 versucht habe, in Berlin Freekeh, früh geernteten Dinkel, Molokheya, eine Gemüsepflanze, die auf deutsch Gemüsejudenpappel heißt, und Mograbieh, Riesen-Couscous, zu kriegen … das war eine schwierige Angelegenheit. Damals bot der Supermarkt Azzam auf der Sonnenallee, wo heute auch hervorragendes Hummus und Fatteh serviert werden, nicht gerade die frischesten Produkte an. Inzwischen hat sich viel getan: Wöchentlich lassen die Besitzer leckere Zutaten aus ihrer Heimat einfliegen. Endlich kann man all die kniffligen Gerichte aus Yotam Ottolenghis „Jerusalem"-Kochbuch ohne deutsche Ersatz-produkte nachkochen. Der Supermarkt Baraka Inter Food (Sonnenallee 39) hat in seiner Metzgerei sogar die fettlose Fleischpaste, die man für einen Kibbeh-Teig braucht! Und wer das nächste Mal in der Gegend ist, sollte auch in der Konditorei Damaskus (Sonnenallee 135) vorbeischauen, wo die besten syrischen Süßigkeiten angeboten werden. I remember try-ing to get my hands on freekeh (smoked green cracked wheat), mulukhiya (a green leaf called Jew's mallow in English), and mograbieh (giant couscous) in 2013 in Berlin. It was a sad affair. At the time, Azzam, the supermarket on Sonnenallee, wasn't exactly selling the freshest of produce. Nowadays the quality has excelled: the owners are flying their produce in fresh on weekly basis, and Azzam and other markets have become a celebration of Middle Eastern culinary tradition. Now you can complete all those tricky dishes from Yotam Ottolenghi's cookbook "Jerusalem" without the German substitutions. Baraka Inter food supermarket (Sonnenallee 39) even has the fatless meat paste in their butcher shop that you need for kibbeh dough! And next time you're in the area stocking up your Middle Eastern kitchen cabinet, don't forget to visit Damaskus pastry shop (Sonnenallee 135) serving the finest in Syrian sweets.

Text: Kavita Meelu / Photos: Daniel Faró

Azzam Lebensmittel
Sonnenallee 54, 12045 Berlin-Neukölln
Mon-Sat 8:00-24:00

EXPERIMENTELLE KÜCHE FÜR GOURMETS EXPERIMENTAL COOKING FOR GOURMET DINERS

Schon am Eingang des Restaurants Industry Standard grüßen eine große, offene Küche, viel Arbeitsfläche und hohe Regale mit Einweckgläsern: eingelegte Dillgurken (die besten meines Lebens), kleine Pilze (hocharomatisch) – alles, was den Köchen gerade so ins Glas kommt, wird hier verarbeitet. Verantwortlich fürs Kochen sind Ramsés Manneck aus Mexiko und der Engländer Daniel Remers, beide mit langjähriger Erfahrung in den besten Küchen Europas. Barkeeper Alonso Maldonado setzt die Kräuteressenzen für seine außergewöhnlichen Drinks (Mia Farrow!) selbst an. Eine bunt gemischte Truppe also, mit einem Ziel: authentischen Geschmack aus besten Produkten zu zaubern. Das Angebot wechselt nach Marktlage – Auster auf Mexikaner (feuriger Shot, superfrische Auster) oder Tartar vom Rind (cremig und vielschichtig) stehen zum Beispiel auf dem Menü. Als Weinhändler empfehle ich dazu natürlich ein Glas von ihrem ausgezeichneten Naturwein! The open kitchen greets you at the entrance to Industry Standard, with multiple work surfaces and shelves holding glasses of sour cucumbers and dill (the best I've ever had), small mushrooms (highly aromatic), and everything else you'd need to inspire a chef. Responsible for all of this is Ramsés Mannek from Mexico and Englishman Daniel Remers, both with long years of experience in Europe's finest establishments. Barkeeper Alonso Maldonado produces hand-crafted herb essences for his unusual drinks (the Mia Farrow!). The rest of the team is a motley group with the same goal: authentic taste for the best products. What's on offer changes with the market – for example, Oyster and Mexikaner (fresh oyster, fiery shot) or Beef Tartare Industry Style (creamy and complex). As a wine merchant, naturally I recommend that you try a glass of their excellent wine.

Text: Holger Schwarz / Photo: Daniel Faró

Industry Standard
Sonnenallee 83, 12045 Berlin-Neukölln
Wed-Sun 19:00–24:00
industry-standard.de

VOM KRANKENHAUS ZUM RAUM FÜR KRITISCHE KUNST FROM HOSPITAL TO CRITICAL ART VENUE

Bis in das Jahr 1970 fungierte der Kunstraum Kreuzberg/Bethanien als Krankenhaus, das 1847 von Theodor von Stein im Auftrag Friedrich Wilhelms IV entworfen wurde. Als der Abriss fast beschlossene Sache war, rettete eine Bürgerinitiative das historische Gebäude, das Sozial-bauten hätte weichen sollen. Heute ist der Kunstraum ein vielseitiger Ausstellungsort für zeitgenössische Kunst mit besonderem Fokus auf soziokulturellen Fragen rund um die Themen Diversität und Identität. Gezeigt werden Künstler wie der Maler Hans Baluschek, berühmt für seine realistischen Porträts und Darstellungen des städtischen Lebens, sowie Kreuzberger Urgesteine wie der Expressionist Erich Büttner, Luise Grimm, eine Schülerin Baluscheks, und der zeitgenössische türkische Künster Hanefi Yeter. Up until 1970 the Kunstraum Kreuzberg Bethanien was a hospital, designed by Theodor Stein at the order of Frederick William IV in 1847. When the building's existence was threatened by a plan to demolish it in favor of social housing, the initiatives of local citizens were able to save the site. Today, Kunstraum Kreuzberg Bethanien is a versatile exhibition space for contemporary art, focus-ing on sociocultural issues such as cultural diversity and identity. Among the artists on show is Hans Baluschek, famed for his realistic portraits and depictions of urban landscapes, and Kreuzberg natives such as expressionist painter Erich Büttner, Luise Grimm, a student of Baluschek, and contemporary Turkish artist Hanefi Yeter.

Text: Victoria Pease / Photos: Daniel Farò

Kunstraum Kreuzberg/Bethanien
Mariannenplatz 2, 10997 Berlin-Kreuzberg
Daily 11:00-20:00
kunstraumkreuzberg.de
kunstquartier-bethanien.de

EXTRA TIP

In der Kottbusser Straße 10 findet man das Künst-lerhaus Bethanien: Neben Werkstätten, Büros und Ateliers gibt es hier auch Platz für Ausstellungen. At Kottbusser Straße 10 you'll find the Künstlerhaus Bethanien: there's room for exhibitions here next to the workshops, offices, and ateliers.

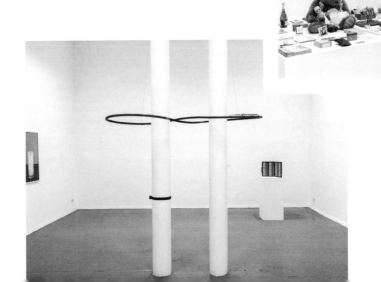

ACTIVITIES

1. Badeschiff at Arena Berlin (E9)
Alt-Treptow / Eichenstraße 4 / Page: 154

2. Flatowturm (H1)
Potsdam / Park Babelsberg 12 / Page: 257

3. Gärten der Welt (A10)
Marzahn / Eisenacher Straße 99 / Page: 159

4. Goldhahn und Sampson (E2)
Charlottenburg / Wilmersdorfer Straße 102-103 / Page: 192

5. Habermannsee (E10)
Mahlsdorf / Kressenweg Page: 159

6. Harry Hurtig (A1)
Waren (Müritz) / Am Seeufer 24 / Page: 151

7. Körnerpark (H8)
Neukölln / Schierker Straße 8 / Page: 85

8. Müggelturm (H10)
Müggelheim / Straße zum Müggelturm / Page: 256

9. Müritzhof / Müritz-Nationalpark (A1)
Waren (Müritz) / Page: 151

10. Park am Gleisdreieck (F5)
Kreuzberg / Möckernstraße 26 / Page: 29

11. Pfaueninsel (H1)
Wannsee / Nikolskoer Weg / Page: 261

12. Sacrower See (H1)
Potsdam / Seepromenade 99 / Page: 212

13. Schöneberger Südgelände (H5)
Schöneberg / Prellerweg 47-49 / Page: 168

14. Sonder 54 (A7)
Mitte / Rheinsberger Straße 54 / Page: 191

15. Spreehafen Burg (H10)
Spreewald / Am Hafen 1 Page: 155

16. Über den Tellerrand kochen (G4)
Schöneberg / Roßbachstraße 6 / Page: 192

17. Urbanhafen (F7)
Kreuzberg / Carl-Herz-Ufer to Planufer Page: 149

18. We make it (A4)
Wedding / Malplaquetstraße 17 / Page: 190

19. Zionskirche (B7)
Mitte / Zionskirchplatz Page: 249

BARS

20. Allan's Breakfast Club and Wine Bar (B8)
Prenzlauer Berg / Rykestraße 13 / Page: 127

21. Bar Milano (B7)
Mitte / Brunnenstraße 11 Page: 110

22. Bar Zentral (E3)
Charlottenburg / Lotte-Lenya-Bogen 551 Page: 233

23. Basalt (A4)
Wedding / Utrechter Straße 38 / Page: 246

24. Bellman Bar (F8)
Kreuzberg / Reichenberger Straße 103 / Page: 73

25. Bergschloss (H8)
Neukölln / Kopfstraße 59 Page: 49

26. Bravo Bar (C6)
Mitte / Torstraße 230 Page: 65

27. Briefmarken Weine (C9)
Friedrichshain / Karl-Marx-Allee 99 / Page: 127

28. Buck and Breck (B6)
Mitte / Brunnenstraße 177 Page: 233

29. Das Hotel (E8)
Kreuzberg / Mariannenstraße 26a / Page: 198

30. Jaja (G8)
Neukölln / Weichselstraße 7 / Page: 127

31. Kumpelnest 3000 (E5)
Tiergarten / Lützowstraße 23 / Page: 247

32. Mandy's Cocktailbar (F8)
Kreuzberg / Reichenberger Straße 61 / Page: 140

33. Mendy & Edeltraut (G8)
Neukölln / Weserstraße 43 Page: 58

34. Neontoaster (A4)
Wedding / Seestraße 106 Page: 127

35. Paloma Bar (E8)
Kreuzberg / Skalitzer Straße 135 / Page: 243

36. Schwein (B6)
Mitte / Elisabethkirchstraße 2 / Page: 127

37. Südblock (E7)
Kreuzberg / Admiralstraße 1-2 / Page: 231

38. Vagabund Brauerei (A4)
Wedding / Antwerpener Straße 3 / Page: 49

39. Viniculture (E3)
Charlottenburg / Grolmanstraße 44 / Page: 127

40. Weinbar Les Climats (E5)
Tiergarten / Pohlstraße 75 Page: 87

41. Weinbar Rutz (B6)
Mitte / Chausseestraße 8 Page: 171

42. Wild Things (G9)
Neukölln / Weserstraße 172 / Page: 127

CAFÉS

43. Black Sheep Café (F9)
Alt-Treptow / Bouchéstraße 15 / Page: 132

44. Bonanza Café at Oderberger Straße (A7)
Prenzlauer Berg / Oderberger Straße 35 Page: 124

45. Bonanza Roastery Café (E8)
Kreuzberg / Adalbertstraße 70 / Page: 51

46. Bravo Bravko Kuchenwerkstatt (E8)
Kreuzberg / Lausitzer Straße 47 / Page: 180

47. Café Eule im Gleisdreieck (E5)
Schöneberg / Bülowstraße 68 / Page: 31

48. Café-Restaurant Wintergarten im Literaturhaus (E3)
Charlottenburg / Fasanenstraße 23 / Page: 152

49. Café zum Löwen (A10)
Gerswalde / Dorfmitte 7 Page: 150

50. Concierge Coffee (F8)
Kreuzberg / Paul-Lincke-Ufer 39-40 / Page: 124

51. Distrikt Coffee (B6)
Mitte / Bergstraße 68 Page: 210

52. Father Carpenter Coffee Brewers (C7)
Mitte / Münzstraße 21, backyard / Page: 70

53. Fine Bagels (D9)
Friedrichshain Warschauer Straße 74 Page: 136

54. Five Elephant Coffee Roastery and Cake Shop (F9)
Kreuzberg / Reichenberger Straße 101 / Page: 124

55. Friedl Rösterei & Kekse (A7)
Prenzlauer Berg / Pappelallee 35 / Page: 124

56. Gordon Café & Recordstore (H8)
Neukölln / Allerstraße 11 Page: 42

57. Hallesches Haus (E6)
Kreuzberg / Tempelhofer Ufer 1 / Page: 195

58. Hofcafé bei Mutter Fourage (H1)
Wannsee / Chausseestraße 15 / Page: 260

59. House of Small Wonder (C6)
Mitte / Johannisstraße 20 Page: 39

60. Kaffeebar (F7)
Kreuzberg / Graefestraße 8 / Page: 109

61. Kaffeekirsche Roastery (E8)
Kreuzberg / Adalbertstraße 23 / Page: 50 & 124

62. Laden Buchholz-berlin (C7)
Mitte / Joachimstraße 20 Page: 165

63. Liquid Garden (A7)
Prenzlauer Berg / Stargarder Straße 72 / Page: 269

64. Mamecha Green Tea Café (C7)
Mitte / Mulackstraße 33 Page: 40

65. No.58 Speiserei (G8)
Neukölln / Weisestraße 58 Page: 216

66. Oliv Eat (E5)
Tiergarten / Potsdamer Straße 91 / Page: 46

67. Ora (E7)
Kreuzberg / Oranienplatz 14 / Page: 129

68. Silo Coffee (D10)
Friedrichshain / Gabriel-Max-Straße 4 / Page: 70

69. The Barn Coffee Roasters (B7)
Prenzlauer Berg / Schönhauser Allee 8 / Page: 124

70. Two Planets (G8)
Neukölln / Hermannstraße 230 / Page: 136

71. Westberlin Coffeebar & Mediashop (E6)
Kreuzberg / Friedrichstraße 215 / Page: 183

CULTURE

72. 401contemporary (E5)
Tiergarten / Potsdamer Straße 81b / Page: 117

73. Acud Macht Neu (B7)
Mitte / Veteranenstraße 21 Page: 234

74. Akademie der Künste (C4)
Tiergarten / Hanseatenweg 10 / Page: 252

75. Amerika-Gedenkbibliothek (F6)
Kreuzberg / Blücherplatz 1 Page: 197

76. Anna-Catharina Gebbers Bibliothekswohnung (C6)
Mitte / Ziegelstraße 2 Page: 236

77. Blain | Southern (E5)
Tiergarten / Potsdamer Straße 77-87 / Page: 87

78. Bumiller Collection (E8)
Kreuzberg / Naunynstraße 68 / Page: 134

79. Carlier | Gebauer (E6)
Kreuzberg / Markgrafenstraße 67 / Page: 184

80. Chert (E7)
Kreuzberg / Ritterstraße 2a / Page: 254

81. City Kino Wedding (A4)
Wedding / Müllerstraße 74 Page: 62

82. Contemporary Fine Arts (E3)
Charlottenburg Grolmanstraße 32-33 Page: 206

83. District Berlin (H5)
Schöneberg / Bessemerstraße 2-14 / Page: 168

84. Edition Block (F3)
Wilmersdorf / Prager
Straße 5 / Page: 164

85. Ehemaliges Stumm-
filmkino Delphi (A8)
Weißensee / Gustav-
Adolf- Straße 2 / Page: 61

86. Frankfurt am Main
(G9)
Neukölln / Wildenbruch-
straße 15 / Page: 126

87. Freiluftkino Hasen-
heide (G7)
Neukölln / Im Volkspark
Hasenheide / Page: 83

88. Fsk - Das Kino am
Oranienplatz (E7)
Kreuzberg / Segitzdamm 2
Page: 130

89. Galerie Barbara
Thumm (E6)
Kreuzberg / Markgrafen-
straße 68 / Page: 184

90. Galerie Patrick
Ebensperger (A5)
Wedding / Plantagen-
straße 30 / Page: 53

91. Galerie Tanja Wagner
(E5)
Tiergarten / Pohlstraße 64
Page: 9

92. Galerie Thomas
Fischer (E5)
Tiergarten / Potsdamer
Straße 77-87 / Page: 87

93. Gillmeier Rech (E5)
Tiergarten / Körner-
straße 17 / Page: 247

94. HAU 1 – Hebbel am
Ufer (E6)
Kreuzberg / Stresemann-
straße 2 / Page: 142

95. Il Kino (F8)
Neukölln / Nansenstraße
22 / Page: 62

96. Insitu (E5)
Tiergarten / Kurfürsten-
straße 21-22 / Page: 126

97. Jarmuschek + Partner
(E5)
Tiergarten / Potsdamer
Straße 81b / Page: 117

98. Kapelle auf dem
Dorotheenstädtischen
Friedhof I (B6)
Mitte / Chausseestraße
126 / Page: 139

99. Käthe-Kollwitz-
Museum (E3)
Charlottenburg / Fasa-
nenstraße 24 / Page: 152

100. Kleine Humboldt
Galerie (C6)
Mitte / Unter den Linden 6
Page: 126

101. Konzerthaus Berlin (D6)
Mitte / Gendarmenmarkt
Page: 241

102. Künstlerhaus Betha-
nien (F7)
Kreuzberg / Kottbusser
Straße 10 / Page: 283

103. Kunstraum Kreuz-
berg/Bethanien (E8)
Kreuzberg / Mariannen-
platz 2 / Page: 283

104. Lichtblick Kino (B7)
Prenzlauer Berg / Kasta-
nienallee 77 / Page: 141

105. Liebermann-Villa am
Wannsee (H1)
Wannsee / Colomier-
straße 3 / Page: 157

106. Max Liebermann
Haus (D5)
Mitte / Pariser Platz 7
Page: 157

107. Museum für
Naturkunde (B5)
Mitte / Invalidenstraße 43
Page: 187

108. Neues Off (G8)
Neukölln / Hermann-
straße 20 / Page: 141

109. Non Berlin – Asia
contemporary art plat-
form (B6)
Mitte / Chausseestraße 11
Page: 126

110. Sammlung Scharf-
Gerstenberg (H2)
Charlottenburg Schloß-
straße 70 / Page: 86

111. Savvy Contemporary
(A5)
Wedding / Plantagen-
straße 31 / Page: 52

112. Schaubühne am
Lehniner Platz (E1)
Charlottenburg / Kurfürs-
tendamm 153 / Page: 88

113. Sexauer Gallery (A8)
Weißensee / Streustraße
90 / Page: 60

114. Smac (B7)
Mitte / Linienstraße 57
Page: 48

115. Studio Niculescu (E7)
Kreuzberg / Oranien-
straße 163 / Page: 59

116. Tchoban Foundation –
Museum für Architektur-
zeichnung (B7)
Mitte / Christinenstraße
18a / Page: 258

117. Theaterdiscounter
(C7)
Mitte / Klosterstraße 44
Page: 142

118. The Feuerle
Collection (E5)
Kreuzberg / Hallesches
Ufer 70 / Page: 134

119. Uqbar (A4)
Wedding / Schweden-
straße 16 / Page: 126

120. Villa Schöningen (H1)
Potsdam / Berliner
Straße 86 / Page: 213

MISCELLANEOUS

121. 25hours Hotel Bikini
Berlin (E3)
Charlottenburg
Budapester Straße 40
Page: 125

122. Barbershop Kücük
Istanbul (G8)
Neukölln / Flughafen-
straße 15 / Page: 36

123. Bootsbau Köpenick
(H10)
Friedrichshagen / Müg-
gelseedamm 70 (im Was-
sersportzentrum Berlin)
Page: 68

124. California Pops (E9)
Kreuzberg / Falckenstein-
straße 4 / Page: 145

125. Das Stue (D4)
Tiergarten / Drakestraße 1
Page: 125

126. Eispatisserie Hokey
Pokey (A7)
Prenzlauer Berg / Stargar-
der Straße 73 / Page: 269

127. Fichtebunker (F7)
Kreuzberg / Fichtestraße
6 / Page: 277

128. Fortuna's Feast
Private Dining (G9)
Neukölln / Weserstraße 58
Page: 209

129. Glut & Späne (A10)
Gerswalde / Dorfmitte 11
Page: 150

130. Loftus Hall (F8)
Neukölln / Maybachufer
48 / Page: 133

131. Markthalle Neun (E8)
Kreuzberg / Eisenbahn-
straße 42-43 / Page: 278

132. Michelberger Hotel -
The Hideout (E9)
Friedrichshain
Warschauer Straße 39-40
Page: 125

133. Mineralogische
Sammlungen der Tech-
nischen Universität (D3)
Charlottenburg / Ernst-
Reuter-Platz 1 / Page: 188

134. Neu West Berlin (F6)
Kreuzberg / Yorckstraße
86 / Page: 244

135. Nomads Apt. (A7)
Mitte / Rheinsberger
Straße 32 / Page: 125

136. Schwuz (G8)
Neukölln / Rollbergstraße
26 / Page: 231

137. Tresorhonig (D8)
Mitte / Köpenicker
Straße 70 / Page: 249

138. Wallyard Concept
Hostel (C4)
Moabit / Lübecker Straße
46 / Page: 125

139. Wild Heart Free Soul
Bazaar (B6)
Mitte / Elisabethkirch-
straße 13 / Page: 20

140. Woltersdorfer
Straßenbahn (H10)
Rahnsdorf / S-Bahnhof
Page: 56

RESTAURANTS

141. 3 Minutes Sur Mer (B6)
Mitte / Torstraße 167
Page: 106

142. Akroum Snack (G8)
Neukölln / Sonnenallee 45
Page: 26

143. Alpenstück-Manu-
faktur (B6)
Mitte / Schröderstraße 15
Page: 176

144. Alsancak Simit
Sarayi (F6)
Kreuzberg / Gneisenau-
straße 3 / Page: 245

145. Arirang Two (F8)
Kreuzberg / Reichenber-
ger Straße 125 / Page: 32

146. Aroma (E2)
Charlottenburg / Kant-
straße 35 / Page: 242

147. Beuster Bar (G8)
Neukölln / Weserstraße 32
Page: 118

148. Bosco (E9)
Kreuzberg / Wrangel-
straße 42 / Page: 274

149. Brasserie Lamazère
(E1)
Charlottenburg / Stuttgar-
ter Platz 18 / Page: 119

150. Café am Neuen See
(D4)
Tiergarten / Lichtenstein-
allee 2 / Page: 200

151. Café Einstein
Stammhaus (E4)
Tiergarten / Kurfürsten-
straße 58 / Page: 76

152. Caligari Bistro (H8)
Neukölln / Kienitzer
Straße 110 / Page: 202

153. Cevicheria (E7)
Kreuzberg / Dresdener
Straße 120 / Page: 28

154. Chicha (F8)
Neukölln / Friedelstraße
34 / Page: 28

155. Der Goldene Hahn
(E8)
Kreuzberg / Pückler-
straße 20 / Page: 82

156. Dóttir (C6)
Mitte / Mittelstraße 40-41
Page: 33

157. Eins44 (G9)
Neukölln / Elbestraße
28-29 / Page: 58

158. Einsunternull (C6)
Mitte / Hannoversche
Straße 1 / Page: 63

159. Good Friends (E2)
Charlottenburg / Kant-
straße 30 / Page: 242

160. Gotcilla (G8)
Neukölln / Weserstraße 31
Page: 140

161. Hallmann & Klee (H9)
Neukölln / Böhmische
Straße 13 / Page: 177

162. Häppies (A8)
Prenzlauer Berg
Dunckerstraße 85
Page: 137

163. Industry Standard
(G8)
Neukölln / Sonnenallee 83
Page: 282

164. James Biergarten
(A10)
Panketal/Zepernick
Hobrechtsfelder Dorf-
straße 30a / Page: 200

165. Jimmy Woo (F8)
Neukölln / Friedelstraße
24 / Page: 181

166. Joseph Roth Diele
(E5)
Tiergarten / Potsdamer
Straße 75 / Page: 87

167. Kanaan (A7)
Prenzlauer Berg
Kopenhagener Straße 17
Page: 42

168. Knödelwirtschaft (F9)
Neukölln / Fuldastraße 33
Page: 137

169. Le Bon (F8)
Kreuzberg / Boppstraße 1
Page: 108

170. Le Petit Royal (D2)
Charlottenburg / Grolman
straße 59 / Page: 206

171. Let it be (G9)
Neukölln / Treptower
Straße 90 / Page: 132

172. L'eustache (G8)
Neukölln / Weisestraße 49
Page: 216

173. Lode & Stijn (F8)
Kreuzberg / Lausitzer
Straße 25 / Page: 23

174. Louis Pretty (E7)
Kreuzberg / Ritterstraße 2
Page: 255

175. Madame Ngo (E2)
Charlottenburg / Kant-
straße 30 / Page: 22

176. Manzini (E3)
Wilmersdorf / Ludwig-
kirchstraße 11 / Page: 164

177. Momos (B7)
Mitte / Fehrbelliner
Straße 5 / Page: 258

178. Mozzarella Bar (C7)
Mitte / Auguststraße 34
Page: 166

**179. Nobelhart &
Schmutzig (E6)**
Kreuzberg / Friedrich-
straße 218 / Page: 169

180. Ojo de Agua (E3)
Wilmersdorf / Ludwig-
kirchstraße 10a / Page: 88

181. Osmans Töchter (A7)
Prenzlauer Berg / Pappel-
allee 15 / Page: 17

**182. Panama Restaurant
& Bar (E5)**
Tiergarten / Potsdamer
Straße 91 / Page: 45

**183. Parma di Vini Bene-
detti (A5)**
Wedding / Utrechter
Straße 31 / Page: 246

184. Pastificio Tosatti (A8)
Prenzlauer Berg / Schlie-
mannstraße 14a / Page: 18

185. Platz doch! (E8)
Kreuzberg / Manteuffel-
straße 48 / Page: 163

**186. Restaurant Moos
(A5)**
Wedding / Gerichtstraße
35 / Page: 53

187. Rosa Caleta (E8)
Kreuzberg / Muskauer
Straße 9 / Page: 82

**188. Speiselokal Tulus
Lotrek (F7)**
Kreuzberg / Fichtestraße
24 / Page: 277

**189. Standard – Serious
Pizza (B7)**
Mitte / Templiner Straße 7
Page: 266

190. Stella (G9)
Neukölln / Weserstraße
166 / Page: 208

**191. Superfoods &
Organic Liquids (B7)**
Mitte / Weinbergsweg 23
Page: 156

**192. Teehaus im
Englischen Garten (D4)**
Tiergarten / Altonaer
Straße 2 / Page: 80

**193. Thai Window Asia
(C7)**
Mitte / Torstraße 22
Page: 105

**194. The Klub Kitchen
(C7)**
Mitte / Mulackstraße 15
Page: 156

195. Tin Tan (B6)
Mitte / Chausseestraße
124 / Page: 138

**196. Tommi's Burger
Joint (B6)**
Mitte / Invalidenstraße 160
Page: 234

197. YamYam (C7)
Mitte / Alte Schönhauser
Straße 6 / Page: 114

198. Zenkichi (C6)
Mitte / Johannisstraße 20
Page: 39 & 236

```
┌─────────────┐
│   SHOPS     │
└─────────────┘
```

199. Alex Valder (F8)
Kreuzberg / Urbanstraße
64, 2nd backyard
Page: 122

200. Amore Store (F8)
Neukölln / Sanderstraße
12 / Page: 215

**201. Andreas Murkudis
Möbel + Architektur (E5)**
Tiergarten / Potsdamer
Straße 77 / Page: 116

202. Anna Badur (G9)
Neukölln / Donaustraße
83 / Page: 122

203. Aura (F8)
Neukölln / Sanderstraße
13 / Page: 276

**204. Azzam Lebensmittel
(G8)**
Neukölln / Sonnenallee 54
Page: 280

205. Bäckerei Hacker (A8)
Prenzlauer Berg
Stargarder Straße 69
Page: 199

**206. Baraka Inter Food
(G8)**
Neukölln / Sonnenallee 39
Page: 281

207. Bartmann Berlin (F8)
Kreuzberg / Hasenheide
12 / Page: 122

208. Bazar Noir (F6)
Kreuzberg / Kreuzberg-
straße 78 / Page: 272

209. Bender Keramik (G8)
Neukölln / Reuterstraße
90 / Page: 186

210. Blomeyer's Käse (D1)
Charlottenburg
Pestalozzistraße 54a
Page: 211

211. Bohazel (H8)
Neukölln / Kienitzer
Straße 111 / Page: 20

212. Candy on Bone (F7)
Kreuzberg / Planufer 92b
Page: 215

213. Chrome Store (F8)
Neukölln / Lenaustraße 10
Page: 276

**214. Damaskus Kondi-
torei (G9)**
Neukölln / Sonnenallee
135 / Page: 281

215. Felicious (B6)
Mitte / Schröderstraße 14
Page: 176

**216. Feuer Zeug Keramik
(E8)**
Kreuzberg / Mariannen-
straße 48 / Page: 186

217. Framepunk (E8)
Kreuzberg / Manteuffel-
straße 48 / Page: 121

218. Frank Leder (E2)
Charlottenburg / Kant-
straße 139 / Page: 173

**219. Geckeler Michels
Industrial Design (G9)**
Neukölln / Treptower
Straße 22 / Page: 122

**220. Happy Shop Global
Alliance (B7)**
Mitte / Torstraße 67
Page: 263

221. Harry Lehmann (E2)
Charlottenburg / Kant-
straße 106 / Page: 74

222. Ic! Berlin (C7)
Mitte / Max-Beer-Straße 17
Page: 121

**223. Jacks Beauty
Department (A7)**
Prenzlauer Berg / Kasta-
nienallee 19 / Page: 172

224. La Cucina (B7)
Prenzlauer Berg / Schön-
hauser Allee 187 / Page:
264

225. Lager Lager (F8)
Neukölln / Pflügerstraße
68 / Page: 181

226. Livia Polidoro (A7)
Pankow / Berliner Straße
80–82 / Page: 179

227. Lunettes Selection (B6)
Mitte / Torstraße 172
Page: 121

**228. Mariusz Malecki /
Studio Ziben (A7)**
Prenzlauer Berg
Kopenhagener Straße 66
Page: 122

**229. Michael Sontag
Shop (E8)**
Kreuzberg / Muskauer
Straße 41 / Page: 161

230. My Kilos (D6)
Mitte / Leipziger Straße 65
Page: 123

231. Mykita (C7)
Mitte / Rosa-Luxemburg-
Straße 6 / Page: 121

232. New Tendency (E8)
Kreuzberg / Adalbert-
straße 6a, 1st backyard
Page: 123

233. Peppikäse (G8)
Neukölln / Weichsel-
straße 65 / Page: 211

**234. Piñateria – Die
Piñata Manufaktur (F8)**
Kreuzberg / Schönlein-
straße 8 / Page: 268

**235. Purwin & Radczun
(E5)**
Kreuzberg / Tempelhofer
Ufer 32 / Page: 175

236. R.T.CO (F8)
Neukölln / Sanderstraße 6
Page: 121

237. Ryoko (F8)
Neukölln / Friedelstraße 11
Page: 38

238. Schwarzhogerzeil (B6)
Mitte / Torstraße 173
Page: 106

239. Soto Store (B7)
Mitte / Torstraße 71 & 72
Page: 214

240. Spezialschön (D1)
Charlottenburg / Nehring-
straße 34 / Page: 86

**241. The Bread Station
(F8)**
Neukölln / Maybachufer 16
Page: 199

242. The Good Store (F8)
Neukölln / Pannierstraße
31 / Page: 133

**243. The Store x Soho
House Berlin (C7)**
Mitte / Torstraße 1
Page: 103

```
┌──────────────────┐
│ ONLINE & OTHER   │
└──────────────────┘
```

Accidental Concrete
Page: 178

Atelier Haußmann
Page: 123

Christian Metzner
Page: 123

Fjord Coffee Roasters
Page: 70 & 124

Nutsandwoods
Page: 122

Objekte unserer Tage
Page: 122

Projekt Samsen
Page: 121

Rainer Spehl
Page: 123

**Und Gretel
Naturkosmetik**
Page: 172

Vava Eyewear
Page: 121

A – Z

Künstlerliste / List of artists

35
Unten / bottom:
Jasmin Müller, Sean Landers

46
Tanya Aguiñiga
Adrien Missika
Björn Dahlem
Kerim Seiler
Dieter Detzner

47
Oben / top:
Julius von Bismarck

48
Oben / top: Knut Eckstein
Unten / bottom: Jens Hausmann,
Alexej Meschtschanow

52 / 53
Links / left: Georges Adéagbo
Mitte / center: Nathalie Mba
Bikoro
Rechts / right: Buhlebezwe
Siwani

60 / 61
Unten links / bottom left:
Futo Akiyoshi
Oben / top: Jay Gard
Unten rechts / bottom right:
Andreas Golder

126
Im Uhrzeigersinn / clockwise:
Non Berlin – Asia Contemporary
Art Platform: Satoshi Fujiwara
Kleine Humboldt Galerie: Maria
Anwander
Uqbar: Diana Artus
Frankfurt am Main: Grayson
Revoir
Insitu: Aurora Sander

135
Links / left:
Gilbert Mc Garragher
Rechts / right: Zeng Fanzhi

138 / 139
James Turrell

164
Links / left: KP Brehmer
Rechts / right: Alicja Kwade

168
Rechts / right: Miryana Todorova

214
Rechts / right: Frank Thiel

234 / 235
Mitte unten / center bottom:
Willem de Rooij / Mario Pfeifer

252 / 253
Oben / top: Tony Cragg

283
Unten / bottom: Anselm
Schenkluhn

Fotos / Photos

Cover
Im Uhrzeigersinn / clockwise:
The Store: Daniel Farò
Hallesches Haus: Daniel Farò
Cee Cee Pop Up Shop: Andreas
Alexander Bohlender

35
Oben / top: Courtesy of Dóttir

48
Unten / bottom: Courtesy of
Alexej Meschtschanow & Jens
Hausmann

53
Oben / top: Courtesy of Savvy
Contemporary

59
Unten / bottom: Courtesy of
Studio Niculescu

60 / 61
Oben links und unten rechts /
top left and bottom right:
AnneLiWestlBerlin

63 / 64 / 65
Courtesy of Einsunternull

86
Bpk | Nina Straßgütl,
Bpk | David von Becker

110 / 111
Mitte und oben rechts / center
and top right: Courtesy of Bar
Milano

117
Courtesy of Andrea Murkudis

121
Im Uhrzeigersinn / clockwise:
Lunettes Selection: Jonas Hegi
Framepunk: Courtesy of
Framepunk
Vava Eyewear: Courtesy of Vava
Eyewear
Ic! berlin: Courtesy of Ic! berlin
Projekt Samsen: Courtesy of
Projekt Samsen
Mykita: Courtesy of Mykita
R.T.Co: Courtesy of R.T.Co

122 / 123
Im Uhrzeigersinn / clockwise:
Bartmann Berlin: Studio Amos
Fricke
Rainer Spehl: Daniel Farò
My Kilos: Courtesy of My Kilos
New Tendency: Courtesy of
New Tendency
Atelier Haußmann: Courtesy of
Atelier Haußmann
Christian Metzner: Courtesy of
Studio Amos Fricke
Mariusz Malecki / Studio Ziben:
Courtesy of Mariusz Malecki /
Studio Ziben
Geckeler Michels Industrial
Design: Haw Lin Services
Alex Valder: Courtesy of Alex
Valder
Objekte Unserer Tage: Courtesy
of Objekte Unserer Tage

Anna Badur: Courtesy of Anna
Badur
Nutsandwoods: Courtesy of
Nutsandwoods

124
Im Uhrzeigersinn / clockwise:
Five Elephant Coffee Roastery
and Cake Shop: Courtesy of Five
Elephant Coffee Roastery and
Cake Shop
Friedl Rösterei & Kekse: Daniel
Farò
Kaffeekirsche Roastery: Daniel
Farò
Concierge Coffee: Daniel Farò
Bonanza: Daniel Farò
Fjord Coffee Roasters: Daniel
Farò
The Barn: Courtesy of The Barn

125
Im Uhrzeigersinn / clockwise:
Michelberger Hotel Hideout:
Courtesy of Michelberger Hotel
Das Stue: Courtesy of Das Stue
25hours Hotel Bikini Berlin:
Courtesy of 25hours Hotel
Bikini Berlin
Nomads Apt.: Courtesy of
Nomads Apt.
Wallyard Concept Hostel:
Courtesy of Wallyard Concept
Hostel

126
Im Uhrzeigersinn / clockwise:
Non Berlin - Asia Contemporary
Art Platform: courtesy of Non
Berlin.
Kleine Humboldtgalerie:
Courtesy of Kleine
Humboldtgalerie
Uqbar: Courtesy of Diana Artus
Frankfurt am Main: Andrea
Rossetti
Insitu: Markus Georg

127
Im Uhrzeigersinn / clockwise:
Wild Things: Courtesy of Wild
Things
Neontoaster: Daniel Farò
Allans Breakfast Club and Wine
Bar: Daniel Farò
Briefmarken Weine: Courtesy of
Briefmarken Weine
Viniculture: Courtesy of
Viniculture
Schwein: Courtesy of Schwein
Jaja: Courtesy of Jaja

135
Links / left:
Gilbert Mc Garragher, Courtesy
of The Feuerle Collection
Rechts / right: Courtesy of
Zeng Fanzhi and The Feuerle
Collection

138
Courtesy of Florian Holzherr

142 / 143
Unten links und oben rechts /
bottom left and top right:
Courtesy of Hebbel am Ufer

151
Courtesy of Tourismusverband
Mecklenburg-Vorpommern

157
Courtesy of Max Liebermann
Gesellschaft

184
Oben / top: Courtesy of
Westberlin Coffeebar &
Mediashop

234 / 235
Courtesy of Acud Macht Neu

258 / 259
Courtesy of Tchoban Foundation

269
Courtesy of Blinking Pigs

272 / 273
Courtesy of Hidden Fortress

Backcover
Im Uhrzeigersinn / clockwise:
Postbahnhof, Friedrichshain:
Andreas Alexander Bohlender
Dóttir: Daniel Farò
Michael Sontag: Daniel Farò
Habermannsee: Daniel Farò

ARTISTS & COURTESY

PUBLISHING DETAILS

Herausgeber & Konzeption / Editor & Concept
Cee Cee Creative
Nina Trippel & Sven Hausherr

Chefredakteurin / Editor-in-Chief
Nina Trippel

Redaktion / Editor
Laura Storfner

Art Direktion / Art Direction
Sven Hausherr

Grafik Design / Graphic Design
Sandra Andriani Bitz, Jessica David, Daniel Farò, Anna Lind Haugaard

Fotografie & Bildredaktion / Photography & Photo Editor
Daniel Farò

Projekt Management / Projekt Management
Cee Cee: Gwendolyn Becker
DISTANZ Verlag: Frederik Kugler

Redaktionsassistenz / Editorial Assistance
Esmé Rocks, Nicolene van der Walt

Übersetzung / Translation
Massimo Hartmann, Esmé Rocks, Laura Storfner

Lektorat Deutsch / Copy Editing German
DISTANZ Verlag: Frederik Kugler, Antonia Berner

Lektorat Englisch / Copy Editing English
Jenna Krumming (Foreword, Intro), Rei Matsuoka (Foreword, Intro), Antonia Harris, Esmé Rocks

Lektorat Karte / Copy Editing Map
DISTANZ Verlag: Frederik Kugler, Antonia Berner
Cee Cee: Nicolene van der Walt, Nella Beljan

Vorwort / Foreword
Christoph Amend

Texte über die Gastautoren / Texts about the guest writers
Celina Plag, Nina Trippel

Autoren / Authors
Helen von der Höden, Veronika Aumann, Ben Barlow, Nella Beljan, Joachim Bessing, Eva Biringer, Sandra Andriani Bitz, Astrid Bruckmann, Mason Dean, Daniel Farò, Stephanie Franzius, Chloë Galea, Fee Gross, Sonja Gutschera, Deniz Julia Güngör, Leonie Haenchen, Ferdinand Hamsch, Antonia Harris, Massimo Hartmann, Sven Hausherr, Kirsten Hermann, Christina Hoffmann, Brigitta Horvat, Hilda Hoy, Daniela Ihrig, Stephanie Johne, George Kafka, Isabelle Kagelius, Milena Kalojanov, Julia Knolle, Rei Matsuoka, Leif Henrik Osthoff, Victoria Pease, Katharina Pencz, Celina Plag, Esmé Rocks, Elizabeth Rushe, Elisabeth Schotte, Holger Schwarz, Lorena Simmel, Janar Siniloo, Mira Starke, Caroline Stephenson, Laura Storfner, Nina Trippel, Michaela Wölfel, Claudia Maria Zenk

Gastautoren / Contributing Authors
Sara Chahrrour, Victoria Eliasdóttir, Christian Falsnaes, Lisa Feldmann, Philip Gaedicke, Herbert Hofmann, Vladimir Karaleev, Kavita Meelu, Christian Metzner, Cristian Niculescu, Angie Ziehmann

Porträtaufnahmen / Portrait Photography
Pascal Rohé

Stadtaufnahmen (Doppelseiten) / Street Photograpy (Spreads)
Andreas Alexander Bohlender

Fotografie / Photography
Hirofume Abe, Jochen Arndt, Thomas Aurin, Andreas Alexander Bohlender, Mani Bakhshpour, Kilian-Davy Baujard, Chiara Bonetti, Marco Borggreve, Markus Braumann, Johann Clausen, Arno Declair, Jochen Drewes, Lee Edward, Daniel Farò, Filine Fink, Stephanie Franzius, David Gauffin, Markus Georg, Caterina Gili, Moritz Grünke, Sonja Gutschera & Leif-Henrik-Osthoff, Emma Haugh, Sven Hausherr, Jens Hausmann, Roland Halbe, Jonas Hegi, Steve Herud, Florian Holzherr, Jonas Klock, Malene Korsgaard Lauritsen, Daniel Kula, Anna Küfner, Philipp Langenheim & Corina Schadendorf, Robbie Lawrence, Anton Roland Laub, Tabea Mathern, Manfred Mayer, Gilbert McCarragher, Alexej Meschtschanow, Son Ni, Julia Luka Lila Nitzschke, Lotte Ostermann, Ludger Paffrath, Patricia Parinejad, Magnus Pettersson, Caroline Prange, Jacob Pritchard, Sarah Radowitz, Tim Richards, Pascal Rohé, India Roper-Evans, Andrea Rossetti, Steffen Roth, Elizabeth Rushe, Ana Santl, Marcus Schneider, Marko Seifert, Janar Siniloo, Nina Straßgütl, Nic Tenwiggenhorn, David von Becker, Helen von der Höden, Uwe Walter

Papier / Paper
Amber Graphic

Schriften / Fonts
Apercu by Colophon
Courier New by Monotype
Dutch 801 by Bitstream

Produktion / Production Management
DISTANZ Verlag, Sonja Bahr

Gesamtherstellung / Production
Livonia Print, Riga

Vertrieb / Distribution
GESTALTEN, Berlin
gestalten.com
sales@gestalten.com

ISBN 978-3-95476-153-1
Printed in Europe

Erschienen im / Published by
DISTANZ Verlag
distanz.de

Kontakt / Contact
Cee Cee Creative
Cee Cee Trippel Hausherr GbR
Leipziger Straße 66
10119 Berlin-Mitte
berlin@ceecee.cc
ceecee.cc
ceeceecreative.com

Danke allen Lesern, Autoren, Gastautoren und Helfern, die Cee Cee jede Woche möglich machen und wachsen lassen sowie jenen, die mitgeholfen haben, dieses Buch zu realisieren.
Thanks to all of the readers, writers, guest writers and helping hands involved in bringing Cee Cee to life week after week, and to the people who helped realize and develop this book.

Besonderen Dank an unser Buch-Team
Special Thanks to the team of the book

Andreas Alexander Bohlender / Anna Lind Haugaard / Daniel Farò / Esmé Rocks / Gwendolyn Becker
Jessica David / Laura Storfner / Nicolene van der Walt / Pascal Rohé / Sandra Andriani Bitz

Dank geht außerdem an
Thanks to

Alexander Trippel / Antonia Berner / Antonia Harris / Barbara Hausherr / Brigitte Trippel / Claudia Trippel
Chloë Galea / Christian Boros / Christoph Amend / Frederik Kugler / Ira Bolsinger / Jule Escherhaus
Matthias Birkholz / Milena Kalojanov / Nella Beljan / Rei Matsuoka / Sonja Bahr / Uta Grosenick